Francis Ottiwell Adams, C. D. Cunningham

The Swiss Confederation

Francis Ottiwell Adams, C. D. Cunningham

The Swiss Confederation

ISBN/EAN: 9783337179687

Printed in Europe, USA, Canada, Australia, Japan

Cover: Foto ©ninafisch / pixelio.de

More available books at **www.hansebooks.com**

THE SWISS CONFEDERATION

THE SWISS CONFEDERATION

A map of
THE CANTONS OF
SWITZERLAND
Scale of English Miles
GERMANY
AUSTRIA
GRISONS
TICINO
VAUD
VALAIS
NEUCHÂTEL
FREIBURG
BERN
SOLOTHURN
AARGAU
BASEL
ZÜRICH
THURGAU
ST GALLEN
APPENZELL
LUZERN
ZUG
SCHWYZ
GLARUS
URI
UNTERWALDEN
ITALY
Basel
Liestal
Aarau
Solothurn
Schaffhausen
Frauenfeld
St Gallen
Herisau
Appenzell
Zürich
Zug
Luzern
Schwyz
Glarus
Sarnen
Stanz
Altdorf
Chur
Neuchâtel
Freiburg
Lausanne
Geneva
Sion
Locarno
Bellinzona
Lugano
L. CONSTANCE
L. Zürich
L. Neuchâtel
Lc. OF GENEVA
L. Como
L. Thun
L. Brienz
R. Rhine
R. Thur
R. Aar
R. Reuss
R. Doubs
R. Saane
R. Rhone
R. Arve
R. Ticino
R. Adda
R. Inn
Iller R.
Lech R.
Oglio R.
Maggia
2° Longitude East of Greenwich 8°
London Macmillan & Co.

THE
SWISS CONFEDERATION

BY

SIR FRANCIS OTTIWELL ADAMS
K.C.M.G., C.B.
LATE HER MAJESTY'S ENVOY EXTRAORDINARY AND
MINISTER PLENIPOTENTIARY AT BERN

AND

C. D. CUNNINGHAM

WITH A MAP

London
MACMILLAN AND CO.
AND NEW YORK
1889

THIS VOLUME

IS DEDICATED BY SPECIAL PERMISSION

TO HIS EXCELLENCY

THE PRESIDENT OF THE SWISS CONFEDERATION

AND THE OTHER

MEMBERS OF THE FEDERAL COUNCIL

PREFACE

In this work the authors have endeavoured to give a succinct account of the rise and progress of the Swiss Confederation through the seven phases of its development, and of the legislative, executive, and judicial authorities which exercise the Federal sovereignty under the amended Constitution of 1874. The nature of the Referendum, or popular vote, whether Federal or cantonal, which is an institution peculiar to Switzerland; the right of Initiative granted to a single voter or body of voters to set on foot proposals for new legislation or for the alteration or abolition of existing laws; and the Communes, which are the basis of Swiss republican institutions, are treated in separate chapters. The Cantons and their Tribunals, the organization of the Army, the system of Education, Religion, Agriculture, Commerce, and some few other subjects, are also dealt with, and in Chapter XIX we have attempted a short comparison between the political institutions of the ancient Swiss Confederation and the more modern Republic of the United States of America.

We have thought that a work treating of more serious subjects than those usually to be met with in publications of the guide-book class might be found acceptable to many of our countrymen, whether as students at home or as travellers in Switzerland, especially at the present time. Democracy has made undoubted strides at home, and it may be well for Englishmen to devote a little time to the study of the institutions of a singularly democratic country abroad.

We have been particularly fortunate in the assistance we have obtained during the performance of our task. In the first place, we cannot prize too highly the gracious permission accorded to us by the President of the Confederation and the other members of the Federal Council to dedicate our book to them. We have besides obtained the sanction and approval of Federal-Councillor Numa Droz, head of the Department of Foreign Affairs, as far as relates to the political chapters, and we beg to thank him most sincerely for his valuable suggestions and for his ready permission, of which we have availed ourselves largely, to make use of his *Instruction Civique*, a manual of great intrinsic worth. Federal-Councillor Ruchonnet, head of the Department of Justice and Police, has also been kind enough to supply us with useful information upon various points requiring elucidation.

To Professor Dr. König, a jurist of European reputation, who has been for many years Legal Adviser to Her Majesty's Legation at Bern, we are indebted for constant assistance in numerous legal and other matters, given with equal readiness and acumen; while M. Charles Boiceau, a lawyer of distinction at Lausanne, and formerly a member of the cantonal government of Vaud, who combines superior legal attainments with a thorough knowledge of our language, has contributed materially to our pages, especially with reference to the Tribunals of his Cantons.

We wish also cordially to acknowledge assistance kindly afforded to us by the following Swiss citizens: Lieutenant-Colonel Albert von Tscharner, of the General Staff, with reference to points connected with the Army; the late Professor Dr. A. Vögelin, who was a member of the National Council; Herr Alfred Frey, Secretary of the Swiss Association for Commerce and Industry; Herr Heinrich Schneebeli, of the School of Agriculture, Zürich; Herr Kaspar Grob, Secretary to the Department of Education, Zürich; and Herr Theodor Curti, member of the National Council.

We close this list of those who have rendered us assistance in Switzerland with a hearty expression of thanks to Mr. H. Angst, Her Majesty's Consul at Zürich, who has been unwearying in his endeavours, upon all occasions, to supply us with the fullest information upon a variety of matters connected with his native country.

We should also not omit to mention that in our comparison of Swiss and United States institutions we were fortunate enough to be able to consult the Honourable Boyd Winchester, United States Minister at Bern.

We have also had very material help at home, and we desire, in the first place, to tender our sincere thanks to the eminent jurists, Mr. James Bryce, M.P., Regius Professor of Civil Law at the University of Oxford, and

for some time Parliamentary Under Secretary of State for
Foreign Affairs, and Mr. A. V. Dicey, Vinerian Professor
of English Law at the same University. They have both
been good enough to take a most kindly interest in our
work, and have cheerfully given invaluable advice and
assistance, especially with reference to the constitutional
and political chapters, and to the comparison between
Swiss and American political institutions.

The chapter upon the Army has, with the full con-
currence of Lieutenant-General H. Brackenbury, R.A.,
C.B., Director of Military Intelligence, been subjected to
the careful supervision of Colonel C. W. Bowdler Bell,
D.A.A.G., Intelligence Division, War Office ; and we
have also had the advantage of consulting Major E. T.
H. Hutton, of the King's Royal Rifle Corps, Brigade-
Major at Aldershot, whose name is well known in con-
nexion with the organization of mounted infantry.

Both these distinguished officers have lately visited
Switzerland, the former with the object of studying the
Swiss Army system, the latter on the occasion of the
manœuvres in September 1887.

In our chapter upon Education we have received
much assistance from Mr. James Blaikie, of the Scotch
Education Department, Whitehall, late one of Her
Majesty's Inspectors of Schools for Scotland.

The Reverend William Cunningham, B.D., Vicar of
Great St. Mary's, Cambridge, and brother of one of the
authors, has been of essential use to us, especially in our
chapter on Religion.

Mr. Wynnard Hooper, the writer of the exhaustive

article upon Statistics in the new edition of the *Encyclopædia Britannica*, has been kind enough to furnish us with interesting particulars relating to Commerce.

To our friend Mr. W. E. Davidson, Legal Adviser to the Foreign Office, who was for many years Honorary Secretary of the Alpine Club, we owe a heavy debt of gratitude. His extensive legal acquirements have been of very great assistance to us, whilst his able criticisms have upon all occasions been as readily given as they have been constantly sought by us during the progress of this work.

NOTE

We are indebted to Mr. H. Angst for most of the information respecting Referendum and Initiative, and Political Parties.

ORDER AND DATES OF THE ENTRY OF THE TWENTY-TWO
CANTONS INTO THE CONFEDERATION

	FRENCH NAME.	GERMAN NAME.	
1.	Zurich.	Zürich.	1351.
2.	Berne.	Bern.	1353.
3.	Lucerne.	Luzern.	1332.
4.	Uri.	Uri.	1291.
5.	Schwytz.	Schwyz.	1291.
6.	Unterwalden.	Unterwalden.	1291.
	Le haut.	Obwald.	
	Le bas.	Nidwald.	
7.	Glaris.	Glarus.	1352.
8.	Zoug.	Zug.	1352.
9.	Fribourg.	Freiburg.	1481.
10.	Soleure.	Solothurn.	1481.
11.	Bâle.	Basel.	1501.
	Ville.	Stadt.	
	Campagne.	Landschaft.	
12.	Schaffhouse.	Schaffhausen.	1501.
13.	Appenzell.	Appenzell.	1573.
	Rhodes-Extérieures.	Ausser-Rhoden.	
	Rhodes-Intérieures.	Inner-Rhoden.	
14.	St. Gall.	St. Gallen.	1803.
15.	Grisons.	Graubünden.	1803.
16.	Argovie.	Aargau.	1803.
17.	Thurgovie.	Thurgau.	1803.
18.	Tessin (*It.* Ticino).	Tessin.	1803.
19.	Vaud.	Waadt.	1803.
20.	Valais.	Wallis.	1814.
21.	Neuchâtel.	Neuenburg.	1814.
22.	Genève.	Genf.	1814.

The general principle has been followed of preserving the German names
for the first seventeen Cantons, except in the case of Graubünden, to
which the more familiar appellation of the Grisons has been given, and
urban and rural Basel have been substituted for Basel-Stadt and Basel-
Landschaft. To the eighteenth Canton, its Italian name of Ticino has
been given ; the four remaining Cantons are designated by their French
appellations, except that Geneva has been substituted for Genève.

CONTENTS

CHAPTER I

HISTORICAL SKETCH

CHAPTER II

THE SWISS CONSTITUTION

CHAPTER III

THE FEDERAL ASSEMBLY

CHAPTER IV

THE FEDERAL COUNCIL

CHAPTER V

THE FEDERAL TRIBUNAL

CHAPTER VI

REFERENDUM AND INITIATIVE

CHAPTER VII

POLITICAL PARTIES

CHAPTER VIII

THE COMMUNES

CHAPTER IX

THE CANTONS

CHAPTER X

CANTONAL TRIBUNALS

CHAPTER XI

THE ARMY

CHAPTER XII

RELIGION

CHAPTER I

HISTORICAL SKETCH

It is not proposed in this work to give a detailed account of Swiss history from the earliest times; we shall rather confine our remarks to the seven phases through which the Confederation has passed from the time of its origin in three small communities in 1291 down to the Constitutions of 1848 and 1874.[1]

The seven phases are :—

1. The League of three Communities, *i.e.* the men of the Valley of Uri, the Community of Schwyz, and the Mountaineers of the Lower Valley, which subsequently became part of the Canton of Unterwalden (1291).[2]

2. The Confederation of eight Cantons (1353).

---

[1] See particularly, for much of the information in this chapter, the second part of the late Dr. Dubs's valuable book, treating of the public law of the Swiss Confederation (*Das Oeffentliche Recht der Schweizerischen Eidgenossenschaft*), Droz's *Instruction Civique*, and Magnenat's *Abrégé de l'Histoire de la Suisse.*

[2] The plateau of Urseren, belonging then to the Abbey of Dissentis, became later part of Uri. The so-called Upper Valley became the other part of the Canton of Unterwalden. The two valleys took the names of Obwald and Nidwald, *i.e.* above and below the forest which formed the boundary between them. Towards the end of the fourteenth century they were definitively divided into two States, or half-Cantons. In their Constitutions they are called Unterwalden ob dem Wald and Unterwalden nid dem Wald.

3. The Confederation of thirteen Cantons (1513).
4. The Helvetic Republic (1798).
5. The Act of Mediation, with nineteen Cantons (1803).
6. The Federal Pact, with twenty-two Cantons (1815).
7. The Federal Constitution of 1848, which was revised in 1874.

It is particularly to be borne in mind that the League formed in 1291 was solely German, and that by degrees more German districts joined the first Confederates. It was only in 1803 that the Rhoetian Leagues (Graubünden or the Grisons), where the language was Romansch or Ladin, Italian-speaking Ticino, and French-speaking Vaud, actually became members of the Confederation.

In the earlier times, much of what later became Switzerland formed part of the Holy Roman Empire, and those deemed themselves fortunate who depended directly upon the Emperor, and not indirectly through intermediate lords. The rise in the 13th century of the Habsburgs, a noble family of Aargau, originally of no particular importance, though subsequently destined to become the imperial Austrian House, is well known, and they ruled over much territory in the name of the Emperor. Rudolf of Habsburg was eventually raised to the imperial throne in 1273. Upon his death in July 1291 a short period of anarchy ensued in the Empire.

It was then that the three communities above mentioned felt the necessity of joining closer together in order to defend their common interests. Hence the origin of that Pact which was concluded between them on the 1st August 1291, and which constituted the germ of the Swiss Confederation.

The men of Uri were mostly serfs of the German Crown; the majority of those from Schwyz were freemen, with a few serfs belonging to monasteries and nobles; and most of the Nidwald men were serfs of similar dependence, the freemen being there in the minority. The Pact was termed a perpetual Alliance, and by it the Confederates (called Eidgenossen because they bound themselves together as comrades by oath) did not pretend to throw off their allegiance to the Emperor or to those nobles who possessed land or rights in their territories; their hostility was directed against the despotic power exercised over them by bailiffs or middlemen, and they swore to sacrifice everything in order to remain free, and to afford assistance to each other against all who should do violence or injury to the persons or goods of any of them. The Alliance was in fact a sort of mutual assurance society, at first purely defensive, as each community reserved to itself the right of self-government. The dependence upon the Empire continued, but it was gradually shaken off as the League grew in dimensions and strength. It was only nominal by the end of the fifteenth century, and was finally abolished by the Peace of Westphalia in 1648.

This, then, was the first phase of the Confederation, consisting of what were called the three Forest States, and to this period belongs the legend of William Tell.[1]

Later, on the night of the 17th November 1307, in the little field of Grütli situated below Seelisberg, on the

---

[1] Legend we fear it must be called, although there may well have been some patriot who rose against some oppressor in the shape of an Austrian bailiff. Still the real tradition seems to have come from the far North. We once asked a well-known figure in Bernese society, now no more, whether the hero of Schiller had ever existed. "Not in Switzerland," was the answer. "If you travel in the Hasli district (Meyringen, etc.), you will find a distinct race of men who are of Scandinavian origin, and I believe that their ancestors brought the legend with them."

shore of the Lake of Luzern, it is recounted that Werner Stauffacher of Schwyz, Walter Fürst of Uri, and Arnold of the Melchthal in Unterwalden, each with ten companions, assembled together and took a solemn oath to deliver their soil from the oppressors, and to recover their ancient rights. They were to be "all for each, and each for all."

It was not, however, until several years had passed that the Confederates were called upon to vindicate their oath and to defend their country. In November 1315 Leopold of Austria marched into Switzerland an army of cavalry containing many powerful nobles, and of infantry drawn from cities and towns.[1] On the 15th they reached a defile, above which, upon the heights of Morgarten in Zug, the peasant soldiers were posted. The latter hurled down stones and trunks of trees upon their opponents, throwing them into confusion, and then, descending from the heights, completely routed them.

Some weeks afterwards deputies from Uri, Schwyz, and Unterwalden assembled at Brunnen, on the Lake of Luzern, and on the 9th December concluded a fresh Treaty of perpetual Alliance. One Article declared that whoever had a lord must obey him in what was just and right, but never against the Confederates. By other Articles it was laid down that no one of the confederated States should engage itself to a lord without the consent of the others ; that every external negotiation was to be conducted and terminated in concert ; that all disputes between Confederates should be decided amicably, or according to right ; and that they would assist each other for ever in all matters, internal and external.

---

[1] Zürich, Winterthur, Zug, Luzern, Sempach, and the towns of Aargau, furnished the infantry.

against all outsiders. The sovereignty of the German Empire was, however, acknowledged.

In 1332 Luzern joined the Alliance of the three communities, and thus the League was increased to four Forest States (Vierwaldstätten), the new member being a city.

Bern and Zürich had now, with other cities and towns, become imperial fiefs, and the growing power of the former excited the jealousy of many nobles towards the West. In June 1339 a considerable force laid siege to Laupen in its territory, but on the 21st of that month it was completely routed by the Bernese and their allies under Rudolf von Erlach, and a death-blow was dealt to the feudal nobility of Western Helvetia.

In 1351 the imperial city of Zürich, which had been engaged in hostilities with Austria, joined the Alliance of the four Forest States, who found in it a wall of defence against the Austrians, a market for their material wants, and an important political centre.

In 1352 Glarus and Zug were freed from Austrian rule, and were included in the Alliance, and in 1353 the city of Bern was added to the League, the Confederation thus attaining its second phase of eight States.[1] The sovereignty of each member of the Confederation within its particular limits had now become more clearly defined, while collective interests led to political Acts concluded by the allies in common.

Three such Acts, of material importance, occur in the earlier history of Switzerland :—

1. The Priests' Charter (1370).
2. The Convention of Sempach (1393).
3. The Convention of Stanz (1481).

[1] The word "Canton" had not yet been introduced. But "Canton" and "State" are words used indiscriminately later.

The two latter will be mentioned in their proper chronological place. These three, together with the Pact of 1291, formed the bases of Swiss constitutional law up to the close of the eighteenth century.

The Priests' Charter (Pfaffenbrief) was so called, partly from its contents, but still more from the facts which occasioned it.

The Provost of the Grand-Moûtier or collegial church of Zürich had, in consequence of a personal quarrel, made a sudden attack upon the Avoyer of Luzern, and taken him prisoner. This was an offence against the sovereignty of Luzern, and it was proposed to adopt certain general measures to prevent the recurrence of a similar complication. The Confederates (except Bern and Glarus) therefore concluded a Convention which has gone by the above name, and which contained provisions for protecting the peace of the country, threatened equally by ecclesiastics and laymen. This document is especially remarkable for having introduced the principle of the majority as regards the adoption of new Articles.

In 1386 more fighting ensued, and on the 9th July the army of Leopold of Austria (nephew to the Leopold who was defeated at Morgarten) was routed by the Confederates at Sempach in Luzern, and he himself was killed.[1]

Again, on the 9th April 1388, the Austrians were defeated at Näfels in Glarus by men of that Canton, assisted by some Schwyzers.

---

[1] This victory was attributed to the prowess of a certain Arnold of Winkelried, who, as the legend runs, rushed to the front in the thick of the battle when his countrymen were being worsted, and seizing a number of the enemy's lances, gathered their points and pressed them against his breast, thus opening a way for the Swiss and turning defeat into victory by the sacrifice of his own life.

In 1393 the deputies of the eight confederate States and those of Solothurn, a city allied to Bern, were assembled at Zürich, and there drew up and signed a document whereby the Federal sovereignty was further strengthened. This was called the " Convenant " or Convention of Sempach. It contained a prohibition directed against waging war unnecessarily, together with stipulations respecting military organization. Churches and convents were to be respected. But the enemy could be pursued even into churches. Women were not to be proceeded against unless they acted on the offensive. Hence the Convention was sometimes called Frauenbrief, or the Women's Charter.

The victories achieved by the Confederates in the fourteenth century have caused it to be termed the heroic period of Switzerland. During the first half of the fifteenth century the Confederation increased in dimensions and influence, each State added what it could to its territory, and there was frequently serious danger of troublesome questions arising among the members of the League. Their institutions were not alike. In the three primitive Cantons all the citizens were free and had equal rights. The whole people of each Canton met together, and in their general assemblies (Landsgemeinden [1]) decided upon all important matters. In the territories of the sovereign cities, on the contrary, there were no such popular assemblies, and the burghers ruled, without consulting the opinions of the country people. This unequal situation was aggravated when in 1415, by order of the Emperor, the Confederates invaded Aargau, which belonged to the

---

[1] In the Constitution of Uri this word is spelt " Landesgemeinde " in the singular. In those of the two portions of Unterwalden and Appenzell, as well as in that of Glarus, we find invariably " Landsgemeinde," and competent Swiss authorities are in favour of the latter spelling.

Habsburgs, and annexed its territory. Most of it fell to Bern, but other parts were formed into bailiwicks, and ruled by members of the League. The Confederation thus began to possess subject territories, and, amongst others, Thurgau came under its rule in 1460, and only gained its independence in 1798.

Civil war at last broke out between Zürich, which had concluded an alliance with Austria, and the Confederates. The Federal tie was even in danger, but after a series of conflicts peace was restored in 1450.

In October 1474 the Confederates declared war against Charles the Bold of Burgundy,[1] and they defeated him, first at Grandson on the Lake of Neuchâtel, after he had taken the town by treachery and put the Swiss garrison to death, then at Morat,[2] and finally, on the 5th January 1477, before the walls of Nancy, which was defended by René, Duke of Lorraine, assisted by 8000 Confederates. Charles himself was among the slain.

After these battles the Confederation was once more threatened with the danger of disruption. The unequal distribution of the booty taken at Grandson and Morat had caused much jealousy and irritation on the part of the five rural States (Länder) towards the three cities of Zürich, Bern, and Luzern, who were the remaining members of the League, and several Diets, convoked in order to allay these dissensions, served only to increase them. The dissolution of the Confederation seemed imminent. At last, thanks to the intervention of the hermit Nicholas von der Flüe, an understanding was

---

[1] The causes of this war are fully dealt with in Freeman's Essay on Charles the Bold. It is attributed to French intrigues and gold, and to Bernese diplomacy. Territorial conquest was evidently the main object in the eyes of Bern, and an eagerness for booty was developed later.

[2] Murten, in German.

effected at a Diet held in Stanz (Nidwald), where a "Convenant" or Convention was signed on the 22d December 1481. The three original Forest Cantons, with Zug and Glarus, gave up their opposition to the admission of two more cities, Freiburg and Solothurn, into the Confederation, and these latter became the ninth and tenth States.

By the Convention of Stanz the Federal sovereignty was still further increased. The admission of new States brought with it a more complete development of the Confederation, the partition of booty in war was regulated for the future, all separate alliances between confederate States were prohibited, and the maintenance of public peace was rendered more secure.

In 1501 the cities of Basel and Schaffhausen became the eleventh and twelfth States of the Confederation, and they were followed by Appenzell as thirteenth State in 1513. The territory of the latter, originally the property of the Abbey of St. Gallen, had obtained its independence at the beginning of the fifteenth century.

This was the third phase of the Confederation, which now consisted of thirteen States or Cantons. It lasted till 1798 without modification, and was marked by internal discord, religious wars, and revolts of peasants. Great numbers, too, of Swiss hired themselves out as soldiers to foreign princes, and many members of patrician families served abroad with distinction. The mercenary services, which have often been made a reproach to Switzerland, date from the period of the Burgundian War.[1]

The sixteenth century saw the rise and progress of

---

[1] No doubt the reproach was in a great degree merited. But the spectacle of some 30,000 Swiss troops mounting guard over continental thrones was not without its grandeur, and made the name of Switzerland famous in Europe. See Chapter XI.

Protestantism. Ulrich Zwingli led the van in Zürich, which became the stronghold of the new faith, and thence the Reformation spread to Bern, St. Gallen, part of Appenzell, Schaffhausen, and Basel. Blood was shed, and at the battle of Kappel in Zürich (1531) the men of that Canton were worsted by troops of the Forest States and Zug, and Zwingli was killed.

Still the reformed faith, particularly through the efforts of Bern, made much progress in the west. Geneva, which had been an episcopal city, and later had allied itself with Bern and Freiburg against the oppression of the Duke of Savoy, was delivered by troops of these States from his rule, and declared itself a Republic in 1535. It adopted in 1541 a new civil and ecclesiastical legislation, which was the work of the famous Calvin, and after the Pays de Vaud, long subject to the House of Savoy, was conquered by the Bernese in 1536, many of its citizens became Protestants.

In 1597, owing to religious dissensions, Appenzell was divided into two parts, or half-Cantons—Inner-Rhoden for the Catholics, and Ausser-Rhoden for the Protestants; and in the seventeenth century the Confederates were more and more divided amongst themselves, so that the Federal tie scarcely existed.

Bern, from being originally of less extent than its present Commune, had now become the most powerful of the Cantons. It had extended its territory on all sides: to the south, towards the Oberland and as far as the Lake of Geneva; to the west, to the Lakes of Neuchâtel and Biel, and the Jura; northwards it approached the Rhine; and to the east it touched the confines of Luzern and Unterwalden. The burghers of the city had constituted themselves into one of those close corporations, the nature of which will be explained in our chapter on the Communes; no fresh members were admitted, and the government and all official places were more and more concentrated in the hands of an ever-decreasing number of patrician families of the higher burghers in the close corporation. Similarly in Luzern, Freiburg, and Solothurn, certain families had obtained permanent rule, to the exclusion from power of the mass of the people. These four were the aristocratic Cantons. Zürich, Basel, and Schaffhausen were semi-aristocratic, the burghers having a share in the elections, from which the country people were excluded. The remaining six States out of the thirteen then forming the Confederation were democratic,[1] ruling themselves in the Landsgemeinden.

There were, besides, associated and protected States, and the subject territories of more or less extent belonging to one or more of the Cantons had increased to about twenty in number.

The relations of the associated States (zugewandte Orte) to the Cantons were various. The Valais and the Grisons were democratic Republics; Geneva, Biel, Mülhausen, and the town of St. Gallen were aristocratic Republics; whilst the Principality of Neuchâtel, then belonging to the King of Prussia, the Abbey of St. Gallen, and the Bishopric of Basel were ruled by real lay or ecclesiastical Sovereigns.

The protected States (schutzverwandte) were the domains of the Abbey of Engelberg (Unterwalden), and the diminutive Republic of Gersau on the Lake of Luzern.

From an early date the legislative authority of the Confederation had been in the hands of Diets (Tagsatzungen). Originally the right to convoke what was

---

[1] We use this word in the *Swiss* sense.

called the Federal Sessions—that is, to fix the day (Tag) for assembling to discuss general matters—belonged to each State, and the place of meeting was mentioned in the letter of invitation, or left to the choice of the State which convoked the Diet. The deputies of the States, having met together, communicated to each other their instructions, and sometimes they merely assembled to hear and refer to their governments (*ad audiendum et referendum*), so that the matter to be discussed had to be postponed to a further Session.

This mode of procedure remained essentially unchanged during the epoch of the ancient Confederation. Little by little the meetings came to be held at fixed periods, and the invitations generally proceeded from Zürich, which, as the first in order of rank, was called the Vorort, or directing Canton. It convoked and directed the Diets, transmitted to the Cantons the matters which concerned them, and served as intermediary with foreign States, but it had no power and no initiative. Previous to the Reformation these assemblies generally met at Zürich, but after that event there were for a long time separate Diets for the Catholic and the Protestant Cantons, deputies of the former meeting at Luzern and of the latter at Aarau.

The essential attributes of the Diets were foreign affairs, war, and inter-cantonal disputes and differences, but their authority was, if not entirely at least nearly, annulled by the fact that the Cantons were themselves sovereign at home, and the deputies could only act according to their instructions.

The neighbouring States, especially France, exercised considerable influence upon political affairs in Switzerland during the eighteenth century. Louis XVI concluded a defensive Alliance with the thirteen Cantons in

1777, had many Swiss mercenaries in his service, and his Envoys possessed, up to the Revolution of 1789, great power of action in the Diets and in cantonal matters.

The internal state of the Cantons clearly showed the need of reforms upon all sides. Zürich, Bern, and Basel, though possessing skilful administrations, were often ruled tyrannically, and many abuses were prevalent in the democratic States. The subject territories had particularly to complain of the arbitrary conduct of the bailiffs, who in general seemed only bent upon enriching themselves as quickly as possible, by whatever means. Penal legislation was particularly severe in all parts of the country. Meanwhile, commerce and agriculture became somewhat developed, and trade flourished in Zürich, Basel, and Geneva, and in the mountainous portion of Neuchâtel, where watch-making was introduced. Also, a number of illustrious men testified to the intellectual development of the country.

The striking inequalities, however, which existed between the inhabitants of town and country, and between the bailiwicks and the sovereign States, only required the impetus imparted by the breaking out of the French Revolution to produce an uprising among those who were in fact subjects and not citizens. Then came the intervention of France, and in January 1798, the Pays de Vaud having declared its independence, a French army entered its territory to assist it against the Bernese ; in other parts of Switzerland revolutionary outbreaks occurred, and whilst under Colonel von Graffenried Bernese troops defeated the French at Neueneck (Bern), where an obelisk now marks the spot, another body of French, commanded by the Alsatian General Schauenburg, routed the Bernese under General von Erlach at Fraubrunnen and Grauholz. The neighbouring city of Bern was then taken, and the ancient Swiss Confederation came to an end.

Up to 1798 there had been simply alliances between different Cantons, and no real Federal Constitution existed. The establishment of the Helvetic Republic, one and indivisible, was the first attempt at a Constitution and the fourth phase of the Confederation. It was imposed upon Switzerland by foreign pressure, and offended against all the traditions of that country; the Cantons, from sovereign States, became nothing more than Prefectures, or simple administrative districts.

Some were cut up and divided; others, again, were united into one. The whole country was torn by two hostile factions, who were continually in dispute; the minority consisted of Centralizers, who wished to preserve the Republic, one and indivisible, and to lodge the supreme legislative authority in one central power, and the majority was composed of Federalists, who demanded a return to that Federal form which existed previous to 1798 and under which the Cantons were sovereign.

At last Bonaparte summoned deputies of both parties to Paris, and after long consultation with them he gave to Switzerland, on the 2d February 1803, a new Constitution termed the Act of Mediation. Old names were restored, and in some cases what had been subject lands were incorporated in the League, which now consisted of nineteen Cantons, each having a separate Constitution. The additional six were: St. Gallen, the Grisons, Aargau, Thurgau, Ticino, and Vaud. This was the fifth phase of the Confederation.

A Diet was created, there being one deputy to each Canton, but still with limited powers, for he could only vote according to his instructions. The nineteen deputies had, however, between them twenty-five votes, because

every deputy who represented a Canton with more than
100,000 inhabitants possessed two votes, and there were
six of these Cantons.   The Diet met once a year in June,
by turns at Zürich, Bern, Luzern, Freiburg, Solothurn,
and Basel, the Cantons of which these were the capitals
becoming successively directing Cantons.   Three were
Catholic and three Protestant.   The head of the directing
Canton for the time being was Landammann of Switzerland and President of the Diet.

The Act of Mediation was not acceptable to all
parties, and before Switzerland could become entirely
independent there was to be one more foreign intervention.   The fall of the Emperor Napoleon brought with it
the destruction of his work in that country, the neutrality
and independence of which were recognized by the Congress of Vienna, though upon condition of the maintenance in the Confederation of the new Cantons; and in
1814 the Valais (a Republic allied to the Confederation
from the Middle Ages till 1798), Neuchâtel (which, from
being subject to the King of Prussia, had been bestowed
by Napoleon upon Marshal Berthier), and Geneva (which
had been annexed to France under the Directory in
1798, but was now independent and rendered more
compact by the addition of some territory belonging to
France and Savoy) were added to the existing Cantons.
Finally, the perpetual neutrality of Switzerland and the
inviolability of her territory were guaranteed by Austria,
Great Britain, Portugal, Prussia, and Russia, in an Act
signed at Paris on the 20th November 1815.   Neuchâtel,
however, only really gained its independence in 1857,
when it ceased to be a Prussian Principality.

The Confederation now consisted of twenty-two
Cantons, and a Federal Pact, drawn up at Zürich by the
Diet in 1815, and accepted by the Congress of Vienna,

took the place of the Act of Mediation, and remained in force till 1848. It was in some respects a return to the state of things previous to the French Revolution, and restored to the Cantons a large portion of their former sovereignty. But the Federal tie was firmly maintained. There was a Diet for general affairs, and deputies from each Canton assembled at one of the three (instead of six) directing Cantons, viz. Zürich, Bern, and Luzern, but they could still only vote according to their instructions. Each Canton had one vote. This was the sixth phase of the Confederation.

Then came an epoch of agitation and discord. The Confederation suffered from a fundamental vice, *i.e.* the powerlessness of the central authority. The Cantons had become too independent, and gave to their deputies instructions differing widely from each other.

The fall of the Bourbons in 1830 had its echo in Switzerland, the patricians of Bern and the aristocratic class in other Cantons lost the ascendency which they had gradually recovered since the beginning of the century, and the power of the people was greatly increased. In several months twelve Cantons, among which were Luzern and Freiburg, modified their Constitutions in a democratic sense, some peaceably, others by revolution. Most of the new Constitutions consecrated the principle of the sovereignty of the people, and of the civil and political equality of the citizens. In Basel the refusal to grant to the country people proportional representation ended in bloodshed, and the separation into two States, or half-Cantons—one urban, comprising the city, and the other rural, comprising the country[1] (1833). Between 1830 and 1847 there were in all twenty-seven revisions of cantonal Constitutions.

[1] Basel-Stadt and Basel-Landschaft.

To political disputes religious troubles were added. In Aargau the Constitution of 1831, whereby the Grand Council was made to consist of two hundred members, half being Protestants and half Catholics, was revised in 1840, and by the new Constitution the members were no longer to be chosen with any reference to creed, but upon the basis of wide popular representation, thus giving a numerical advantage to the Protestants. Discontent arose among the Catholics, and eventually some two thousand peasants of that faith took up arms, but were beaten by Protestants of Aargau at Villmergen in January 1841, and the consequence was the suppression of the eight convents in that Canton, and the confiscation of their most valuable property. This measure was generally considered to be a violation of the Federal Pact of 1815, the 12th Article of which guaranteed the existence of convents and chapters, and although the four convents of women were afterwards re-established, the whole matter was destined to lead to very serious consequences.

A first result of the suppression of these convents was the fall of the Liberal government of Luzern, and the advent to power of the chiefs of the Ultramontane party in that Canton. Two years later, the new government convoked delegates of the Catholic Cantons at Rothen, near Luzern, and there, in secret conferences, and under the pretext that religion was in danger, the bases of a separate League or Sonderbund were laid, embracing the four Forest Cantons, Zug, and Freiburg. Subsequently the Valais joined the League, which was clearly a violation not only of the letter but also of the spirit of the Federal Pact.

In 1844 the Grand Council of Luzern voted in favour of the Jesuits' appeal to be entrusted with the direction of superior public education, and this led to hostilities between the Liberal and Ultramontane parties. Bands of volunteers attacked Luzern and were defeated, the expulsion of the Jesuits became a burning question, and finally, when the ordinary Diet assembled at Bern in July 1847, the Sonderbund Cantons declared their intention of persevering in their separate alliance until the other Cantons had decreed the re-establishment of the Aargau convents, abandoned the question of the Jesuits, and renounced all modifications of the Pact. These conditions could evidently not be accepted. It was reported that Unterwalden had begun to erect fortifications at the Brünig Pass, and Uri at the Susten Pass, whilst munitions of war were crossing Ticino for the use of the seven Cantons.

These matters were referred to a committee of the Diet, consisting of the following seven members: Ochsenbein (Bern), Furrer (Zürich), Munzinger (Solothurn), Näff (St. Gallen), Kern (Thurgau), Luvini (Ticino), and Druey (Vaud). This committee considered its powers to be general, and to include all matters relating to the Sonderbund, and it lasted till the refractory Cantons were reduced to submission.

On the 4th November 1847, after the deputies of the Sonderbund had left the Diet, this League was declared to be dissolved, and hostilities broke out between the two contending parties. A short and decisive campaign of twenty-five days ensued, Freiburg was taken by the Federal troops under General Dufour, later Luzern opened its gates, the small Cantons and the Valais capitulated, and the strife came to an end.

Although a question relating to the Jesuits was the pretext, and the Protestant Cantons alleged their fear of the influence of that order upon the education of the youth of Luzern, who would later play a considerable part in the public affairs of Switzerland, there was no doubt a strong and very natural desire on the part of a number of Cantons to obtain a revision of the Federal Pact, which no longer suited the new cantonal Constitutions, modified as they now were in a democratic direction. It is easy to understand, moreover, that the larger Cantons wished to have a greater voice in Federal affairs than those of small dimensions.

As soon as the Sonderbund was dissolved, it became necessary to proceed to the revision of the Federal Pact. Opinions necessarily varied as to the manner in which this should be effected, and four different groups were formed. These consisted of :—

1. Partisans of the maintenance of the *status quo*, who were to be found only in the Canton of Neuchâtel.
2. Partisans of a moderate reform of the Pact of 1815, the bases being preserved, and no representation entrusted to the people. Amongst the leaders of this group, Furrer, Näff, and Munzinger should be particularly mentioned.
3. Partisans of a return to the Act of Mediation. The leader of this group was Casimir Pfyffer of Luzern.
4. Partisans of a complete change, with the Constitution of the United States as a model. This opinion was prevalent in French Switzerland, under the leadership of Druey of Vaud and Fazy of Geneva.

On the 17th February 1848 the task of drawing up a Constitution was confided to a committee of fourteen members, the reporters being Druey and Kern, and the work was finished by the 8th April. The project was submitted to the Cantons, and accepted at once by thirteen and a half; others joined during the summer, and the new Constitution was finally promulgated with the assent of all on the 12th September.

Hence arose the seventh and last phase of the Confederation, by the adoption of a Federal Constitution for the whole of Switzerland, being the first which was entirely the work of Swiss, without any foreign influence, although its authors had studied that of the United States; they were at the same time wise enough to understand that, in their peculiar country, the details must be worked out differently,[1] and they accomplished their arduous task with much success. The new Constitution, as M. Droz well remarks, gave to the Confederation the force which it required, on the one side to maintain order at home, and on the other to represent and defend its common interests with respect to other nations. Two legislative Chambers were for the first time created : the National Council, to which deputies were elected proportionally to the population, thus favouring the larger Cantons and representing the Swiss people as a whole ; and the Council of the States, which resembled the American Senate, each Canton, large or small, contributing two members. The two Chambers constituted the Federal Assembly, and an executive power was created, called the Federal Council. It consisted of seven members, like the committee appointed at the time of the Sonderbund, and five out of the seven became members of it. Dr. Kern, who for so many years worthily represented Switzerland in Paris, was replaced by Colonel Frei-Herosée of Aargau, and M.

---

[1] See Chapter XIX.

Luvini by M. Franscini, also from Ticino. Of the seven original members General Ochsenbein alone survives.

By the Constitution of 1848 the right was reserved to the Confederation of disposing of the troops for the maintenance of internal order and national independence. A great benefit was conferred upon the nation by the unification of such matters as coinage, weights and measures, and posts, all of which came under the control of the Confederation. The Cantons surrendered to it the exclusive right to levy duties at the frontiers of the country, and the monopoly of fabricating war-powder, and they abolished numerous internal dues and tolls, receiving certain indemnities in return.

It was clear that there must now be one Federal capital, and Bern was chosen. It became the seat of the two Chambers, and of the Federal Council.

The Constitution of 1848 was evidently constructed with a view of satisfying both elements, cantonal and national. It was essentially a work of compromise, and the central power created by it naturally resulted in a diminution of the sovereignty of the Cantons, rendering them less independent individually, whilst they evidently gained in compactness so far as their external relations were concerned.

It was natural that, as in process of time commerce and industry were developed, and as the differences between the legislation of the various Cantons became more apparent, a revision of the first really Swiss Constitution should be found necessary. This was proposed both in 1871 and 1872, but the partisans of a further centralization, though successful in the Chambers, were defeated upon an appeal to the popular vote on the 12th May 1872, by a majority of between five and six thousand, and by thirteen Cantons to nine.

The question was, however, by no means settled, and in 1874 a new project of revision, more acceptable to the partisans of cantonal independence, was adopted by the people, the numbers being 340,199 to 198,013. The Cantons were about two to one in favour of the revision, $14\frac{1}{2}$ declaring for and $7\frac{1}{2}$ against it.

This Constitution bears date the 29th May 1874, and has since been added to and altered in certain particulars.

In concluding this historical sketch we may remark that the Swiss Constitution, as at present existing, fulfils the two conditions which Professor Dicey, in his Lectures introductory to the study of the Law of the Constitution, lays down as essential to the formation of a Federal State.[1]

There must exist, he says, in the first place, a body of countries such as the Cantons of Switzerland, the Colonies of America, or the Provinces of Canada, so closely connected by locality, by history, by race, or the like, as to be capable of bearing, in the eyes of their inhabitants, an impress of common nationality. It will also be generally found that lands which now form part of a Federal State were at some stage of their existence bound together by close alliance or by subjection to a common Sovereign. It were going further than facts warrant to assert that this earlier connection is essential to the formation of a Federal State. But it is certain that where Federalism flourishes, it is in general the slowly-matured fruit of some earlier and looser connection.

With regard to Switzerland, we have seen that this condition is amply fulfilled. In 1291 three small communities, closely connected by locality, race, and other

[1] Pp. 128-130. Second edition.

ties, entered into what was termed a perpetual Alliance, and the Confederation of to-day is the slowly-matured fruit of this earlier connection.

A second condition, which Professor Dicey declares to be absolutely essential to the founding of a Federal system, is the existence of a very peculiar state of sentiment among the inhabitants of the countries which it is proposed to unite. They must desire union, and must not desire unity. If there be no desire to unite, there is clearly no basis for Federalism. If, on the other hand, there be a desire for unity, the wish will naturally find its satisfaction, not under a Federal but under an " unitarian," *i.e.* a centralized Constitution. The phase of sentiment, in short, which forms a necessary condition for the formation of a Federal State is that the people should wish to form for many purposes a single nation, yet should not wish to surrender the individual existence of each man's State or Canton. One may perhaps go a little further and say that a Federal government will hardly be formed unless many of the inhabitants of the separate States feel stronger allegiance to their own State than to the Federal State represented by the common government.

Here again Switzerland fulfils the second condition explained by Professor Dicey. The Swiss Cantons, whilst desiring union, do not desire that unity which would lead to the habitual exercise of supreme legislative authority by one central power, such as is found in the British Parliament. The Helvetic Republic, one and indivisible, only lasted from 1798 to 1803. It is certain that at the time of the Sonderbund civil war in 1847 the citizens of Roman Catholic Luzern felt far keener loyalty to their Canton than to the Confederation, and that the same thing held true, perhaps in a less degree, of the men of Protestant Zürich or Bern. The two feelings in a Federal State are no doubt to a certain extent inconsistent, but they must co‑exist. There must be a desire for national union, and at the same time there must be a determination to maintain the independence of each man's separate State.

CHAPTER II

THE SWISS CONSTITUTION

THE internal history of Switzerland clearly shows the
existence of a double sovereignty [1] in the Confederation,
the one Federal and the other cantonal, and instances
abound of their frequent opposition to each other.   The
Swiss Confederation is an agglomeration of Cantons,
containing a medley of races, tongues, sects, and creeds,
within a comparatively small area.   Each of these
Cantons may boast to its heart's content of its sovereignty, but even when the Confederation consisted of
only three small communities in Uri, Schwyz, and
Unterwalden, there was an innate feeling in them that
where it was a question of mutual defence against foreign
foes, each would have to give up something of its
independent action for the common weal.   And so it has
been ever since.   Whenever the Federal tie has been
weakened, the Confederation has been in danger of
falling to pieces.   The two sovereignties must be co-
existing, and the great question is how to balance them
against each other in such a way as to prevent any undue
preponderance of either.   Hence the executive govern-

---

[1] Jurists may consider the term "double sovereignty" to be somewhat inaccurate, on the ground that there can in no State be more than
one sovereign or supreme power.   But it is the term consecrated by
universal usage in Switzerland, and cannot well be replaced by any other.

ment, or Federal Council, established since 1848, is perpetually seeking to effect such compromises on the various questions of the day as will not trench too much upon either sovereignty.

There are times indeed when, for a brief space, the Federal instinct seems almost to extinguish the cantonal. This is eminently the case with regard to external matters. We have high authority for stating that never has the flame of patriotism burnt more brightly than now, and never has there been a more determined feeling to preserve that neutrality which has been guaranteed to Switzerland by the Powers, and which her sons will, should necessity unfortunately arise, undoubtedly fight to the last to maintain. An attack from without, by whatever neighbour, would assuredly cause the Cantons to sink all their local differences at once. Catholics would join with Protestants, German Swiss would fight side by side with French Swiss, Ticino from the south and Schaffhausen from the north would join hands, Zürich and Bern would forget their rivalry, and radical Neuchâtel would fraternise with ultramontane Freiburg.

Again, upon public occasions where all the Cantons are represented, such as the Federal Rifle Meeting, the gala day of an Exhibition, or the inauguration of a public building, a stranger, witnessing the unanimity of feeling, the cordial greetings, the affectionate manner in which each orator addresses his " Dear friends " and " Dear Confederates," would be led to believe that no more united country than Switzerland could exist in the world. When, however, such festive gatherings as above mentioned are over, when the Confederates have drunk their last glass together, when they have bid adieu to each other and have returned home, each to his Canton, the old jealousy breaks out, the interests of the particular

Canton become once more predominant, and the national sentiment of yesterday is no longer apparent. We do not, in these remarks, at all pretend to argue that the mutual jealousy of Cantons is hurtful. On the contrary, it may be affirmed that this feeling infuses additional life and vigour into the component parts, and encourages a healthy emulation and rivalry amongst them, so that Switzerland is materially stronger as a Confederation of Cantons than if she were a centralized State. Still it seems clear that the tendency must be towards the latter, and, as a matter of fact, Federal laws are gradually passed, causing many anomalies to disappear in the various Cantons, their separate laws being abolished in order to give place to uniform legislation for the whole of Switzerland.

Nevertheless it is the fact that each of the two feelings exists in a very remarkable degree. There is a sturdy sentiment of cantonal rights, engendered especially by a long period of self-government; and there is also, when occasion requires, as manifested in patriotic gatherings at home, and in a firm attitude towards the outer world, that aggregate sentiment of nationality without which the Confederation would separate into its several parts and cease to exist as a whole.

It is perhaps difficult for the general reader to understand how it has come to pass that in Switzerland, exposed as she is to powerful influences tending to make union difficult, the national sentiment is yet so firmly rooted. But, notwithstanding all differences in race, language, and religion, the whole Swiss people, knowing full well that they are surrounded by powerful countries possessing mighty armies, cling the more closely to each other as a nation, and there is not one Canton which would exchange its national independence for the rule of its foreign neighbour. We have never heard, for instance, that to-day Ticino, which is Italian in language and climate, and is divided from the rest of Switzerland by a chain of lofty mountains, evinces any real desire to separate itself from the other members of the Confederation, and, giving up its present independence, become a portion of the kingdom of Italy. Nor do we believe that Schaffhausen, situated though it is on the right bank of the Rhine, ever shows any tendency to renounce its ancient traditions as a free State in order to form a minute portion of the German Empire. The very position, then, of Switzerland, in the middle of Europe, strengthens her steadfast determination to preserve that national Union, which exists in a remarkable degree throughout the length and breadth of the land, notwithstanding the variety of interests in the several Cantons of which it is composed.

Dating from the perpetual Alliance of 1291, Switzerland now counts nearly six centuries of republican government. It is therefore hardly necessary to remark that her ancient Republic differs from modern ones, such as those of France and the United States. Indeed the saying of a Swiss in authority is to be remembered: "We love our own Republic, but not the Republics of others."

The first chapter of the Federal Constitution of 1874 contains general provisions, and commences by stating that the people of the twenty-two sovereign Cantons of Switzerland therein named, united by the present Alliance, form as a whole the Swiss Confederation. Three are divided into half-Cantons. Each Canton, and also each half-Canton, is a State in itself. The official order corresponds with the historical dates of their entry into the Confederation, except that Zürich, Bern, and Luzern, after joining the League of small Cantons, were placed at the head.[1]

The object of the Confederation is declared to be to insure the independence of the country against foreign nations, to maintain internal tranquillity and order, to protect the liberty and rights of the confederated citizens, and to increase their common prosperity.

The Cantons are stated to be sovereign so far as their sovereignty is not limited by the Federal Constitution, and, as such, they exercise all rights not delegated to the Federal power. The Confederation guarantees their sovereignty within the limits aforesaid, the liberty and rights of the people, the constitutional rights of citizens, as well as the rights and powers which the people have conferred upon the authorities. The Cantons are obliged to demand from the Confederation a guarantee of their respective Constitutions, which is accorded upon condition that the same do not contain anything contrary to the stipulations of the Federal Constitution, that they insure the exercise of political rights according to republican forms,[2] and that they are accepted by the people, and capable of revision when the absolute majority of citizens demand it.

1. Matters in which the Confederation is supreme.

It has the sole right of declaring war and of concluding peace, as well as of making alliances and treaties with foreign States. It is true that *exceptionally* the Cantons preserve the right to conclude treaties with foreign States respecting matters of public economy,

---

[1] Anciently Luzern took the lead, but when Zürich entered the Confederation as an imperial city in 1351 it displaced Luzern, and two years later Bern joined the League, and obtained the second place.

[2] These may be either representative, as is the case with the greater number, or democratic, i.e. in the form of those primary and general assemblies called Landsgemeinden.

and respecting frontier and police relations, but these treaties must not contain anything contrary to the Confederation or to the rights of other Cantons. This exception is easily understood where a country surrounded by other States has a number of relations of neighbourhood which do not touch general interests, and in such cases agreements can be concluded between Cantons and frontier States, the Confederation only reserving the right of supervision.[1]

It has the control of the Army, and certain Articles regulate its organization and disposition. This subject is treated fully in Chapter XI, and it is sufficient to observe here that there is no standing Army; that no Canton or half-Canton can have more than 300 permanent troops without the authorization of the Federal power; and that in principle every Swiss citizen is bound to perform military service.

The entire postal and telegraphic system of the country (which now includes telephones as well) is completely under Federal direction, and the receipts are paid into the Federal chest.

The Confederation alone has the right of coining money, and the issue and repayment of bank-notes is under its exclusive control. It has the monopoly of the manufacture and sale of war-powder. By a recent law it has also obtained exclusive control over the manufacture and sale of spirituous liquors. It also determines the system of weights and measures. Matters relating to revenue appertain to it. It levies all import and export duties, and these form its principal receipts. The principles which are stated to govern import duties are that articles necessary for the industry

---

[1] For instance, if the Canton of Ticino concludes a treaty with Italy for furnishing salt, this does not affect the Confederation.

and agriculture of the country, and those necessary for life, should be subjected to as low a tax as possible, and that articles of luxury should pay the highest duties. Those upon exports should also be as moderate as possible.

The only direct tax which may be said to be levied by the Confederation is that for exemption from military service, but this is done in agreement with and through the Cantons, who collect the tax. Half the product goes into the Federal chest. It levies no stamp duties.

The Confederation alone can legislate upon matters involving civil capacity,[1] copyright, and bankruptcy, to which patents have since been added. It also legislates concerning measures of sanitary police with reference to epidemics of a dangerous nature.

It has the right to expel from its territory foreigners who compromise the internal or external security of Switzerland.[2] The expulsions are decreed by the Federal Council as being the executive authority of the Confederation, charged with watching over that security, and they are carried out by the proper cantonal authorities.[3]

The Confederation has also an *optional* right, which has not yet been exercised, to create, besides the existing

---

[1] On entering his twenty-first year a citizen acquires the right to bind himself by contract. There are exceptions for lunatics, spendthrifts, persons who voluntarily place themselves under guardianship, and those who are in prison.

[2] No Swiss citizen can be expelled from his native soil. A single exception was made in the case of Mgr. Mermillod. In order to expel him, he had to be regarded as a foreigner, the reason given being that, as Vicar-Apostolic of Geneva, he was the direct though unrecognized agent in Switzerland of the Holy See, which was a foreign government. It was only when, after being thus expelled, he resigned his office of Vicar-Apostolic that he was allowed to return to his native country in his quality of a Swiss citizen.

[3] See Chapter XVI.

Polytechnic School at Zürich, a Federal university and other establishments for superior education, or to subsidize them.

2. Matters in which the Cantons, not being limited by provisions in the Federal Constitution, are sovereign.

Civil law, except as regards the civil capacity of persons; the law of land and land rights; criminal law; administration of civil and criminal justice, including the organization of tribunals; cantonal and local police; the organization of the Communes; public works in general.

The organization of schools, except where the Confederation steps in by virtue of the Constitution. All primary instruction is provided by the Cantons, and it is obligatory and gratuitous in the public schools.

The general administration of justice is left in the first instance to the Cantons, but certain matters are reserved for the exclusive cognizance of the Federal Tribunal.

Although every particular alliance or treaty of a political nature is forbidden to the Cantons, they can conclude conventions with each other, called concordats, respecting matters of legislation, administration, and justice, so long as these do not contain anything contrary to the Confederation or to the rights of other Cantons.

3. Matters which, being properly within the domain of the Cantons, have been placed under the control of the Confederation.

Thus, the Confederation can order at its cost, or encourage by subsidies, public works for the benefit of the whole or of a considerable part of Switzerland. It can enforce expropriations; it has the right of supreme supervision with respect to dykes, and to forests in mountainous regions; it aids in measures for confining

torrents within proper channels, and for replanting
woods at their sources; it can make legislative enactments as to fishing and shooting.

In all these matters the Confederation does not act
directly; it is the Cantons which are charged with the
execution of what is ordained by the Confederation, and
the latter can only interfere where the former neglect or
refuse to fulfil their obligations.

Again, the legislation respecting the construction
and working of railways belongs to the Confederation.
A short account may be given here of the mode of proceeding when a concession is demanded by one or more
individuals, or by a firm or a company. The process is
the same for all railways in Swiss territory, whether confined to a single Canton or running within the limits of
more than one, and of whatever length, from the great
Swiss lines down to the railway up the Rigi and the
little funicular lines, such as those connecting Territet
with Glion, and Biel with the Kurhaus of Magglingen,
which is some 1500 feet above the town. The demand
must in the first place be addressed to the Federal
Council, with the necessary documents and information.
These are at once transmitted to the cantonal government or governments, a portion of the territory of which
it is proposed to borrow for the purpose of the line,
and negotiations take place later between cantonal representatives and the person or persons demanding the
concession, under the presidency of a delegation of the
Federal Council, including the head of the particular
department.

Similarly, when Swiss railways have to be connected
with those in neighbouring States, the Federal Council
consults with the frontier Cantons as to the stipulations
of the conventions to be concluded.

After the Federal Council has settled the terms of a concession, it sends a message, with the text of the proposed conditions, to the Federal Assembly for their consideration. If it disapproves of the concession, the message states the reasons. The Federal Assembly, with which the ultimate decision rests, can grant a concession, even if a Canton opposes it. An instance of this occurred when in 1887 the Bernese cantonal government supported the opposition of the Commune of Interlaken to a line connecting that well-known resort with Grindelwald and Lauterbrunnen, as well as to a funicular railway up to the Schynige Platte, nearly 5000 feet above Interlaken. The reason of the opposition is evident. The guides and keepers of horses and carriages in the Commune, perhaps naturally enough, dislike the making of these lines from a similar feeling to that of the English coach-proprietors, coachmen, and ostlers in the olden days when railways were first being introduced into our own country.

The Federal Assembly can also forbid the concession of any railway which might injure the military interests of the Confederation.[1]

Other articles of the Constitution are as follows :—

All Swiss are declared to be equal before the law.

Imprisonment for debt is abolished.

The freedom of establishing himself upon any point of Swiss territory is guaranteed to every Swiss citizen, upon certain conditions.

---

[1] By the Federal law of 1872 any railway company which pays a dividend of 4 per cent in a year has to give to the Federal chest £2 : 16s. per kilometre, or two-thirds of a mile. If the dividend is 5 per cent, the contribution is £4 ; if 6, it is £8 per kilometre. The purchase of Swiss railways by the Confederation has been much discussed of late, so far without any result.

Liberty of conscience and of belief is declared to be inviolable, and the free exercise of worship is guaranteed within the limits compatible with public order and decency. Other provisions relating to religious matters are treated in Chapter XII.

It is evident that the Federal sovereignty makes itself felt more or less in numerous matters throughout the Confederation, such as foreign relations, the army, public works, weights and measures, means of communication (railways, posts, telegraphs, and telephones), customs, and public instruction. But in most cases its power is limited to a general controlling supervision; the Confederation lays down the principles, and the Cantons provide for the execution of the necessary measures. Posts, telegraphs, telephones, and customs are, however, wholly administered by Federal officials.

The second chapter of the Constitution relates to the three authorities by which the Federal sovereignty is exercised. They are [1]:—

1. The Federal Assembly, or legislative authority.
2. The Federal Council, or executive authority.
3. The Federal Tribunal, or judicial authority.

The third chapter treats of the means by which the Constitution can be revised.

Revision (total or partial) can take place at any time. When one of the Chambers decrees it but the other withholds its consent, or when fifty thousand Swiss citizens having the right to vote demand revision, the question whether the Constitution shall be revised or not is submitted to the Swiss people. If the majority

[1] See Chapters III, IV, and V.

of citizens participating in this popular vote, or Referendum,[1] pronounce in the affirmative, the two Chambers are renewed in order to frame the desired measure of revision, and when this is adopted by them, the popular vote is once more taken.

The revised Federal Constitution comes into force when it has been accepted by the majority of Swiss citizens at the Referendum and by the majority of the States, the vote of a half-Canton being counted as half a vote, and the result in each Canton or half-Canton being considered as the vote of the State.

It may safely be affirmed that the present Constitution meets with general favour in Switzerland. The Roman Catholic population would no doubt be glad to be freer in their relations with their Church, but nevertheless no tendency seems to exist anywhere in the country to return to the old order of things. The Constitution of 1874 is clearly much superior to all that preceded it.

To recapitulate : up to 1798 there were only leagues between Cantons. Then came the Helvetic Republic, one and indivisible, which was created after the old Confederation had come to an end in that year, being imposed upon Switzerland by the executive directory of the French Republic, and, from its nature, only lasting for a short period, viz. till 1803. It was succeeded by Bonaparte's Act of Mediation, which in its turn disappeared with its founder, and gave way to the Federal Pact of 1815. The latter lasted till 1848.

The existing Constitution of 1874 is an improvement upon that of 1848. It is not of course perfect, any more than any other human institution. For instance, as will hereafter be seen, it does not clearly distinguish

[1] See Chapter VI.

between the executive and judicial functions in all cases, and this is particularly to be remarked with reference to certain matters in which the rights of religious bodies are concerned.

But on the whole it is popular in the country. Those who favour centralization regard it as a station on their road, whilst the Federalists consider it to be a wall against the encroachments of centralization. Still it seems certain, as already indicated, that more power must come gradually into the hands of the Confederation. The diversity of legislation in different Cantons is clearly productive of much inconvenience and even confusion, and besides the Federal laws passed since 1874, others destined to effect uniformity in regard to bankruptcy, to criminal matters by means of a code of universal application, and to other subjects of a general character, are either being discussed in the Chambers, or are in contemplation.

CHAPTER III

THE FEDERAL ASSEMBLY

THE two political powers by which the Federal sovereignty is exercised are the Federal Assembly and the Federal Council. By the Constitution of 1874 the supreme authority of the Swiss Confederation is vested in the former, subject to the rights of the people and the Cantons, acting through the Referendum, or popular vote, whether taken with regard to laws and resolutions affecting the whole Confederation, or to the revision of the Constitution. The Federal Council is elected by the Federal Assembly, and, as will be seen in the next chapter, is in the nature of an executive committee for the management of business.

The Federal Assembly consists of two Chambers, viz. the National Council and the Council of the States. The former emanates from the people, the latter from the Cantons, and together they represent the double sovereignty existing in Switzerland. In general they sit separately, but for some special purposes they deliberate in common.

Each Chamber originally met in ordinary session only once a year. But as business increased it was found necessary to have a winter as well as a summer session and in December 1863 it was decided that there should in general be a second session in that month by way of continuation of the ordinary annual one. Again, in December 1873 it was fixed that the Chambers should assemble on the first Monday in June for the first, and on the first Monday in December for the second portion of the ordinary session, and these dates are still rigidly observed. If there is much unfinished business at the close of either portion, the Assembly is adjourned, and an extraordinary session is held in spring or autumn.

The National Council is composed of deputies of the Swiss people, each 20,000 of the whole population electing one member. Fractions above 10,000 are counted as 20,000. The members are the representatives of electoral districts created by Federal legislation within cantonal limits, so that inhabitants of no two Cantons can vote together in the election of any one deputy. Each Canton, and in the three divided Cantons each half-Canton, elects at least one deputy, and the whole Chamber consists at present of 145, apportioned amongst 49 electoral districts. The number of members in a Canton varies from one returned in one district, as in Uri, etc., to twenty-seven returned by Bern in six districts. The basis of representation is fixed according to the Federal census, which usually takes place every ten years. But the present arrangement of districts having given rise to a good deal of discontent and to much discussion in the Chambers, the last census was taken in December 1888 (instead of in 1890), and it is to be hoped that a new law will be adopted including a more satisfactory arrangement than exists at present.

Every Swiss, not otherwise disqualified, is entitled on attaining his twenty-first year to as many votes as there are members for his electoral district, and every lay Swiss who can vote is eligible for the National Council.

Ecclesiastics, although electors, are not eligible for that Chamber. The reason alleged is the fear of acrimonious discussion of a religious nature becoming prevalent in the Chamber and occupying time which ought to be given to political matters and to those of general interest. But this exclusion only applies in reality to Catholics. With them, once a priest always a priest is the rule, whereas in Switzerland Protestant ecclesiastics can, by renouncing their profession, become deputies.[1]

The National Council is elected by ballot for three years, and is renewed integrally on the last October Sunday of the triennial period. It is only in case of a revision of the Constitution that an extraordinary integral renewal of the two Chambers can take place. There are registers in each Commune in which every citizen having a vote must be inscribed. These registers are on view at least two weeks before the day of election, and are closed, at the earliest, three days previous to it.

The process of voting is entirely in the hands of the Cantons, and differs considerably. In one Canton a card from the Commune where each voter is registered is left at his house; in another he has to present himself at the proper office in order to obtain his card, and so on. The place of voting is very often a church.

Candidates must be elected by an absolute majority, *i.e.* half the voters plus one at least at the first ballot, and similarly if a second ballot is required. If a third ballot becomes necessary, the election is decided in favour

[1] In a recent case a citizen belonging to the Bernese clergy sent in his resignation as such upon being elected a member of the National Council, but only for the period during which he might retain his seat in the Chamber. So that if he loses his election in 1890 he may again be admitted to preach the Gospel.

of the candidate or candidates, as the case may be, at the top of the poll.

Upon the meeting of the Chamber, the members whose election is not contested are admitted at once ; where an election is contested, the matter is immediately examined by a committee which generally reports on the following day, and a further inquiry is seldom necessary.

The National Council chooses from among its members a president and a vice-president. During the triennial period there are four different presidents and vice-presidents. These changes give to each Canton a greater chance of being represented from time to time in the two offices. When a president goes out of office, the vice-president generally succeeds him. In voting, if there is a tie the president has the casting vote.

Each member is paid sixteen shillings out of the Federal chest for every day that he is present during the session, but if he does not answer when his name is called he loses his day's pay, unless indeed he comes in later and gives to the secretary of the Chamber a good reason for his tardiness. If, however, there is a vote necessitating a second calling of names (*appel nominal*), or if there is a count out to ascertain whether an absolute majority is present, unless he then answers to his name his day's pay is forfeited. Every member also receives travelling expenses at the rate of 20 centimes a kilometre, say about 2½d. a mile.

The composition of the National Council has changed but little of late. After the elections of 1881 loud complaints were heard that the Radicals, who were in the majority, used their power authoritatively, with small regard for the other parties, and the people proceeded to reject, from time to time, measures presented to them which had been passed by the Federal Assembly.[1] This proceeding was attributed to a desire to record their dissatisfaction with the predominant party, independently of the goodness or badness of the measures themselves. But the elections of October 1884 made hardly any difference in the composition of the new National Council. Great was the disappointment of those whose organs in the press had been loudly proclaiming that the rejection by the popular vote of a series of measures proved that the nation had lost all confidence in the Radical representatives, and who had prophesied a thorough change, which, in their opinion, would alone render useful legislation possible.

There certainly was considerable apathy shown by the mass of electors, but the fact seems clearly to be that the ordinary Swiss voter is to a certain extent indifferent as to the choice of his legislators. He is quite ready to vote again and again for the same candidates; he probably looks upon them as good men of business with a long experience of Parliamentary and Federal affairs, and he knows very well that if measures are passed of which for some reason or other he does not approve, he and his fellows can combine to reject them at the Referendum. This, however, does not prevent him from again voting for the old representatives at the next election, and he will do so, in many instances, time after time.

In October 1887, again, the elections showed that the new National Council would differ but little from its predecessor, and the numerous abstentions in some important places seemed to prove a certain lack of interest in the proceedings. But the power of rejecting all measures which are put to the popular vote is the

[1] See Chapter VI.

people's stand-by, and makes them masters of the situation when they so will.

The Council of the States is composed of forty-four deputies or members. Each Canton is equally represented, and returns two members. Zürich or Bern has thus no preponderance in this Chamber over Uri or Schwyz. In the three cases where Cantons have been split into two, each half-Canton returns but one member, so that when, as often happens in a divided Canton, the two members vote on opposite sides, the whole Canton is neutralized. For instance, the member for the Catholic portion of Appenzell will probably vote one way, and the member for the Protestant portion the other way, in religious questions. The mode of election of the deputies is determined absolutely by each Canton. In most cases they are chosen by the legislative bodies, but in some by the people, either in the Landsgemeinden or by ballot. The functions of the majority of these deputies last for a year like those of the deputies of the old Diets, others are chosen for three years like the deputies of the National Council, but the duration of their functions is left entirely in the hands of each Canton.

The Council of the States chooses from among its members a president and a vice-president in a similar manner to that of the National Council, but neither of these functionaries can be elected from among the deputies of the Canton, a deputy of which was president in the immediately preceding ordinary session. Nor can deputies of the same Canton fill the office of vice-president during two successive ordinary sessions. In voting, if there is a tie the president has the casting vote.

The deputies are paid by their Cantons, except when

they form part of committees during a recess, and then they receive an allowance out of the Federal chest.

A great proportion of the members of the Assembly are men who have held office, first in their Commune and then in their Canton. A certain number are drawn from the mercantile class. Contrary to the custom which prevailed in the Diets, the deputies in both Chambers vote without instructions from their respective Cantons, and they thus occupy a much more independent position than the members of those old assemblies. The subject of political parties is treated in Chapter VII.

The two Chambers, when deliberating together, constitute the Federal Assembly. They elect the members of the Federal Council and Federal Tribunal, the Chancellor of the Confederation,[1] and the General-in-Chief of the Federal Army in time of war; they possess the right of pardon so far as offences against Federal laws are concerned ; they have also a right of amnesty, which was exercised after the termination of the Neuchâtel Revolution in 1856, the Royalist prisoners and deserters being amnestied in 1857. They also pronounce upon conflicts of competency between Federal authorities. The provisions for revising the Federal Constitution have already been given in the previous chapter.

The matters which lie within the competency of the two Chambers, when sitting separately, include the following :—

---

[1] This functionary is head of the Federal Chancery, and countersigns the notes signed by the president of the Confederation in the name of the Federal Council. He is also head of the secretary's office in the Federal Assembly. He is elected for three years, at the same time as the Federal Council, is re-eligible for election, and has been constantly re-elected. There have been only two since 1848. His salary, including a house allowance, is £440 a year.

1. Laws as to the organization and mode of election of the Federal authorities.
2. Laws and resolutions upon matters which the Constitution places within Federal competency.
3. Salaries and indemnities for the authorities of the Confederation and the Federal Chancery.
4. Ratification of alliances and treaties with foreign States.
5. Measures for the external security as well as for the maintenance of the independence and neutrality of Switzerland; declarations of war and conclusions of peace.
6. Guarantee of each cantonal Constitution, and supreme controlling power over the Cantons respecting the due observance of Federal prescriptions.
7. Fixing the annual budget and passing the accounts.
8. A certain control over Federal administration and justice.
9. Railway concessions (see preceding chapter).
10. Examination and discussion of the annual report of the proceedings of the Federal Council.

The Chambers can, upon the interpellation or motion of any member or members, request the Federal Council to adopt a particular foreign policy. In general, discussions upon foreign affairs only occur when the annual report of the proceedings of the Federal Council is being considered by either Chamber. It is not usual to proceed to any formal decision, so that no occasion need arise for disavowing the executive power. The latter is perfectly well acquainted with the opinion of the majority of the Assembly, and will of course take due account of it.

All Federal laws, as well as resolutions of a general

nature which are not declared to be urgent, after having been passed by both Chambers, are submitted for adoption or rejection to the Referendum, if the demand is made either by thirty thousand vote-possessing citizens, or by eight Cantons. All measures accepted by the people become valid upon being published by the Federal Council. There are also Federal resolutions declared, perhaps in some instances rather arbitrarily, to be of an urgent character. These come into operation at once, and are not submitted to the popular vote. As to those which, being of a general nature and not of an urgent character, are therefore liable to the Referendum, it must be confessed that the Chambers have not been always strict in defining them. The best definition appears to be that resolutions are of a general nature when they fix permanent and obligatory rules, either for the citizens or the Cantons, but not when they are taken in special cases, as for instance with reference to a particular appeal, or for granting a subsidy, say with regard to an exhibition, a road, or works in connection with the course of a river.

Neither Chamber can hold a sitting unless those present form an absolute majority of all the members, and in each Chamber the absolute majority of members voting decides.

The right of initiative, exercised particularly as to bills and motions of various kinds, belongs to each Chamber and to each member. Thus, either Chamber can recommend to the Federal Council that it shall draw up and present a bill on a particular subject to the Federal Assembly, or a member can suggest one to his own Chamber, and if accepted it will then be referred to the Federal Council, with a request to draw up the necessary bill for the consideration of the Assembly, or the Federal Council itself presents one upon its own initiative. The Cantons can also exercise the right of initiative by correspondence. It is clearly to be understood that every bill, from whatever source it has originated, must first come into the hands of the Federal Council, and be laid before the Assembly by that body. At the beginning of each session, the business is divided between the two Chambers. When a bill is presented to them by the Federal Council, the Chamber which has first to take it up begins by appointing a committee of members to discuss its provisions, and report upon it. When the committee is unanimous, there is but one report;[1] otherwise there are reports giving the conclusions of the majority and the minority. Then comes the discussion in the Chamber, and the bill is ultimately either passed with or without amendments, or rejected. In the former case it is referred to the other Chamber, where it undergoes similar treatment. If that Chamber accepts the text as presented to it, then the bill, being adopted by the two sections of the Assembly, becomes law, and is published as such by the Federal Council in the *Feuille fédérale suisse*; subject, however, to the Referendum if duly demanded. But if the text is not accepted, then the bill is returned to the other Chamber with any amendments which may have been made, and a second, and sometimes even a third debate takes place. If the amendments are adopted, or if a compromise between the two Chambers is agreed upon, the bill, subject as aforesaid, in its new form becomes law, but if both persist in their divergent opinions it is lost. Sometimes, too, a bill is referred back to the Federal Council for reconsideration, and is subsequently laid before the Chambers in an altered form.

[1] Or one in French and another in German.

After a law, a regulation, or a resolution has been adopted by both Chambers, the Federal Council publishes it officially, stating the date when it shall come into force, if that has not been done already in the text. Generally speaking, this may be expected to be the day of publication. But for those measures which are liable to the Referendum, what is termed a *délai d'opposition* is mentioned, being a period of three months during which the right of appeal to the popular vote can be exercised. If there is no appeal, the measure comes into force after the expiration of the three months.

The separation of powers is not very strictly observed between the Federal Assembly and the Federal Council (nor, indeed, as mentioned in our chapter upon the Federal Tribunal, between the judicial authority and the two Federal political authorities). The duty of the deputies is one of control and criticism, and as they cannot be expected to be thoroughly acquainted with all the minute details of the administration, any attempt upon their part to carry out reforms in that administration must only lead to a confusion of powers. Still it would appear that there is no decision of the Federal Council which cannot be revised by the Chambers. They recommend to that body, by motions called *postulats,* such alterations or reforms as seem to them to be necessary. If the Federal Council does not assent to a particular *postulat* presented to it by one of the Chambers it makes a report to that Chamber, and if the latter insists upon its point of view then a regular proposition is drawn up, and if this is carried in both Chambers the Federal Council is bound to execute its provisions.

When it became necessary to pass a law respecting railways, and the Federal Council proposed that they should be constructed by the State, the Chambers decreed their construction by private enterprise; and, again, in the case of the law passed by the Chambers granting a monopoly to the Confederation in the manufacture and sale of spirituous liquors, they adopted quite a different principle from that originally proposed by the Federal Council. Nevertheless, in both instances, the latter accepted the measures of the Chambers as a matter of course, framed the necessary bills, and loyally executed their provisions after they had come into force.

A notable instance of a *postulat* happened with reference to the revision of the Federal Constitution. In 1869 M. Ruchonnet, then a deputy in the National Council, demanded a partial revision in order to settle the question of mixed marriages between Catholics and Protestants, a subject which had given rise to continual disputes. The motion was enlarged into a demand for a total revision, and in this shape was adopted by the Chamber. In 1872, after the proposed revision had been rejected by the people, a *postulat* voted by both Chambers requested the Federal Council to take up the matter at once, and the result was the Constitution of 1874.

From that time different *postulats,* or motions, have resulted in partial revisions, which are recorded in Chapter VI.

Numbers of such motions respecting laws and other measures upon a variety of subjects have been either adopted or rejected in one session after another.

In 1883, after *postulats* respecting emigration agencies had been presented by two private members in the two preceding years, the Federal Assembly, by a motion of a similar kind, requested the Federal Council to take the necessary steps for remedying certain abuses connected with those agencies, and to propose such legislative modifications as might be found indispensable for attaining the object in view.

Again, in 1886, the Assembly, by another *postulat*, requested the Federal Council to examine whether the Federal laws of 1880 respecting these agencies should not be revised.

The general plan with regard to a measure introducing some innovation is for the Federal Council to be requested, sometimes by means of a suggestion from itself, to present it to the Assembly rather than to take the initiative itself. It is considered that public opinion is better prepared by this mode of proceeding, and if the measure be rejected, the Federal Council need not look upon the rejection in the light of a defeat.

Both Chambers are stated to be of the same political importance, and any preponderance of the one over the other is held to depend entirely upon the capacities of individual members. We cannot, however, help thinking that in practice the National Council has more influence than the Council of the States, and Dr. Dubs observes that with few exceptions the principal political men of the Cantons had in his time come to sit in the National Council, one reason being the absence of a fixed term for these functions in the other Chamber.

It may also be remarked that when the two Chambers unite as one body for joint deliberation, the president of the National Council takes the chair, and as that Chamber contains more than three times as many members as the Council of the States, it can always out-vote the latter, because the majority of votes decides. Still there is no marked rivalry or hostility between the Chambers, so that it cannot be said that the more numerous one really overrides the other. The minority

of Roman Catholics and members of the Centre, or
moderate Liberals, in the Council of the States only help
to increase the comparatively small forces of these parties
in the National Council, and such matters, for instance,
as the nomination of Federal authorities and the decisions on appeals for pardon do not give rise to votes
in which the Chambers would be in serious opposition
to each other.

In the sittings of the Chambers each of the three
national languages can be used. It is curious to hear a
speech in German followed by another in French, or
vice versâ, and sometimes even by one in Italian; and
when a vote is taken by calling out the names, the
alternations of "*Ja*," "*Nein*," "*Oui*," and "*Non*" are
striking to a stranger. If the president is a German
Swiss he naturally speaks in German, but his remarks
are immediately repeated in French by an official at his
side, and with a president who is a French Swiss the
process is reversed. The deputies who speak Italian,
from Ticino and sometimes from the Grisons, understand French or German sufficiently not to require a
special translation into their tongue. But the laws and
resolutions are published in all three languages. The
Constitutions of 1848 and 1874 are also published in
Romansch and Ladin.

The debates are carried on with much decorum.
There is seldom a noisy sitting, even when the most
important subjects are being discussed; interruptions
are few, and scenes such as unhappily have of late
been painfully frequent in our House of Commons do
not exist. It is true that there are but 44 members
in one Chamber, and 145 in the other. But the
sittings strike a spectator as being those of men of
business, though the members are by no means devoid

of eloquence. It is worthy of note that whilst the members of the more numerous Chamber stand up to speak, those of the smaller Chamber speak from their seats. This gives a more familiar air to the proceedings of the latter, and their debates, generally speaking, are shorter than those of the National Council. They devote more time to business matters and juridical questions. Political questions are treated with a greater degree of animation in the National Council than in the calmer atmosphere of the much smaller Council of the States.

The public are generally admitted to the debates in both Chambers, and there are galleries for their accommodation.

The Chambers occupy the two wings of the Federal Palace in Bern. They meet every week - day but Monday at eight or nine o'clock in the morning according to the season, and on Monday afternoons at three. This arrangement is made in order to allow those members who wish to go home for the Sunday to leave on a Saturday afternoon and return on the following Monday. The sittings are over not later than one or two o'clock, when every one hurries off to dinner. There are seldom two sittings in the day, except at the end of a session when there is a press of business. The Federal flag floats over the building during the sittings. The sessions generally last about three weeks. During the recesses committees of one or both Chambers meet, sometimes together with one or more Federal councillors, in different parts of the country, in order to discuss subjects which are brought later before the Federal Assembly. This proceeding lightens the work of the sessions. Objection has been taken to these meetings on the score of the extra expense which they entail, but they have their advantage. They bring members of the

Federal Council and deputies of other Cantons in touch with the authorities of the Cantons in which they assemble. This tends to strengthen the Federal tie, to promote good feeling, and is a satisfaction to cantonal authorities, who feel that after all everything is not done at Bern.

CHAPTER IV

IT has been stated in the preceding chapter that the National Council is elected for a period of three years in the month of October. After the commencement of the session at Bern the following December, the two Chambers meet together and elect the seven members of the Federal Council, or executive government of the Confederation, chosen also for three years from among all Swiss citizens eligible for the National Council. Two citizens of the same Canton of origin cannot be members of the executive at the same time. It has been objected that this rule might exclude statesmen of high merit, and therefore diminish the resources of the Confederation, but in practice we doubt whether this imperfection is ever seriously felt. If, during his three years of office, any member resigns or dies, his place is filled up for the remainder of the triennial period by the Assembly at its next meeting. The majority naturally come from the more populous German Switzerland; Zürich, Bern, and Aargau have long been regularly represented, each by one member, and in the present body two others are citizens of Thurgau and Solothurn. The remaining two come from Vaud and Neuchâtel, thus representing French Switzerland. Other Cantons have had from time to time their turn. The constant, though not invariable, practice since 1848 has been for each member to be chosen out of the Assembly of which he has been elected a deputy by his own Canton. This previous election is considered to be a proof of the confidence and attachment of the voters to a fellow-citizen, and he takes his place in the executive government, holding his office indeed directly from the Assembly, but at the same time invested with popular confidence equally with the other deputies. Supplementary elections are then held in order to fill up the seats vacated by those deputies who have become Federal councillors, as they cannot, during their tenure of office as such, be deputies as well.

The president of the Confederation and the vice-president of the Federal Council are named for one year by the Federal Assembly from among the seven members of the executive. The outgoing president cannot be elected president or vice-president for the ensuing year, nor can the same member be vice-president two years running. The vice-president of one year is usually elected president of the next year. The president receives £540 and each of the other members £480 a year from the chest of the Confederation. It may seem strange that men of talent should be found to accept posts at the same time so laborious and so badly remunerated, and sceptics might even throw a doubt upon the capacity of individual members. One must perhaps have lived in the country in order to understand how this happens. When a place in the Federal Council is vacant, and has to be filled up, say, from French Switzerland, some leading man in one of the French Cantons will be picked out by general consent to be the candidate. He has most probably served his apprenticeship in the administration of his Commune and Canton, and though he may have to give up a lucrative profession which he has followed as well, his patriotism and the interests of his Canton compel him to throw it up, to leave his cantonal residence, and to settle down in Bern with a moderate income for a number of years.

The business of the Federal Council is divided among seven departments, each presided over by one of its seven members, who probably keeps his particular post for several years, and who has for his substitute, during absence, another member of the Council appointed as such by that body. According to the Constitution, the sole object of this departmental division is to facilitate the examination and despatch of business, all decisions emanating authoritatively from the Council as a whole. But now, owing to the continual increase of work, the independent authority of each member, especially in the larger departments, has greatly increased. Nevertheless, matters of importance are discussed and decided at the regular Council meetings, which are generally held twice a week. A decision is not valid unless at least four members are present, and no decision can be reversed except by four out of the seven in a sitting attended by more than four.

Up to the end of 1887 the president for the year had charge of what was called the political department, including foreign affairs. As it was found that since 1848 the business of all the departments, with the exception of the political one, had increased very considerably, particularly those of commerce and agriculture and of finance, it became evident that a reorganization was absolutely necessary, and the scheme drawn up by the Federal Council was accepted by the Chambers on trial, and came into force on the 1st January 1888. The seven departments are now thus divided:—

1. Foreign Affairs.
2. Interior.
3. Justice and Police.
4. Military.
5. Finance and Customs.
6. Industry and Agriculture.
7. Posts and Railways.

Foreign affairs are no longer in the hands of the president of the current year as such, and this is a decided advantage. The head of this department, if he remains in office for several years, as is most likely, will be better able to deal with this important subject, and the work of the foreign representatives will manifestly be thereby facilitated. The new department retains what belonged to the political department, with the exception of the former presidential functions; it is charged with the encouragement of commerce in general, with work preparatory to the negotiation of commercial treaties and co-operation in drawing up the customs tariff; also with matters relating to industrial property, copyright, and emigration. It thus embraces the majority of questions concerning the relations of Switzerland with foreign countries. The new department of industry and agriculture has a less pressure of business than that of commerce and agriculture, which it has replaced, and the work of the finance department is also lightened.

By the actual arrangement, the work of the president of the Confederation has been considerably diminished. He is of course still head of a department, which may no doubt be that of foreign affairs, though he can equally direct one of the others, such, for instance, as war or finance. But his presidential functions have been lessened by relieving him of a number of matters of mere administrative procedure, and of the duty of giving numerous audiences to foreign representatives and other persons. He still opens all correspondence addressed to the Federal Council, distributes the business among the different departments, presides at the sittings of the body, and signs the notes and other official correspondence in its name. He still receives foreign representatives on certain occasions, such as the delivery of letters from the head of their country, and the presentation of their letters of credence and recall. He also continues to take the first place, ranking before his colleagues, upon public occasions. It is thus clear that the president of the Confederation has not a tithe of the power entrusted to the president of the United States. He may, indeed, without any disrespect, be likened to the chairman of a board.

All the members have the right to speak in either Chamber, of which they avail themselves whenever their presence is required, or indeed whenever they wish to take part in the debates, but they cannot vote.

Perhaps the most remarkable sight is that which occasionally occurs when a debate arises in either Chamber upon a question where the difference of opinion of members of the Federal Council is very marked, and it has happened that two of the body have risen in succession to support dissimilar views. The debate once over, no particular friction results between the two colleagues; both victor and vanquished may spend the evening at the same café, continue their discussion amicably or not at all, and they will sit serenely together on the morrow in Cabinet Council as if nothing particular had happened.

The members of the Federal Council are re-eligible,

and in point of fact the same individuals remain in office for a number of years, notwithstanding the existence of well-known differences among themselves and between some of them and a majority in the Assembly.

There have been hitherto only two instances of a member willing to serve not being re-elected, but from time to time some naturally resign, one for a more lucrative post, another to become head of a diplomatic mission, another from a desire to retire into private life.

The Federal Council, having been elected by the Federal Assembly for three years, cannot be dissolved by that body in the interim, any more than it can itself dissolve the Assembly. It does not in any way depend upon the majority in the Assembly. Its members, each in his own department, prepare bills and resolutions either suggested by one of the Chambers, or of their own initiative, and these measures, when agreed to by the Council, or even by a majority of its members, are submitted to the Chambers, who deal with them in the manner already described.

This Council does not consist, as is the general rule in the English Cabinet, of a body of men all holding similar views. The majority at present no doubt belong politically to the Left, which party has the majority in the Chambers, but there are also some who hold more Conservative views, and amongst these one moderate Roman Catholic, who has served for many years. There is also one Old Catholic, but there has never been an Ultramontane Roman Catholic since the creation of the Council in 1848. The practical harmony between the members is secured by the minority giving way to the majority, if the whole body cannot agree among themselves to a compromise.

It will thus be seen that the election of the Federal councillors cannot accurately be termed a purely party business, nor do they represent the majority in the Assembly, otherwise they would now be all either Democrats or Radicals. There is a certain understanding, one might almost say a certain feeling of fair-play, which leads the majority in the Chambers to concede the principle that other parties should at least be represented in the executive government; and again, a Conservative vice-president, who is almost certain in any case to be elected president for the ensuing year, often succeeds to that office by an almost unanimous vote.

Collisions between the Federal Council and the Federal Assembly do not exist. If any measure proposed by the former is rejected by both Chambers, or by one, and thus does not become valid, the Federal Council, as seen in the preceding chapter, accepts the rejection; it asks for no vote of confidence, nor does anything ensue in the shape of what we should call a ministerial crisis. Similarly, there is no question of a dissolution of the Chambers when the people reject measures passed by them. The Federal authorities, whether legislative or executive, being chosen for a fixed term, remain at their posts during that term.

In 1882, a measure relating to education, which will be more particularly dealt with in Chapter XIII, and which was avowedly the work of one member of the Federal Council, had passed both Chambers with some modifications, but was nevertheless rejected when submitted to the Referendum. There was, however, no question of its author giving in his resignation, as might well have been expected by many foreigners. So far, indeed, from this being the case, an influential Swiss

newspaper, totally opposed to him in politics, remarked
that it was lucky the parliamentary system did not exist
in Switzerland, as otherwise there would have been an
immediate resignation of a capable, honest, and devoted
administrator. Nor did the Chambers for one moment
entertain the idea of a dissolution consequent upon the
people's adverse decision.

With respect to foreign affairs the Federal Council
possesses a real power, being independent of the Cantons.
It watches over the interests of the Confederation abroad,
and is entrusted generally with all that concerns foreign
relations.[1]

With respect to internal affairs, it watches over the
due observance of the provisions of the Constitution,
and of Federal laws and resolutions, and provides for
the execution of the decisions of the Federal Assembly,
of the judgments of the Federal Tribunal, and of divers
matters where disputes arise between Cantons. It has
to examine whether the articles of the various cantonal
Constitutions are in harmony or not with the principles
laid down in the Federal Constitution, and it reports
upon them to the Federal Assembly; it has also to
examine laws passed by the Cantons in order to judge
whether they are in accordance with the Federal Constitution and do not conflict with Federal laws. But
herein lies an imperfection which, we are assured, is
readily acknowledged by all sound Swiss statesmen. If
a cantonal government chooses to adopt a measure
which the Federal Council, when appealed to, considers
to be unconstitutional, and if it declines to submit to
that Council's order to cancel or revoke such measure,
the latter has no direct way of enforcing its order. If

---

[1] For the mode of proceeding in the Chambers respecting foreign
affairs, see the preceding chapter.

the Canton continues refractory, it can certainly send a special commissary to the spot to negotiate with the cantonal authorities, but should he be unable to settle the matter amicably, he becomes powerless. The Canton, however, generally gives way when the Federal Council, upon the failure of its commissary, threatens to quarter troops upon it from another Canton, thus saddling the offending Canton with a heavy expense which it is prone to avoid. So the Federal Council indirectly gets its way.

We may give the following instance of a case in point :—

On Sunday the 26th October 1884, the triennial elections for the National Council were held all over Switzerland. Immediately before the closing of the electoral registers for the district of Lugano, three days previous to the polling day, certain Conservative citizens applied to their municipality, who were of a Radical hue, to make some considerable changes in the lists. To this the municipality agreed only in part, whereupon the citizens appealed to the cantonal government of Ticino at Bellinzona, who were of their way of thinking in politics. The cantonal government considered that the changes were lawful, and ordered the municipality to make them, under a penalty of £100. This was on Saturday the 25th, the day before the elections, and the municipality, alleging that there was no time to reopen the lists, appealed to the Federal Council by telegraph against the cantonal order. The elections took place on the unaltered lists upon the following day.

The Federal Council now requested the cantonal government to submit their views, and meanwhile to suspend action against the municipality. This request was repeated several times by telegraph and in writing during the next fortnight, but the cantonal government, setting the Federal Council at defiance and declaring their perfect competency in the matter, summoned the municipality to pay the fine, and on their refusal ordered the Prefect of Lugano to take possession of a garden belonging to one of the municipal officers and have it sold by public auction.

The Federal Council thereupon despatched a member of the National Council as their commissary to Bellinzona. He was politely received, but could not alter the views of the Ticino government, and although he telegraphed to the Prefect of Lugano to stop the sale, the garden was actually sold by public auction.

The Federal Council, being informed of this, at once sent word to the cantonal government that if they persisted in their disobedience force would be resorted to, and that a battalion of Luzern troops had been ordered to hold itself in readiness to be called out at any moment, and would be sent into Ticino, where the soldiers would of course be quartered at the Canton's expense.

This threat was successful. The cantonal government, whilst still protesting against the action of the Federal Council, ordered the sale to be annulled and the amount of the fine to be remitted.

Another plan to which the Federal Council has had resort when a Canton is refractory is to keep back subsidies which are to be provided for local objects out of the chest of the Confederation, and this has been found efficacious.

Similarly, if the Federal Council has to proceed against trespassers in the case of royalties belonging to the Confederation, it can threaten to have them tried before a Federal jury convoked *ad hoc* (*i.e.* for the occasion), with all the necessary judicial apparatus. This is a very expensive procedure, and being so, the simple threat is likely to end, as in the case of the Canton, in the speedy submission of the trespassers.

Again, as the Federal Council has no means of executing the judgments of the Federal Tribunal, it is obliged to resort to cantonal machinery for the purpose, so that these judgments have in reality to be executed by the cantonal authorities. Still this does not appear to give rise to any difficulty.

Other attributions of the Federal Council consist in watching over the external and internal security of Switzerland, the maintenance of her independence and neutrality, and the preservation of tranquillity and order. It is also entrusted with the administration of the finances, it proposes the budget, and renders an account of receipts and expenditure. Besides an annual report of its proceedings, it sends frequent messages to the Assembly upon a variety of subjects for consideration and decision.

The members of the Federal Council, we will venture to affirm, yield to no other government in Europe in devotion to their country, in incessant hard work for a poor salary, and in thorough honesty and incorruptibility. A diplomatist, who knew them well and appreciated their good qualities, aptly remarked that they reminded him of a characteristic industry of their own country—of watch-making. For, having to deal with very minute and intricate affairs, their attention is unremittingly engaged by the most delicate mechanism of government, by the wheels within wheels of Federal and cantonal attributes, by the most careful balancing of relations between contending sects and Churches, and by endeavours to preserve the proper counterpoise between two (French and German), not to say three (the third being Italian) nationalities. Their task is thus essentially one of constant vigilance and careful supervision.

From what we have written in this chapter it would follow that there are three points in which the Swiss Federal Council differs from other executive governments :—

1. It is elected by the legislative Assembly and its members take part in the debates of both Chambers, but cannot be removed by the Assembly during the triennial period.

2. Although elected by the Assembly it cannot dissolve that body.

3. It is not a purely party government; it is rather an executive committee for the management of business than a real executive power such as exists in other countries.

CHAPTER V

On the 21st September 1886, the new Federal Palace of Justice was inaugurated at Lausanne in the presence of representatives of the Federal authorities, the diplomatic body, and most of the Cantons, as well as of delegates representing the law faculties and the universities.

The site is on the height of Montbenon, whence there is a charming view of the lake and of the rugged mountains on its opposite side.

Upon the steps M. Cuénoud, Syndic of Lausanne, formally handed over the building to the Federal authorities, and M. Ruchonnet, head of the Federal department of justice and police, in an eloquent speech, accepted it on the part of the Confederation. The official personages then proceeded to the large room destined for the sittings, where M. Ruchonnet, on his part, delivered the building over to the Federal Tribunal, the gift being duly acknowledged on behalf of the judicial body by its president, M. Olgiati.

The Federal Tribunal was instituted by the Constitution of 1848. Its first rudiments, according to Dr. Dubs, are to be found in the alliances of 1291 and 1315 between the three primitive Cantons, and by the latter of the two it was provided that the best and wisest should meet together, and put an end to war or discord between the Confederates, amicably or according to right. But when Zürich joined the League in 1351 it was agreed that disputes should be decided by tribunals of arbitrators, and until 1848 the only mode of settling inter-cantonal quarrels was by means of arbitration, a system which could not always be satisfactory.

Up to 1874 this supreme Tribunal, established since 1848, had no permanent seat in any one particular place. It met in different towns, and in general for short periods. But when, upon the adoption of the Constitution of 1874, its functions were materially increased and it rose considerably in importance, a permanent abode had to be chosen for the highest Court of Justice. After considerable discussion Lausanne was fixed upon by the Chambers, and on that town was imposed the obligation of supplying the necessary buildings. This decision was a concession to the feeling of French Switzerland, and it was also perhaps thought well that the Federal Tribunal should not be in contact with the political atmosphere of Bern. The present structure is vastly superior to that in which the sittings were previously held.

The judges are appointed by the Federal Assembly, care being taken that the three national languages are represented. Every Swiss citizen eligible for the National Council can be a judge of this court, but he cannot while holding such judicial office be a member of the Federal Assembly or of the Federal Council, nor an official appointed by either of those bodies, nor accept any other post either in the service of the Confederation or of a Canton, nor indeed follow any profession.

The Constitution of 1874 having been adopted, a

Federal law was drawn up fixing the organization of the Federal judiciary, the number of its members and substitutes, the duration of their functions, their salaries, and other matters. It bears date the 27th June of that year.

The members of this judiciary are nine in number, and they are elected for six years by the Federal Assembly, which appoints the president and vice-president out of the nine every two years. The judges can be, and often are, re-elected at the expiration of their term of office. Nine substitutes are chosen to serve in case of necessity, also for six years. The term of service for these judicial posts is thus double that of the members of the Federal and National Councils. The salary of the president is £440 and that of each of the other judges £400 a year. In all cases an uneven number of judges must sit, including the president, who takes part in the deliberations and in the voting.

No judge or substitute can exercise his functions where he, his wife, his betrothed, a relation in the direct line, or in the collateral line up to and including his first cousin, or the husband of his wife's sister, has a direct or indirect interest; or in matters where his ward is concerned, or in which he has already been engaged in some other capacity; or where his Canton of origin or his Commune is a party; or where appeals are brought against the legislative authorities or the government of his Canton.

Since 1874 the Federal Tribunal has been not only a court of civil and of criminal justice, but it also deals with questions of public law. Its attributions comprise criminal, civil, and political matters, and its proceedings are governed by certain articles of the Federal Constitution, and by the organization law of the 27th June 1874 already mentioned.

The different attributions of the Federal Tribunal are the following :—

1. As a court of civil justice.

It is competent to decide upon disputes respecting civil rights: (*a*) between the Confederation and one or more Cantons; (*b*) between Cantons; (*c*) between corporations or individuals as plaintiffs and the Confederation as defendant; (*d*) between Cantons on the one part and corporations or individuals on the other, but it is only when one of the parties demands it that a suit in this category can be heard before the Federal Tribunal at once.

The matter in dispute in the last two cases must amount to £120 at least, in order to be judged by the Tribunal. In all four the suit is brought directly before it, and not on appeal from a cantonal court.

The Federal Tribunal is alone competent to decide disputes between Communes of different Cantons concerning citizenship, where one Commune contends that a certain individual is not its citizen, and that it is therefore not obliged to acknowledge and provide for him as such; ordinary disputes between two or more Communes of the same Canton are, however, submitted to the local courts.

Questions relating to Heimathlosat,[1] expropriations for the construction of railways and other works of public utility, civil questions between the Confederation and railway companies, and the winding-up of the latter, go directly before the Federal Tribunal. The provisions with respect to railway companies are, however, to be regarded in the light of an exceptional measure, and as

---

[1] Homeless persons. Those who have no home comprise not only foreigners who have lost their nationality of origin without having obtained another, but also natives who are not burghers of any Swiss Commune.

such are expressly mentioned in the law of organization.[1]

The Tribunal is also bound to judge the following two cases : (*a*) those which by the constitution or the legislation of a Canton are entrusted to its competency—such provisions are only valid if they have been ratified by the Federal Assembly ; (*b*) those which are brought before it by agreement between the parties, where the matter in dispute amounts in value to £120 at least.

2. As a court of appeal.

In cases where Federal laws have to be applied by cantonal tribunals, and the amount of the matter in dispute is £120 at least, or cannot be estimated, either party has, by virtue of an article in the organization law, the right to have recourse to the Federal Tribunal against the judgment of the highest cantonal Tribunal.[2]

To this category now belong the Federal laws respecting contracts (other than those relating to real estate), copyright, protection of trade marks, and divorce and nullity of marriage.

Contracts relating to the sale and purchase of land, easements, mortgages, etc., are governed by the law of each Canton. In general, questions as to the devolution of property by will or upon intestacy are regulated by the ordinary cantonal courts, and are not within the competency of the Federal Tribunal, even upon appeal.

3. As a court for the administration of criminal justice.

The Federal Tribunal, assisted by a jury, takes cog-

---

[1] The winding-up of any other company, where the value amounts to £120 at least, comes before the Federal Tribunal upon appeal.

[2] The parties can also mutually agree that a judgment given by the lower cantonal Tribunal may be referred at once to the Federal Tribunal without passing through the cantonal Court of Appeal.

nizance of the following cases : (*a*) high treason against the Confederation, such as being concerned in an attempt to overthrow the Federal Constitution by force; (*b*) revolt or violence against Federal authorities ; (*c*) crimes and offences against international law ; (*d*) crimes and political offences which are the cause or the consequence of troubles occasioning an armed intervention by the Federal authority ; (*e*) charges against officials appointed by a Federal authority, when the latter makes application to the Federal Tribunal.

For the administration of criminal justice the Federal Tribunal is divided by the organization law into three sections.   There is a Chamber of Accusation with three ordinary members and three substitutes ; a Criminal Chamber with the like number, which takes part in all the sessions of the Federal Assizes ; and a Court of Criminal Appeal (*Tribunal de Cassation*) with five members and three substitutes.   One of the former must be the president for the time being of the Federal Tribunal.   Sentences are only valid when the court consists of five judges.

The Federal Assizes are composed of the Criminal Chamber and a jury of twelve elected in the Cantons by the people, and drawn by lot from the list of the district in which the Assizes are to be held.   The territory of the Confederation is divided into five assize districts.   There is one juror for every 1000 inhabitants in four districts comprising the Cantons and portions of Cantons where French or German is the national language, and one for every 500 in Ticino and the Italian Communes of the Grisons, which together constitute the fifth district. With certain exceptions, every citizen having the right to vote in Federal matters is eligible as a juror.   Those are exempt who are of the full age of sixty, whose names

were placed on the previous list of jurors, or who are
incapacitated by sickness or infirmity. The lists of
jurors are renewed every six years.

When the Assizes are to be held, the Criminal
Chamber causes the names of all the jurors of the
district to be placed in an urn, and fifty-four are drawn
by lot. The *Procureur général*, chosen by the
Federal Council for the particular case, has the right
to refuse twenty, and the accused twenty also. The
remaining fourteen are summoned, and two of this
number are selected by lot to act as substitutes in case
of need, so that the jury consists of twelve, as mentioned
above. In order to acquit or condemn a prisoner there
must be a majority of at least ten out of the twelve,
otherwise a fresh trial must take place with another
jury.

These Federal Assizes are not of frequent occurrence.
The principal ones which have been hitherto held were
at Geneva in 1864 with reference to a conflict between
two parties, Radicals and Independents ; at Zürich in
1871 after disturbances consequent upon a banquet
organized by Germans inhabiting that town in order to
celebrate the proclamation of the Empire at Versailles ;
at Neuchâtel in 1879, when an anarchist was condemned for a crime against international law (instigation
to the assassination of sovereigns).[1]

4. As a court to decide upon questions of public law.

Its powers were very considerably enlarged in 1874.
By the Constitution of 1848, all appeals in such questions were brought before the Federal Council, and
there was a further appeal to the Federal Assembly. If
the two Chambers agreed their decision was final, other-

---

[1] Most of the details respecting the Federal Assizes, etc., are taken
from Droz's *Instruction Civique*, p. 194.

wise the decision of the Federal Council prevailed.
The examination and discussion of these appeals
occupied a large portion of the time of the Chambers,
and it was found very difficult to establish an uniform
jurisdiction, because political questions and questions of
public law could not easily be separated. It was therefore a great step in the way of progress to place the
constitutional rights of Cantons and citizens, by way of
appeal, under the guarantee of the judicial authority,
and by virtue of Article 113 of the Constitution of 1874,
together with certain provisions in the organization
law, the Tribunal has now cognizance of: (*a*) conflicts of competency between Federal and cantonal
authorities; (*b*) such disputes between Cantons as are
within the domain of public law; (*c*) claims for violation of rights of citizens or corporations guaranteed
by the Federal or by a cantonal Constitution; (*d*)
Federal laws which have been passed in execution
of the Federal Constitution; (*e*) claims of individuals
or of corporations for violation of concordats between Cantons, as well as of treaties with foreign
countries.

By this Article what are termed "administrative
disputes" were reserved to be dealt with by Federal
legislation, and accordingly the organization law enumerated certain of these matters which were to be
treated, not by the judicial authority, but by one or
other of the two political authorities of the Confederation. Among them are disputes respecting public
primary schools of the Cantons, liberty of commerce
and trade, rights of established Swiss, and some
religious matters to be presently mentioned.

The competency in administration disputes does
not therefore belong entirely either to the political

authorities or to the judicial authority, and, according to Dr. Dubs, it is difficult to trace any guiding principle in this separation of powers. He considers that all disputes between the Confederation and the Cantons as to the limits of their reciprocal sovereignty should be left absolutely to the Federal Tribunal, whatever the subject might be, and he draws attention to the fact that certain religious matters are included under the head of "administrative disputes."

When the question of revising the Constitution of 1848 was being discussed, the competency to be given to the political and judicial authorities in religious matters was debated at much length, and it was ultimately settled by the Federal Assembly that both political authorities should in general have cognizance of religious disputes relating to matters of public law, whilst those within the domain of private law should be relegated to the Federal Tribunal. The Article respecting the interdiction upon Swiss soil of the Jesuits and societies affiliated to their order was particularly left to be dealt with by the political authorities.

It surely would have been better, as that great authority Dr. Dubs ardently desired, to have given to the Federal judiciary cognizance of all these religious disputes, whether in the domain of public or of private law, than (as sometimes happens) that the Federal Assembly, which is a legislative body, should be transformed for the nonce into a sort of religious tribunal, where such matters are apt to rouse political passions, and to be decided by a majority simply upon party lines rather than upon legal principles.

It has already been mentioned in Chapter IV that by the Constitution of 1874 the Federal Council has to provide for the execution of the judgments of the

Federal Tribunal, and that these must be carried out by means of cantonal authorities.

The deliberations of the Federal Tribunal are public, except in the case of juries and of the Chamber of Accusation. Each judge records his vote in public, but he is permitted to deliver his judgment in his own language, whether French, German, or Italian. The fact, stated above, that no judge can sit on a matter which concerns his own Canton, may on occasion cause anomalous results, inasmuch as in two similar cases the majority may decide one way in one case and another way in another.

It can hardly be expected, considering that the judges are appointed by the Federal Assembly out of all citizens eligible to the National Council, that the Federal Tribunal should consist of the best jurists in the land. Political appointments of inferior individuals might easily be made; the present judges, however, are stated to be men of good legal attainments.

This chapter gives the actual constitution and powers of the Federal Tribunal, but the Federal Council has announced its intention of presenting before long a new law which will introduce extensive modifications. Amongst the contemplated changes it will probably be proposed to increase the number of judges to thirteen, to divide the Tribunal into two sections, one for civil and the other for criminal cases, and when the two sections sit together to give them power to act as a court of appeal in criminal matters, and to entertain and determine other cases which are not under the jurisdiction of one or other of the sections alone.

CHAPTER VI

REFERENDUM and Initiative are two political institutions peculiar to Switzerland. They are the children of democracy, whose powerful weapons they have become.

1. Referendum means the reference to all vote-possessing citizens either of the Confederation or of a Canton, for acceptance or rejection, of laws and resolutions framed by their representatives.[1]

The Referendum is of two kinds, compulsory and optional. It is compulsory in certain Cantons where all laws adopted by the Grand Council or other representative body of a Canton must be submitted to the people, and optional where limited to those cases in which a certain number of voters demand it.

In earlier times, before any Referendum had been actually introduced, the people in Cantons comprising cities, such as Zürich, Bern, and Luzern, where there was no Landsgemeinde, were nevertheless from time to time formally consulted by their governments upon various matters.

After 1830 several Cantons introduced a popular

---

[1] In the time of the old Swiss Confederation, the delegates of the thirteen independent States of which it was composed had to *refer* to their governments for the confirmation of the decisions taken by the Federal Diet. Hence the name of Referendum. See Chapter I, p. 12.

veto, which paved the way for the Referendum. The first was St. Gallen by its Constitution of 1831. This contained an article declaring the sovereignty of the people, and stating that they had therefore the right of passing their own laws, and that every law was subject to the sanction of the people, who could, after a fixed period, refuse to adopt it. They could thus exercise a right of veto.

In Federal matters there are now two Referendums. The first was established by the Constitution of 1848, and was limited to one point, viz. the revision of that Constitution. All such revisions became subject to a compulsory appeal to the people, and the articles relating to this matter were reproduced in the revised Constitution of 1874. But, as we have seen, the latter also contains an article, extending the exercise of the popular vote, when demanded by thirty thousand citizens or eight Cantons, to all Federal laws and all resolutions of a general nature which have been passed by the Chambers. These two Referendums, the one compulsory and the other optional, are exercised by the collective vote of the citizens of the whole Confederation. By the cantonal Referendum, whether compulsory or optional, many important local matters are submitted to the collective vote of the citizens of the particular Canton interested, and the institution is now to be found all over Switzerland except where there is still a Landsgemeinde, and in Freiburg, where the Ultramontane majority are perhaps a little prone to deprecate changes.

The Referendum has struck root and expanded wherever it has been introduced, and no serious politician of any party would now think of attempting its abolition. The Conservatives, who violently opposed its introduction, became its earnest supporters when they found that it undoubtedly acted as a drag upon hasty and radical law-making. It has given back to the people of Switzerland rights originally possessed by them in most of the old Cantons, but partly or wholly lost in the course of time. Previous to the French Revolution, as mentioned in our first chapter, the governments of different States of the Confederation had gradually fallen into the hands of a limited number of aristocratic families. That Revolution introduced the idea of really representative government, but the period of reaction following the Napoleonic era was unfavourable to the development of popular institutions. Since 1830, whilst the share of the people in the management of affairs has gradually increased, the imperfections of the purely representative system have been brought more clearly to light. It was considered by the Radical party that delegates elected by universal suffrage were not always true interpreters of the popular will, and that class interests were mostly paramount in various matters, such, for instance, as the framing of laws and the levying of taxes. They therefore brought forward the idea of the Referendum, through which they hoped to recover for the people the right to that direct share in legislation which they had lost when government by representation alone was established in most of the Cantons.

A sufficient period has elapsed to allow the people of Switzerland to form an opinion of the working and results of the popular vote. As regards the former, nothing could be more simple. All the voter has to do is to deposit in the urn his voting paper with either "Aye" or "No" written upon it. As to the moral effect which the exercise of this institution has had upon the people, we are assured that it is admitted to be salutary even by adversaries of democratic government. The consciousness of individual influence, as well as the national feeling, is declared to have been strengthened, and the fact of a large and, on several occasions, increased participation of the people in the vote is quoted as tending to prove that their interest in political questions is growing keener.

The application of the Referendum as worked in Switzerland and the issues raised by it are so easy to understand, and in most cases, at all events, are so independent of party manœuvres, that public opinion acquiesces at once in the result, and the general feeling entertained in the country with reference to a particular question finds its accurate and, for the time, final expression. Extreme measures, whether radical or reactionary, have no chance whatever of being accepted by the people, who, while in a manner fulfilling the functions of a second Chamber, have infinitely more weight than any such body usually possesses, even if it be thoroughly representative and chosen by universal suffrage.

It would seem that, of the two forms of Referendum existing in Cantons, the compulsory is more practical than the optional. Such an eminent authority as M. Droz considers that where the latter is in force, the agitation occasioned in procuring the necessary signatures produces too much excitement, diverting the thoughts of voters from the real question at issue, and thus giving an undue bias to public opinion. Hence any calm discussion of the proposed measure becomes an impossibility, and there is every chance of its being rejected without due examination; whereas the system which subjects all laws voted by the cantonal legislative bodies regularly to the popular vote is free from any such inconvenience.

2. Initiative is the exercise of the right granted to any single voter or body of voters to initiate proposals for the enactment of new laws, or for the alteration or abolition of existing laws. It is essentially a powerful engine in a democratic direction. By means of it legislative bodies, mostly composed of persons belonging to the well-to-do class, can be compelled by the people to take up and put to a vote matters which, without it, would in all probability never be brought to the front. But it is an institution still in its infancy and requiring development. Those who belong to the above class have no special desire for reforms which would principally be used against what they deem to be their interests, whilst those in a lower sphere are not yet sufficiently well organized to make effective use of their right to initiate legislation. There is, moreover, great difficulty in embodying this right in a form at once simple and efficacious.

It is an important fact, which cannot too strongly be insisted upon, that both Referendum and Initiative are institutions which have grown up gradually in the Cantons, spreading from one to another, till all, with the exceptions already mentioned, possess either a compulsory or an optional Referendum, and in two instances both, whilst a number have introduced Initiative.

Although the Referendum does not, in strictness, exist in the Cantons with Landsgemeinden, most important business, as we shall show with reference to Uri,[1] is settled by the people in those primary assemblies.

The compulsory Referendum exists in the seven Cantons of Zürich, Bern, Solothurn, the Grisons, Aargau,

---

[1] Chapter IX.

Thurgau, and the Valais, and in the rural half-Canton of Basel. In Schwyz and Vaud both forms have been introduced.

In Zürich, where the institution has been most fully developed under the cantonal Constitution of 1869, the popular vote must be taken upon all changes in the Constitution, new laws, concordats, and the vote of a single sum exceeding £10,000, or an annual expenditure exceeding £800. The power of the cantonal Council is thus limited financially, and in practice it submits to the Referendum many other matters, although they are within its own competency. Its power is further limited by the Initiative. Any voter, if supported by one-third of the members present at its next sitting, or any 5000 voters may demand the passing, alteration, or abolition of a law or of a decision of the Council, and if the demand is not accepted by the latter, the question is submitted to the people, sometimes together with an amended text framed by the Council. That body may undertake the revision of the Constitution at any time after two separate deliberations and an affirmative popular vote. If the revision is demanded by the Initiative of 5000 voters and is accepted by the people, a fresh cantonal Council must be elected to frame the new law.

Such are the popular institutions in the democratic Canton of Zürich, where there are many citizens who would even increase the preponderating power of the people by diminishing the number of the legislative body from over two hundred to thirty or forty, and thus turn it into a kind of committee, the most important business of which would be limited to preparing measures for submission to the Referendum.

A few words must be added upon these important subjects with reference to other Cantons.

In the rural portion of Basel, as early as 1831, the Referendum was made compulsory for all laws, resolutions, and conventions, and an Initiative and a vote respecting revision was established, upon the demand of 1500 citizens.

Similar provisions exist in Bern, Solothurn, the Grisons, Aargau, and Thurgau, and also in Schwyz and Vaud, with variations in the number of voters required for an appeal to the people, and in the manner of carrying out revision. In the Valais there is only a Referendum for financial matters. Solothurn, the Grisons, Aargau, and Thurgau each possess an Initiative upon the demand of voters varying from 1500 to 5000. In Bern and the Valais there is none.

In all these Cantons one of the matters submitted to the Referendum relates to a proposal for a single item of expenditure, or for a certain fresh annual sum.[1]

In both Schwyz and Vaud there is also an optional Referendum ; in the former, upon the demand of 2000 voters, for concordats and for various resolutions emanating from the cantonal Council, and in the latter for any law, upon the Initiative of 6000 voters.

There remain seven Cantons and one half-Canton possessing only an optional Referendum. These are Luzern, Zug, Schaffhausen, St. Gallen, Ticino, Neuchâtel, Geneva, and the urban portion of Basel. Generally

---

[1] The following are the gradations :—

Bern	£20,000 at least.
Schwyz	£2000, or over £400 a year.
Solothurn	£4000 at least, or over £800 a year.
Grisons	£4000, or £800 for each of five consecutive years.
Aargau	Over £10,000, or over £1000 a year.
Thurgau	£2000 at least, or over £400 a year.
Vaud	£20,000, not comprised in the budget.
Valais	£2400, or an average of £800 during the period of three years.

speaking, laws, concordats, and sometimes resolutions of cantonal councils are submitted to the optional Referendum. It exists for financial matters in different gradations in Luzern, Zug, and Schaffhausen.[1] There is an Initiative in Zug, Schaffhausen, Neuchâtel, and in the urban portion of Basel. Revision is put to the popular vote in all upon certain conditions.

Since the adoption of the Federal Referendum in 1874 for laws and general resolutions passed by the Chambers, many such measures have been accepted by the Swiss people without a vote. Others have given rise to much discussion and difference of opinion, some being ultimately sanctioned and some rejected by the popular vote. The following nine instances occurred between 1875 and 1879[2] :—

> 23d May 1875. *Modification of right of voting.* *Rejected* by 207,263 to 202,583.
>
> *Marriage law.* This abolished cantonal regulations and rendered civil marriage compulsory throughout the Confederation. *Accepted* by 213,199 to 205,069.
>
> 23d April 1876. *Bank-notes law.* *Rejected* by 193,253 to 120,068.
>
> 9th July 1876. *Indemnities payable to the Confederation by citizens dispensed from military service. Rejected* by 184,894 to 156,157.
>
> 21st October 1877. *Another law on the last subject. Rejected* by 181,363 to 170,223.
>
> *Factories law. Accepted* by 181,204 to 170,857.

[1] Luzern   At least £8000, or at least £800 a year.
Zug   £1600, or £200 a year.
Schaffhausen   £6000 at least, or £600 a year.

[2] See the table at the end of Curti's *Geschichte der Schweizerischen Volksgesetzgebung.*

> 21st October 1877. *Political rights.* *Rejected* by 213,230 to 131,557.
>
> 19th January 1879. *Subsidies to Alpine railways.* This had especial reference to the great St. Gothard line. *Accepted* by 278,731 to 115,571.
>
> 18th May 1879. *Capital punishment.* Modification of the law on a proposal for a revision of the Federal Constitution. *Accepted* by 200,485 to 181,588, and by fifteen Cantons.

Next came a period when the conservative and cantonal tendencies of a great number of the people evidently produced a feeling of alarm at the progress of centralization and the frequency of Federal intervention. It seemed as if the majority of the nation had determined to reject whatever, as the saying was, came from Bern, without much consideration or inquiry.

On the 31st October 1880 they *rejected*, by 260,126 to 121,099, a law for the *Monopoly of Bank-notes*, which was proposed by way of a total revision of the Federal Constitution. The measure was rejected by $17\frac{1}{2}$ Cantons.

On the 30th July 1882 they rejected a law *respecting certain epidemics* by the immense majority of 254,340 to 68,027, and a *Patent* law, proposed as a revision of the Federal Constitution, by 156,658 to 141,616.[1]

---

[1] The defeat of the Patent law was attributed to the fact of both these measures being presented on the same day, and to the great unpopularity of the compulsory vaccination clause in the law on epidemics, numbers voting against both. This may perhaps be considered an exception to the general rule that questions submitted to the Referendum receive from the people their accurate, and, for the time, final expression. A Federal Patent law has since obtained the sanction of the people.

Again, on the 26th November 1882, the people *rejected*, by 318,139 to 172,010, a law authorizing the appointment of a Federal secretary of education, upon grounds which are mentioned in Chapter XIII.

On the 11th May 1884 no less than four measures which had been adopted by the Chambers were rejected by the popular vote. One was for the creation of a special secretary in the Federal department of justice and police, with an annual salary of from £220 to £280 ; another granted an annual salary of £400 for a secretary to the Swiss Legation at Washington ; a third was to exempt native commercial travellers from taxation which those of other countries had not to pay ; and the fourth would have given large powers to the Federal Council to remove criminal cases from a cantonal to a Federal Tribunal, whenever confidence in the independence or impartiality of the former was shaken in consequence of political excitement.

The two measures requiring additional expenditure were refused by the largest majorities, owing mostly to the fact that the people grudge giving their sanction to the outlay of money in which they discern no particular advantage to themselves. A peasant cannot see why a Federal or a cantonal functionary, whom he looks upon as his paid servant, should draw what in his idea is an extravagant salary, and he thinks it monstrous that the whole expense of a legation, which already amounts to £2000 a year, should be increased by £400 more. The measure for relieving native commercial travellers from a particular tax was certainly not rejected upon its merits, and the remaining one was said to owe its defeat to the disinclination of the Swiss people to leave to the discretion of a political power the honour and good faith of the cantonal tribunals.

The following were the numbers :—

	For.	Against.
1. Secretary in department of justice and police	149,729	214,916
2. Secretary of Legation at Washington	137,824	219,728
3. Commercial travellers' tax	175,192	189,550
4. Increase of criminal jurisdiction of Federal Council	159,068	202,773

Two modifications in the Federal Constitution have since been accepted by the Swiss people.

One, on the 25th October 1885, introduced an alteration in the law respecting the manufacture and sale of spirituous liquors, thereby granting a monopoly to the Confederation ; and on the 10th July 1887 the people, reversing their former decision, gave their sanction to a Patent law for Switzerland.

There are of course opponents of the Referendum. They argue that a number of measures which can properly and advantageously be discussed and settled in the Chambers are of such a nature that they ought not to be left to the decision of all the vote-possessing citizens. For instance, they consider a law treating of higher education, or establishing a Federal code of bankruptcy, as much too abstruse to be laid before the whole people, and they would prefer to leave such subjects to be dealt with by the two Federal Chambers at Bern. There is no doubt that the Federal Referendum has diminished the importance of the discussions upon laws and general resolutions in the Chambers, and of those bodies themselves in the eyes of the people. It would not be surprising if the deputies were to feel at times less earnestness in their work, since they know that, after all, the measures adopted by them, however necessary, are at the mercy of the popular vote, so that their decision need not be final, and all their time and trouble may be thrown away.

The Referendum does not extend to foreign relations, and there would clearly be a difficulty in referring a treaty with another country to the vote of the people.

It is a question for us Englishmen to consider whether it would be possible and advantageous to introduce the Referendum at home. For instance, it might well be that such a vexatious question as Home Rule for Ireland could once for all be settled one way or the other by a vote of the whole electoral body in the United Kingdom. We merely throw out this as a suggestion, but of course the conditions of Great Britain are very different from those of Switzerland, where the nation is so eminently democratic, and where the Referendum has been habitually employed for a variety of local matters.[1]

[1] The provisions of the Free Libraries Acts have introduced into British legislation a principle very like that of the Referendum.

See, too, the notice in the *Times* of the 8th January 1889, page 11, of the Referendum introduced by the Municipality of Cluny with regard to a loan, and the adoption by the Paris Municipal Council of a proposal to consult the population as to the advisability of constructing a metropolitan railway.

CHAPTER VII

POLITICAL PARTIES

In this chapter we have endeavoured to place before our readers as accurate an account as we have been able to obtain from trustworthy native sources of the state of political parties in Switzerland. We are fully conscious that the subject is a difficult one, but since it has never, so far as we are aware, been treated at any length in an English work, we feel that it ought not to be passed over by us.

It cannot be said that Switzerland is divided into distinct and large political parties, though the two broad currents of Liberal and Conservative opinion exist there as elsewhere. The thorough Centralizers mentioned in Chapter I, who aimed at the complete unification of the country, no longer exist, and the forcible abolition of the Cantons, which was by many considered possible, nay, even desirable, after the turmoil of the French Revolution, is no longer within the range of practical politics in Switzerland. The Centralizers of the present day are men who, with due regard for cantonal susceptibilities, try gradually to strengthen the central power, *i.e.* the Confederation. The existence of the twenty-two Cantons, with a population composed of four different nationalities speaking as many languages, prevents that broad distinction of parties of which there has been a striking example in Great Britain. Government by party would be impossible in Switzerland, and this fact finds its outward expression in the Federal Chambers, where there is no regular division into Ministerialists and Opposition, the members being in reality seated with little reference to their political creed.

The average Swiss citizen will usually think first of his Commune and then of his Canton, and his vote is often influenced more by local and cantonal than by general Federal interests. Still, if he be a *fervent* Roman Catholic, he is bound to consider his faith first of all, and this, combined with the ancient organization of their Church, has made the Roman Catholics the only party who possess real cohesion.[1] The Ultramontane Catholics all over Switzerland, irrespective of Cantons, race, or language, are ever ready to oppose the Protestants and Liberal Catholics upon any Federal question which may clash with their religious feelings, or relate even in a somewhat remote degree to their faith. But they have at times been equally ready to join with what may be denominated *Conservative Protestants* against Radical measures.

The Federal Assembly consists of three political divisions—the Right, the Centre, and the Left.

1. The Right.—There are Roman Catholics in each of the other two divisions, but the *clerical* section form one separate party called the Right, and number at present thirty-five members in the National Council and eighteen in the Council of

---

[1] The working men are beginning to be organized, but they cannot yet be called a parliamentary party, as no genuine labour representative has so far sat in the Federal Assembly.

the States. Two shades of opinion are observable
in this party, one led by members from rural districts of the Canton of Luzern, the other mostly by
members from Freiburg. The former represent rather
the views of the Swiss Catholic *laymen;* the latter
decline to subordinate the rights of their Church
to those of the State, and they have often proved the
stronger of the two among the rural population, where
the influence of the parish priests can be more actively
exerted. In the Chambers the Right, in spite of frequent domestic quarrels at home and lively polemics in
their own newspapers, generally give a solid vote, and
always where religious matters are concerned.

2. The Centre is now reduced from the phalanx of
the once omnipotent Liberal party to a handful of
members—fourteen in the National Council and five in
the Council of the States. Still, through their intimate
relations with the Federal Council (several of whose
members have been taken from their ranks), and the
control of old-established newspapers, they command a
considerable amount of public attention, and have a
large body of supporters in the country. In fact, the
Centre may be roughly described as representing the
political *traditions* of the Liberal majority of the Swiss
people. This position they owe also to their conciliatory
attitude in Federal, and more especially in religious
questions ; the latter being considered by the Centre as
of minor importance, to be used chiefly for tactical purposes in the Chambers. The Centre see their principal
strength in the solution of questions of political
economy. They are mild adherents of the Manchester
school and sympathize to a certain extent with the ideas,
as well as the interests, of financiers and capitalists ;
they may be likened to the moderate Liberals in England.

3. The Left, or Radical Democratic party, comprising all shades of Liberal, Radical, and Democratic opinions, from those held by men whose more advanced ideas have drawn them away from the Centre to those of the extreme section called Young Democrats, are the most numerous in the Assembly. They now count ninety-six in the National Council and twenty-one in the Council of the States, so that they can command the absolute majority. There are Centralizers as well as Federalists in this party—the former being recruited principally from the German Cantons, the latter from the French. As a whole they are pledged to support political and social progress, but what may be denominated *Radicals proper*, forming the great bulk of the Left, have evinced little initiative of late. They seem, in the opinion of many, to show a disposition to rest on the laurels won by their party years ago in the arduous struggle with church, aristocracy, and privileges of all kinds.

The Radicals from the German portion of Switzerland are strong upholders of the Federal Constitution, which, as revised in 1874, conferred upon the Confederation rights not previously existing. They would advance resolutely upon the road to centralization, and their war-cry is, in fact, " One law and one army." The greater centralization of the army and the partial unification of civil law are principally due to them, though it is only fair to add that in these matters they have been well seconded by the Centre.

The Radicals from the French part of Switzerland, besides being Federalists, mainly perhaps from some apprehension of losing their national independence by being *germanized*, have a somewhat authoritative tendency. They look upon the emancipation of the lower classes as a task to be undertaken from above, *i.e.* in their meaning, by an enlightened government with a strong hand.

The outspoken Radicals of both tongues agree, generally, in their political methods. They look upon the Roman Catholic Church and the orthodox clergy of the two Protestant communions [1] as the great enemies of progress. An exception should be made in the case of Vaud, where the majority of the members sent to the Federal Assembly profess to be stanch supporters of the National Church of the Canton, and are thus in unison with the sentiments of the rural population. Radicals of the above stamp still favour the representative and parliamentary system, which they consider to be the bulwark of intelligence against the numerical superiority of democratic masses insufficiently instructed and therefore easily misled. They would prefer themselves to regulate the measure of progress in the country, and they view with scepticism or distrust any further attempt in the direction of a greater participation of the people in legislation and government.

The extreme wing of the Radical Democratic party is formed by the Democrats. They are a small but influential body, who profess to work not only *for* but *through* the people and in full sympathy with their wants and aspirations. This group made its first appearance after 1860 on the occasion of a popular demand for a revision of the Federal Constitution, and became more important in consequence of the democratic movement in the Canton of Zürich (1867-1869). The Democrats are the exponents of a growing desire among the masses for social as opposed to political legislation.

[1] The Reformed Churches of Zwingli and Calvin.

This small knot of politicians, more especially the section known as *Young Democrats*, declare social reform to be now the most pressing mission of the Confederation. The social aims of the Democrats find supporters among the Right. The leaders of the Freiburg deputation to the Federal Assembly, and, in particular, one ardent Roman Catholic from the Grisons, are earnest advocates of all measures tending to substitute social for political legislation, and having for their object the amelioration of the condition of the labouring class. They naturally endeavour to gain over to their side Roman Catholics of this class.

The Democrats are in favour of Federal monopolies, but with the active co-operation of the Cantons, in order to procure the means necessary for carrying out great social improvements. They are the authors of the law establishing a Federal monopoly in the manufacture and sale of spirituous liquors which, adopted by the people in 1885, came into operation two years later. Some time ago one of the leaders of the Young Democrats, with the consent of his colleagues, put forth the following programme for Federal legislation of the near future :—

1. Extension of labour legislation.
2. General compulsory insurance against sickness, accidents, and death ; also against the damages caused by hail-storms, which latter was for the special benefit of the peasantry.
3. Federal monopolies for the issue of bank-notes, for tobacco, matches, and playing cards.
4. Purchase by the Confederation of the different Swiss railways, now mostly in the hands of private companies.

    5. Development of elementary education, and gratuit-
ous distribution to all children of school-books
and writing materials.

As regards the *modus operandi* of the parties in the
country and in the Chambers, the Centre, the Radicals
proper of the Left, and the moderate elements of the
Right have their centre of gravity in the Federal
Assembly itself. Believing in the efficiency and vitality
of the parliamentary system, they consider the Chambers
as their real field of action. The leaders and spokesmen
of these sections enjoy the confidence of the Federal
Council, and with their followers they form together by
means of a tacit understanding what may be denominated a kind of government party. The Democrats,
the Ultramontane members of the Right, and the
Radical Intransigeants (who do not agree with the
moderation shown by the Federal Council in religious
matters) stand aloof from this combination. The
Democrats, who have to a great extent lost faith in
the old parliamentary system, seek their support more
in the country by attending public meetings and supplying the popular public press with stirring appeals.
It is a remarkable fact, which goes far to prove how
little the parliamentary system introduced into Switzerland from abroad is still understood, or rather appreciated, by the people, that voters as a rule are satisfied
with general declarations of policy on the part of their
representatives, without requiring from them detailed
and clear utterances concerning the great political questions of the day. The knowledge which the people
possess that the ultimate decision with reference to
measures passed by the Federal Assembly rests with
them, works in the same direction. As for personal

canvassing, or pledges by candidates at election time, little was known of either until quite lately. The people, too, are supposed to take so little interest in the debates at Bern that the Federal Council have not deemed it necessary yet to have *verbatim* reports printed of the proceedings in the Chambers. The want of such reports is often felt as a serious drawback, and has been much commented upon of late by the press of various political shades.

There is no special class of politicians in Switzerland such as is to be found in the United States. The Caucus in the English and American sense of the word is unknown. On the other hand, there exist a few political associations which advocate different sides, such as the democratic (or, so far as the leaders are concerned, *social* democratic) Grütliverein and the conservative Eidgenössische Verein. The former is composed almost exclusively of working men, and thus represents the masses; whilst the latter is recruited from the Protestant classes. Although neither of these two associations, whose political aims are directly opposed to each other, is a regular parliamentary organization, they both exercise considerable influence at some elections and in the case of Federal Referendums. A new and more advanced party, with distinctly socialistic aims, is now in course of formation, and may be destined to have a marked influence in Swiss politics. It is more particularly mentioned in our concluding chapter.

Journalism, which in France has so often opened the door of ministries to clever writers, has not as yet achieved any such success in Switzerland, but several journalists are coming to the front now, both in the country and in the Chambers.

In some of the ancient democratic Cantons a few

families who were at the head of affairs centuries ago have still preserved their local influence, though there, as well as in the larger Cantons, the old patrician element may be considered as politically dead. "I had," a Swiss statesman once told us, "as colleagues in the National Council at the same time a Reding from Schwyz and a Wirz from Unterwalden, each belonging to an ancient family in his Canton. I think that a great reason of old families remaining at the head of affairs in some democratic Cantons is owing to the principle of the places not being largely salaried. The people look down upon those they pay, and honour those who render them, so to speak, gratuitous services. The first magistrate in the primitive Cantons, elected only for a year, but re-eligible, is paid a very small salary. Hence he must be in easy circumstances in order to accept the place, and the people have the feeling that he sacrifices his time and his convenience to them, and they repay him and his family by their gratitude."

This traditional preference for men of certain families in the disposal of elective offices where birth carries with it no legal privilege whatever is commented upon in Freeman's *Growth of the English Constitution*. The election by the Landsgemeinden year after year of members of ancient families to the functions of first magistrate is no doubt well suited to raise up in those families a succession of men fitted to hold the high offices in their own Cantons. "A man," Mr. Freeman remarks,[1] "of the favoured house knew that if he were at all worthy of a certain post of honour, he would be chosen to it before any other man; but he also knew that, if he showed himself unworthy of it, he might either fail to attain it at all or might be peacefully removed

[1] Page 27, fourth edition.

from it at the end of any twelvemonth. Such an one was surely under stronger motives to make himself worthy of the place which he hoped to fill than either the man who has to run the risk of an unlimited competition, or the man who succeeds to honour and authority by the mere right of his birth."

In what were aristocratic Cantons, such as Bern, Freiburg, and Solothurn, on the contrary, the old families have been swept away. They pay for what are considered to have been the faults of their ancestors, who enjoyed privileges not allowed in these days. For instance, since 1830 the patricians of Bern have retired from, or been ousted out of, public affairs; and in October 1884 the sole representative in the Federal Assembly of that ancient governing class in the Canton was defeated at the elections for the National Council. This aristocratic class has given place to citizens who cannot boast of their birth; what may be called a new order has sprung up, in which are to be found citizens of smaller towns, such as Biel and Olten, and also rich peasants. The same change is on the increase in Zürich, and even in Luzern.

In the new Cantons, which only date from the Act of Mediation (1803), or from 1814, there are now no historical families in power. Thus in Vaud the ancient nobility of Savoy were removed from participation in public affairs from the time when that country came temporarily under the sway of the flourishing Canton of Bern.

CHAPTER VIII

IN the beginning of the thirteenth century many cities, such as Zürich, Bern, Freiburg, and Solothurn, as well as a number of towns of lesser note, had already been endowed with important privileges, and were becoming centres of liberty and independence. The lower classes were more and more enfranchised, and the old feudal system fell into decay and was finally abolished. Even in feudal times Communes were already in existence, though they were largely controlled by superior lords, but that communal system which is peculiar to Switzerland spread gradually and surely till it ultimately embraced the whole country, and it can truly be called the basis of Swiss republican institutions.

The Communes have certainly played a very important part in Swiss history, and by their resistance to the feudal system they contributed largely to the foundation of public liberty. The independence which they achieved is justly considered to be the school and cradle of the political liberties of the people. Swiss legislation has its starting-point from the principle that institutions are only really free and popular when the Communes are free, and a Swiss citizen will contend that the normal development of political liberty is only possible when it is based upon that of the Communes, when it ascends from the lowest organization to the highest, progressing from the simple to the composite.[1] The Commune is the base, a number of Communes make up a Canton, and twenty-two Cantons form the Confederation.

A Swiss Commune is an assemblage of individuals and families inhabiting a certain defined portion of national territory, and possessing intimate relations of neighbourhood, as well as common interests regulated by a common administration.[2] It is in fact a kind of miniature of the State (Canton), and has been described as one of the cells of which the social body is composed. All the Communes are by no means of one unvarying type. Some are rich and extensive, others are poor and small in size. Rules and regulations differ, but each Commune is free and independent in itself, subject, however, to the supervision of the State. That authority must naturally have the right to exercise a certain control over communal administration, so that the latter may be prevented from exceeding its powers or abusing its liberty.

A Commune provides for all the public services within its limits much after the manner of a Canton ; it generally possesses a sort of local police, which keeps order day and night in its territory, is present at fairs and markets, has an eye to public-houses, and watches over rural property. There are also communal officials who maintain the public buildings, roads, and fountains, look after the lighting, take measures against fires,

---

[1] See the preface to a little pamphlet published at Thun in February 1871 by the Société d'Utilité Publique. It is called "Souvenir de la Suisse," and was addressed to the French soldiers of Bourbaki's army then in Switzerland, and distributed among them. The object was to show in a few pages the real nature of the Swiss Republic, and to hold it up as a pattern to the French at the time they were establishing their Republic.

[2] Droz's *Instruction Civique*, p. 108.

superintend schools and religious matters, and supply necessary aid to the poor both in sickness and in health.

The organization of a Commune depends much upon its extent. If its territory be small, a communal or municipal council may be sufficient. This is composed of several members, and is presided over by an official called in different Cantons either syndic, maire, or president. In larger Communes there are generally two councils, one legislative and the other executive, and there are frequently special committees charged with the inspection of schools or hospitals, or again with the superintendence of buildings in course of erection.

Every citizen belongs to some Commune. In France a citizen is first a member of the Commune in which he is born, but if later he establishes his principal domicile in another Commune, he becomes a member of it when he has resided there for a certain time. In Switzerland this is not so. The place of a citizen's birth or domicile does not necessarily alone determine to which particular Commune he belongs, but he must possess a Commune of origin, which in French is called "bourgeoisie," and in German "Burgergemeinde," and which in English may be denominated "Burgher-Commune," being that in which he, his father, or his ancestor has acquired certain personal advantages, and particularly the right of receiving aid in case of poverty. He thus obtains citizenship in a particular locality; this makes him a citizen of the Canton in which the locality is situated, and hence, according to Article 43 of the Federal Constitution, a Swiss citizen.

The Burgher-Communes are an ancient institution

in Switzerland, and some particulars as to their origin may be interesting.[1]

Originally the Communes in Switzerland, as elsewhere, possessed vast fields, pasturages, and woods which were held in common by all the inhabitants. But later, as population increased, the share of each inhabitant naturally diminished, and the tendency of members of poor Communes was to establish themselves in more prosperous ones. This immigration was naturally displeasing to the members of the latter, and they therefore constituted themselves into close corporations. Hence the origin of these Burgher-Communes, to the members of which the communal property was limited, the remaining inhabitants being excluded from participation in it, as well as in the local administration. The Burgher-Communes were bound to receive their own members at all times, and to give them aid if required. The right of burghership, as already indicated, passed from father to son. Each burgher must be inscribed in the books, and when going to be married or changing his residence to some other place, must obtain his Act of origin, *i.e.* a document certifying to his Commune of origin.

As time went on, trade became developed, increased facility of communication rendered a change of domicile much easier, and so it came to pass at last that in most Communes the majority of the inhabitants were not burghers. Now it was necessary to raise taxes to meet the public expenditure, and it was not admissible that the burghers alone should administer the Commune, while the rest of those who dwelt within its limits should have nothing to say to its administration. This would have been contrary to the principle of equality.

[1] Droz's *Instruction Civique*, pp. 110, 111.

On the other hand, the burghers were averse to giving up their property, and thus allowing the other inhabitants to have a share in it. Hence in a number of Cantons there came to be a double Commune: that of the burghers, who kept their property and only looked after the interests of their own members, especially of those who were poor, and that of the inhabitants, forming the municipality, embracing the whole of the population, and providing for the public service.[1]

The relations between the two kinds of Communes have no doubt been a source of trouble in some Cantons, and this duality has given rise to much political discussion and difference of opinion between Radicals and Conservatives. The former desire to abolish the Burgher-Communes and to establish what is termed an "unique" Commune of all the inhabitants, but to this Conservatives of all shades are strongly opposed.

Some Communes also contain guilds (Zünfte), all the members of which must be burghers of the particular Commune.

We will now proceed to give some account of the communal organization in one particular Canton, *i.e.* that of Bern.[2]

In each Canton a greater or less number of Communes form a district.[3] Bern contains thirty such districts (Amtsbezirke), each presided over by a prefect (Regierungsstatthalter). He represents the cantonal government, the seat of which is at Bern, and he has various officials attached to him.

---

[1] *Commune des bourgeois* or *Burgergemeinde*, and *Commune des habitants* or *Einwohnergemeinde*.

[2] See the pamphlet "Souvenir de la Suisse," and the general cantonal law of the 9th December 1852.

[3] These districts are, of course, quite distinct from the electoral districts.

The Commune of Bern possesses, within the limits of the city, no less than thirteen Zünfte or guilds, including the tanners, the butchers, the carpenters, the weavers, the blacksmiths, and one all the members of which belong to patrician families.

Now the number of burghers is very small, and has remained almost stationary, whilst the population of the city has increased rapidly. The non-increase of burghers is attributed to the amount charged for admission into their close corporation. He who aspired to be a burgher of Bern must not only be received into the Burgher-Commune, but also simultaneously into one of the thirteen guilds.[1]

In future, however, owing to changes voted by the Bernese burghers on the 23d April 1888, an individual may become a burgher without belonging to any of the guilds. He must have been established two years in Switzerland, and prove that he possesses £400 free from all debt or obligation ; if he has been established in the country for ten years he need only possess £200. The price of admission is fixed at £20, half of which is to go to the burghers' hospital, and half to their orphanage. If the candidate elects not to be a member of a guild, he must also pay £20 for the poor, and £4 for each of his children. If he is a foreigner, he will be charged an additional twenty-five per cent upon the total of the above sums.

The administration of each Commune in this Canton is divided between two governing bodies—the communal Assembly, which is the legislative, and the communal Council, which is the executive authority. There are also parish officials for religious matters.

The principal qualifications which entitle every

[1] Compare the older constitution of the City of London.

citizen within the Commune who possesses them to a vote in the communal Assembly are the following: he must have attained his twenty-first year; he must have the right to administer his own property, not being under guardianship, *i.e.* in technical phraseology *sui juris;* he must be in full enjoyment of the general civil and political rights of a citizen, and must also be under no temporary civil or criminal disability, such, for instance, as arises in the case of a person otherwise entitled to vote but at the moment undergoing a sentence of imprisonment as a criminal, or being an undischarged bankrupt; he must pay either a public direct tax or one destined to be applied towards the general expenses of the communal administration ; or, if he pay neither of the above taxes, he must be a burgher of the locality, or have been established for two years in the Commune.

It is a curious fact that although women having the free administration of their property and paying communal taxes have the right to vote, they can only exercise the suffrage through their male representatives.

Paupers, and those who have not paid their taxes, cannot vote. Those, too, who from intemperate habits have been prohibited for a limited period from frequenting public-houses are not allowed to vote during that period. This punishment is inflicted by the communal authorities with the sanction of the prefect of the district, and a notice thereof is put up in all the public-houses of that district.

There is a register in each Commune of all citizens who have the right to vote. It is open to the inspection of the public, and, if demanded, is placed upon the table at communal assemblies.

The following branches of local administration are

within the exclusive jurisdiction of the communal Assemblies: election of the president, secretary, and members of the communal Council; creation of permanent and salaried places, and determination of the salaries to be attached thereto; acceptance or modification of all communal regulations; foundations of churches, charitable institutions, hospitals, school-houses, and prisons; levy of communal taxes; erection of buildings, where the cost exceeds the sum fixed by the communal regulations, and similarly in the case of the sale and purchase of landed property, where the estimated value exceeds the fixed sum; loans to be contracted in the name of the Commune; certain judgments in legal matters where the communal Council is not competent; fixing the annual budget and passing all the accounts.

There are ordinary and extraordinary meetings of the Assembly—the former being held at fixed periods, the latter whenever required.

A communal Council is composed of a president and at least four other members. They are elected by the Assembly, and the president is the head official of the Commune both in administrative and police matters. Every citizen is eligible to the communal Council who is domiciled in the Commune, and is personally capable of voting in the communal Assembly. Any decision of this Council, in order to be valid, must be taken in the presence of at least half the members, besides the president or his substitute, and by an absolute majority. The president has a casting vote.

In general every citizen of the Commune must serve two years in any office to which he is elected, unless he can give a valid excuse, such as the fact that he already exercises other public functions, that he is sixty years old, or in bad health.

The principal matters assigned to the direction of the communal Councils are :—

1. Local police, *i.e.* the duty of watching over public security and tranquillity, and managing all matters concerning residence and establishment in the Commune. Non-members of the Commune, if Swiss citizens, have within it equal rights with those who are born there, excepting in respect of the communal property.

2. Guardianship. It is the duty of the communal Councils to take care of orphans and of those who are not capable of managing their own property. They are responsible for the affairs of such persons, and must furnish accounts of their stewardship once a year.

3. Poor. When a Commune possesses insufficient funds or no fund at all for the poor, the latter are relieved by voluntary contributions, and this matter is in such circumstances left as much as possible to charitable associations, the establishment of which the communal authorities must endeavour to promote. The communal Councils can also institute special committees for charitable purposes (Armen oder Spendcommissionen).

4. Public instruction. The primary schools are administered by the Communes, which appoint the teachers and pay their salaries, the State granting a subsidy.

5. Administration of communal property. The expenses of the Communes are covered, in so far as the revenues of the communal property are insufficient to meet them, by taxes levied upon landed property, capital, and revenue.

All the Communes and communal authorities in a Canton are placed under the supervision of the cantonal government. The communal accounts are submitted to it for investigation, and for correction if need be. Where great irregularities have been committed, it has even the right (which has been exercised on at least one occasion) to put a Commune under guardianship, by appointing some one, probably a lawyer, to set its affairs in order. A Commune might indeed under certain circumstances become bankrupt.

Having thus given some account of the principles underlying the organization of the Bernese Communes in general, we will proceed next to consider that of some particular Commune, and we have thought that we could not do better than choose one which must be well known to a number of our readers, and which is especially associated in our own minds with the recollection of many pleasant visits during a course of years. We mean Grindelwald, where we have stayed under the roof of the far-famed hostelry of the "Bear," managed with such friendly consideration and true courtesy towards their guests by the Boss family. In conversations with members of that family, especially with Herr Fritz Boss, himself one of the Bernese Grand Council, and with the obliging assistance of Pfarrer Strasser, who, from his constant devotion to all that concerns the welfare of his parishioners, is an admirable example of what a country pastor ought to be, we have compiled the following particulars.[1]

The Commune of Grindelwald is in the district of Interlaken. The original name of the little village was Gydisdorf, *i.e.* Gydi village, and it is supposed to have derived its title from a certain Gydi, one of the first

---

[1] Much, no doubt, of the particulars respecting Grindelwald applies to a number of other Communes. We give the information just as we obtained it upon the spot.

inhabitants.   At the present time only a portion of the village, round and about the "Aigle Noir," has retained this name.   The Commune is divided into eight districts : Scheidegg, Grindel, Holzmatten, Bach, Bussalp inner Orts, Bussalp ausser Orts or Burglauenen, Itramen, and Wärgisthal.   It extends on the one side down the valley towards Zweilütschinen, and on the other over the great Scheidegg in the direction of Rosenlaui.   On the south it is bounded by huge mountains of the Oberland and by glaciers.   To the north it reaches right up to the Faulhorn, and towards the west it extends as far as the little Scheidegg and the Männlichen.

The Commune contains over 3000 inhabitants living in 600 houses.   All are Protestants, and there is a parish Assembly and a parish Council.   The only schools are primary, and of these there are seven, accommodating about 600 children.

Grindelwald possesses a communal Assembly and a communal Council.   The former consists of all who are entitled to a vote ; the latter is the executive, and is chosen by the former by ballot.

The communal Assembly has three ordinary meetings every year : on the fourth Monday in March, the first Monday in May, and the second Monday in October.   The matters generally treated at these meetings are :—

In March all the accounts are passed, officials who have the care of the poor are elected as vacancies occur, and a treasurer of the Commune is chosen ; in May places are filled up in the communal Council and upon the school committee ; and in October the budget is examined and the taxes are fixed for the ensuing year.

Extraordinary meetings are held either on the demand of the prefect, of the communal president (who presides over both the Assembly and the Council), of the communal Council, or of thirty qualified voters.

Every member of the Assembly has a right to speak his mind freely upon any subject which is discussed, and to make proposals. This must be done in a clear and orderly manner. Members who wander from the subject, or use improper or insulting language, are called to order by the president, and if they do not at once submit to his ruling, they can be stopped from speaking. If any member can prove that grave irregularities have taken place in the proceedings, the prefect of the district, on being appealed to, can declare those proceedings to be null and void, and another Assembly must be held.

The communal Council consists of the president, eight councillors, and a secretary. One councillor is elected out of each of the eight districts. A father and son, a father-in-law and son-in-law, a brother and half-brother, cannot be members at the same time. Nor can the president and secretary be in any such relationship to each other. The Council meets as a rule on the first Monday in every month. It provides for the administration of guardianship matters, of deeds relating to landed property, and of local police. It only has competency in affairs of the estimated value of £8 or less. Where the value is greater, the matter has to come before the communal Assembly. The president is paid £4, each member of the Council 16s., and the secretary £24 annually. The members remain in office for two years, and service of their first term of office is, with certain exceptions, compulsory. They can be re-elected, but are not obliged to serve a second term in succession, *i.e.* for four years running.

The communal officials are subject to the supervision

and control of the government of the Canton of Bern, which is exercised on their behalf by the prefect of the district. This functionary resides at Interlaken, and, amongst other important duties, has to audit and approve all the accounts of the Commune.

One cantonal Landjäger (policeman) is stationed at Grindelwald, but he is under the control of the communal Council. The regular public road from the lower end of the Commune in the valley up to the village church is a cantonal road, constructed and kept up at the expense of the Canton. A Wegmeister (road-master) may often be seen working upon it. He belongs to the Commune, but is appointed and paid by the Canton, as are any other men who are employed occasionally for cleaning away the snow, repairing damage caused by floods, and so forth. The communal authorities are bound to see that this is properly done at the right time. If the Wegmeister neglects his duty, the communal Council reports him to the district engineer at Interlaken. All the other roads and paths are kept in order at the expense of the Commune.

The communal property consists of some small woods, buildings, and money. There is a reserve of £64, called Burgergut, for journey-money in case of war, to assist the men who have to join for service at headquarters.

Each homestead has a right, in return for a small payment, to a certain amount of wood annually, but it must be strictly for home use. Where there are several families residing in the same house, each has this right. Any one not belonging to the Commune, whether a Swiss or a foreigner, who resides in a homestead situated within its limits, is also entitled to his share, but at a greater proportional rate of payment, so

that if the communal householder pays half a crown for
his wood, a Swiss from another Commune or a foreigner
would pay about four shillings. The money is expended
in the salaries of the foresters (here called Bannwärte,
which was the name of the earliest forest officials), in
planting new trees, etc. Curiously enough, there is no
pasture in common in Grindelwald. The water-rights
of those who possess land are strictly defined by the
deeds under which they hold the property.

When the head of a family dies, the youngest son
has the privilege of taking the house and adjoining plot
of ground at the estimated value, paying over to the
rest of the family their due shares. Should he decide
not to take this property, and should the family not be
able to come to any private arrangement respecting it,
then it must be sold by public auction. Any other land
or property which belonged to the father, as to which
no such private arrangement can be made, is also sold
publicly. In practice, if at the auction a member of the
family makes one of the highest biddings, the property
is, as a general rule, adjudged to him. This is due to
a traditional feeling ingrained in the community that
the same family should retain its homestead and land, if
possible, from generation to generation.

The communal taxes vary according to the communal expenditure from about half a crown to four
shillings per £40 of capital. In 1888 they amounted to
3 francs 25 centimes, or about two shillings and seven-
pence. The cantonal tax is calculated *ad valorem* at
the rate of one-fifth per cent, and includes fire-insurance,
which, on buildings of over £4 in value, is obligatory.[1]

The poor are relieved in three different ways. For

---

[1] The metal plates of insurance companies to be seen on many houses
indicate that the furniture is insured.

the regular paupers (Notharmen) there is a cantonal official who comes up from Interlaken, makes his inspection, and pays for their maintenance out of cantonal funds; other less necessitous persons and poor people passing through the Commune are relieved by one special committee; while yet another provides for the wants of the sick poor. In 1887 Grindelwald expended £48 for the poor.

The Commune has also the right to several beds in the district hospital at Interlaken, where those who have been very seriously injured, or who are suffering from some complicated illness, are taken in for treatment, if they do not themselves possess sufficient means to ensure proper nursing at home. If a case is still more serious, and the man is poor, he can be provided with a certificate from the communal Council, and be sent to Bern to be in hospital under the best medical advice.

There are fire-engines in different parts of the Commune, and if a fire does break out, which seems very seldom the case, bells are rung, men are despatched on horseback to rouse the population by blowing horns, and the fire-brigade and the inhabitants generally are soon on foot.

A curious custom prevails in the Commune with respect to the supply of the necessary firewood in winter for the schoolrooms. Every boy or girl must contribute a piece. Visitors in winter may constantly see children tearing down hill, each with a log of wood tied to his little sledge, as his contribution to the school fire.

The inhabitants seem to be a contented quiet race, whose ambition in general does not soar higher than the making of a sufficiency for their few wants, and who are gifted with much perseverance and much capacity for hard continuous work. They will themselves confess to a considerable ingredient of stubbornness in their nature, and they are easier to lead than to drive. Among them are a set of guides who are the most faithful, attentive, good-tempered fellows that can be conceived, who become your friends, from whom you part with regret, and whose hands you clasp with pleasure when you meet them again.

Apart from what is earned by the guides and porters, by employment in the hotels, and by the sale of milk, eggs, etc., for the visitors, farming and raising cattle are the principal means of living. According to information given to us at Easter 1888, there were then 519 homesteads with their plots of ground, a few inhabitants possessing from twelve to twenty-four head of cattle (valued from £10 to £16 each), and a number with one or more cows each. In the whole Commune it was reckoned that there were 2630 cows, 1443 goats, 1343 sheep, 442 pigs, 169 horses, and 99 hives of bees.

A farm labourer's annual earnings, food and lodging being supplied to him, may be reckoned at from £10 to £12; a day labourer gets a franc, say tenpence, and his food. It is the custom of tradespeople to come to their employers' houses. A shoemaker will bring his tools and make a pair of shoes at any one's house, the material being found for him; a tailor is accustomed to do the same. They, as well as carpenters, joiners, and others, are paid about one shilling and eightpence a day and their food; a mason gets half a crown and his food. The women make the homespun clothing worn by the men, and a few girls earn a little money by silk-weaving. A maid-servant is paid from eight shillings to fourteen shillings and sixpence a month, and is given in addition one pair of shoes a year.

In conclusion we may remark that the communal

system, as it exists in Switzerland, does not allow of that extent of personal liberty which is found in England. In a Swiss Commune every inhabitant must be inscribed at the police office, and must have his papers in order, so as to show that he is really a member of the Commune, contributing to its taxes and sharing in its advantages. If he removes to another Commune he must take his papers with him, and they must be satisfactory to the local police, or he will not be allowed to remain there; that is to say, he will not be allowed to become an inhabitant of the Commune if there is any chance of his becoming a burden to it. One Commune has no idea of permanently supporting vagrants or beggars who belong to another, and it views the immigration of strangers with a certain amount of jealousy and suspicion.[1]

[1] This feeling has increased of late in some parts of Switzerland owing to the large influx of poor Germans, many being mere tramps who have no serious intention of seeking work.

CHAPTER IX

IT has been mentioned in Chapter II that each Canton, and each half-Canton, is a State in itself, every single one being sovereign, except where it has ceded to the central power attributions of a general nature in which all the States of the Confederation are equally interested. Matters in which the sovereignty of the Cantons is either absolute or limited by the Federal power have been enumerated, as well as the conditions upon which the cantonal Constitutions are guaranteed by the Confederation. When a Canton is charged with a breach of its Constitution, the case is generally brought before the Federal Tribunal. If the breach is proved, the Federal Council has.to provide for the judgment of the Court being properly carried out, and it could, no doubt, order forcible measures to be taken for this purpose, *manu militari*, but such a proceeding has never been found necessary, because the Cantons always submit to the judgments of the supreme Federal Court.

In old days their rights were much more extensive than now. They could send representatives to foreign powers, and *vice versâ*. The religious disputes occasioned by the Reformation gave rise to several of these missions.

In 1631 King Gustavus Adolphus of Sweden accredited the Knight Rasche as special ambassador to Zürich, with the object of inducing the Protestant Cantons to enter into an alliance with His Majesty.

In 1689 a special ambassador, Thomas Coxe, arrived at Zürich, charged by King William III to promote the friendly relations existing between the Protestant Cantons and Great Britain.

In 1529 envoys from Luzern, Uri, Schwyz, Unterwalden, and Zug made a special treaty at Feldkirch (Vorarlberg) with the Austrian delegates, the so-called "Ferdinandische Bund." The treaty was directed against the Protestant Cantons.

Again, in 1578, the town-clerk of Luzern, Rennwald Zysat, was sent by his government to the Duke of Savoy to conclude an alliance.

Of course Cantons, such, for instance, as the Valais, the Grisons, and Geneva, which did not belong to the old Confederation of thirteen States, and were merely its allies, could negotiate freely with foreign countries, and even in 1815 the Grisons, although already a member of the Confederation, had special delegates at the Congress of Vienna, in opposition to the envoys of the Federal Diet.

Besides, each Canton had its own coinage, possessed its own little army, and hired out, on its own account, troops to foreign rulers. Till very lately most of the Cantons levied duties on wine and spirits imported into their territory. That privilege too is gone. Formerly there existed what was termed *la traite foraine*, being a tax levied upon every kind of property which left the territory of the Canton, whether by the emigration of a citizen or the departure of a foreigner, or through inheritance, donation, or sale. This tax varied, and sometimes reached 10 per cent.

The sovereignty of the Cantons resides in the people of each State, and at the commencement of their Constitutions words clearly enunciating this principle are inscribed. According to the first Article of the Constitution which Zürich adopted in 1869, the power of the State rests upon the totality of the people, and is exercised directly through the vote-possessing citizens (Aktivbürger), and indirectly through the authorities and officials. Similar articles, with variations in their respective texts, are to be found in the Constitutions of the other Cantons.

The cantonal Constitutions are of various kinds. The ancient Landsgemeinden, those open-air assemblies held in the spring, and composed of all the people possessing votes, still exist in Uri, in the two half-Cantons of Unterwalden, in those composing Appenzell, and in Glarus. In 1848 they were abolished in Schwyz and Zug. Uri may be taken as an example. There, on the first Sunday in May, the people assemble in a meadow at Bözlingen an der Gand, not far from Altdorf. The Landammann,[1] after having duly attended mass in the village church, proceeds in procession to the place of meeting. He is accompanied by ushers in antique costumes of black and yellow, the colours of the Canton. There is an ancient banner with the arms of Uri (a bull's head on a yellow ground), and there are old wild bulls' horns which year after year are borne upon poles by men in front. The Landammann seats himself at a table in the centre of the meadow with another official (Land-schreiber), and the people, standing or sitting, range themselves around him as in an amphitheatre. The

---

[1] This is the spelling in the Constitution.

Landammann makes his opening speech, and reviews the events, domestic and foreign, of the previous year. Then there is silence over the whole assembly, every one offering up a prayer, and after that the real business commences. Each man speaks his mind when and for as long as he pleases; every subject is discussed with decorum, and finally, when all other matters have been settled, the officials for the following year are chosen. The out-going Landammann (who may be, and generally is, re-elected for another year) delivers up his charge with an affirmation that he has injured no one voluntarily, and he asks pardon of any citizen who may think himself aggrieved. The new Landammann takes the prescribed oath, and the whole people swear to obey him, to serve their country, and to respect the laws. Other officials are then elected by show of hands, and the meeting is over.[1]

We ourselves were present, with Mr. Angst, Her Majesty's consul at Zürich, on the 6th May 1888, at the General Assembly of the people of Uri. It was a brilliant day, and through the kindness of Herr Gustav Muheim, the Landammann, we obtained front seats in the ring of people, and we watched the proceedings with much interest. Above the meadow there is a green eminence rising towards the east, and upon its slopes women in various-coloured garments and children were picturesquely grouped, and above the eminence, on the horizon, are snow-clad peaks.

The meeting was more important than usual, for a new Constitution was to be proposed by the authorities,

---

[1] The whole scene is vividly described by Count Bernard d'Harcourt, formerly French ambassador at Bern, in a pamphlet called "Une République qui dure," published originally in the *Revue de France*. See too the eloquent passages in Freeman's *Growth of the English Constitution from the Earliest Times*, Chapter I.

and much opposition was expected. This was especially
the case with regard to a reform abolishing certain
secular privileges in the higher region known as the
Valley of Ursern, or Urseren.[1] This district has hitherto
virtually formed a real Canton within a Canton. It
was not to be expected that the mountaineers of Uri
(as the inhabitants of Urseren are termed) would give up
their ancient rights without a struggle, and the debate
was long and serious. First the Landammann stood
up, and, taking off his hat, demanded if any one was
desirous of addressing the Assembly, and this he repeated after every speech. There was no lack of
orators. We do not pretend to have understood the
local *patois*, but the excitement of the Urseren men
was very visible, and our consul helped materially to
make us understand the general drift of the arguments.
Finally the Landammann himself spoke in favour of
the new Constitution, and then there was a show of
hands. This was peculiar. Each voter not only held
up his hand, but he moved the fingers quickly up and
down, accompanying the motion with a low moaning
sound, which was in fact a kind of subdued cheer. The
effect to us was very startling.

The new Constitution was adopted by a large majority, and although a protest from the side of Urseren
was addressed to the Federal Assembly, it has obtained
the necessary guarantee of the Confederation. The
elaboration of this Constitution will no doubt take a
considerable time. The Canton possesses an executive
power (Regierungsrath) and a representative legislative
power (Landrath). The matter was first referred to the

---

[1] The district of Ursern, as it is spelt in the old Constitution, is there
stated to form only one political Commune—the Valley Ursern—with
its four subdivisions of Andermatt, Hospenthal, Realp, and Zumdorf.—
Andermatt being the seat of the district authorities.

former body, which then prepared its message to the latter. All measures which may be adopted will be duly presented to the sovereign people. The Landrath has always the power of convoking an extraordinary meeting of the Landsgemeinde.

In the other Cantons, where no Landsgemeinde exists, the form of government is of course somewhat different, and these general assemblies are replaced by representative bodies, the executive authority being exercised by another body, each member of which presides over a particular department.

We propose to give a sketch, by way of example, of some of the provisions of the Constitution of the Republic and Canton of Geneva, which, drawn up particularly under the auspices of the celebrated James Fazy, was accepted by the citizens on the 24th May 1847, and has since been modified in certain particulars.[1]

It begins with an article defining the political state of the Canton, and declaring that the sovereignty resides in the people, and that all the political powers and public functions are only a delegation of its supreme authority.

This is followed by articles relating to individual rights. All Genevese are equal before the law. Individual liberty, inviolability of domicile and property, except in cases of expropriation, are guaranteed, as well as liberty of the press, which, however, must not be abused. The same is the case with respect to the right of establishment in the Canton, to freedom of trade, worship, education, and petition. No corporation or congregation can be established in the Canton without the authorization of the Grand Council or legislative

---

[1] See Gavard's *Genève et ses Institutions*, which is bound up with Droz's *Instruction Civique*.

body. Genevese citizens can now vote after attaining their twenty-first year, and Swiss citizens of other Cantons of the same age have a vote, provided they have become domiciled in the Canton after three months of establishment or residence. Those of either category may be deprived of their political rights who have been convicted of some heinous offence, who are under the control of a *conseil judiciaire,* who exercise political rights outside the Canton, or who are in the service of a foreign power. The law can pronounce the suspension of a portion of the political rights of those who are passing through bankruptcy.

The sovereignty of the Genevese people is exercised either directly by them, assembled in a General Council, or in their name by the cantonal authorities acting through one of three distinct channels : the Legislative, or Grand Council, the Executive, or State Council, and the Judicial, or Courts of Law.

1. The General Council consists of the whole electoral body. It was originally a deliberative assembly, offering a certain analogy to the Landsgemeinden, but in the present century its deliberative functions were abolished, though it still appoints the members of the State Council, thus differing from the practice in the majority of Cantons. It also votes upon all the changes and additions proposed either in the Federal or the cantonal Constitution. There is an optional Referendum.[1]

Until the year 1886 the citizens of the whole Canton forming the General Council were obliged to resort to the electoral building in the town of Geneva in order to vote. This system no doubt entailed expense and trouble upon the country electors. It was also supposed to open the door to fraud in the way of personifi-

---

[1] See Chapter VI.

cation, as all the citizens could not be known at the polling places where they recorded their votes. A party question arose, the Conservatives starting an opposition to the existing system, whilst the Radicals supported it as being in their eyes an efficacious means of effecting a greater unity in the manifestations of the popular will. The Conservatives were so far successful some years ago that twenty-four electoral districts were created for the elections of deputies to the National Council at Bern and to the Grand Council at Geneva.

But in September 1886 the *vote à la Commune*, as it is called, was extended to other elections, including those to the State Council. No one residing in the rural districts of the Canton will therefore now be put to the trouble and expense of going to Geneva to vote, and that this change was desired by the greater portion of the country people is evident from the fact that in almost all the twenty rural districts there was a majority in favour of the alteration in the law. In each of the four town districts it was rejected.

2. The Grand Council is composed of one hundred deputies[1] chosen in the three electoral districts (*collèges d'arrondissement*) by *scrutin de liste*[2] and by the majority of votes, provided that such majority is not less than one-third of the voters. All lay citizens having a right to vote are eligible after attaining their twenty-sixth year. The members are appointed for two years and are re-eligible. The elections take place on the second Sunday in November. The whole Council is renewed at

---

[1] Thirty-seven for the city, twenty-three for the right bank, and forty for the left bank of the lake and the Rhone.

[2] By this system each elector has as many votes as there are members for his particular district. There are always lists published previous to an election by the two principal parties, called Democrats and Radical-Liberal. One or more names may figure in both lists.

the same time. There are two ordinary sessions a year, and sometimes an extraordinary one is convoked.

Among other matters this legislative body nominates the judicial magistrates, pronounces on the validity of the elections of its own members, prepares bills and resolutions, and adopts, rejects, or amends those presented to it either by the State Council, by one or more of its members, or by a special committee. Urgency may be demanded. It exercises the right of pardon, and of granting general or particular amnesties. It receives the annual report of the State Council, refers it to a committee, and deals with it after the committee has presented its report. It votes the taxes, decrees expenditure, loans, and expropriations, and passes the State accounts. It names the deputies to the Council of the States at Bern. The members have the right of Initiative. Each receives six francs, or about four shillings and tenpence, a sitting.

3. The State Council provides for the general administration of the Canton. It consists of seven members, chosen every two years on the second Sunday in November by the electoral body. The election takes place in the year in which there is no election of the legislative body. To be eligible, the members must be laymen who have attained their twenty-eighth year and do not hold any other paid public office. The president receives a salary of £240, and each of the other councillors of £200 a year. Each member presides over one of the seven departments into which the administration of the State is divided—viz. military, public instruction, finance and commerce, public contributions, justice and police, interior, and public works.

The State Council elects its president every year (who is only re-eligible after an interval of a year) and its vice-president. Among other matters it regulates the organization of the seven departments; it exercises a legislative Initiative concurrently with the Grand Council, and presents bills or legislative resolutions to the latter. It publishes those of either sort which have been adopted by the Grand Council and submits them to the Referendum if duly demanded, except when urgency has been declared. It promulgates the laws, and is charged with their execution. It presents the budget of receipts and expenditure annually to the Grand Council, as well as an annual account of the administration and of the finances.

As the State Council emanates directly from the people, it has a greater degree of independence than those executive authorities in other Cantons which are appointed by the legislative bodies. Several other Cantons follow the same system as Geneva, the authorities charged with making the laws and with their execution being appointed directly by the people.

In Zürich the executive government consists of seven members, chosen every third year by the people of the whole Canton, forming one electoral district. In Zug the people have the direct election of the members of the executive government. Similar powers are given to the people in the rural half-Canton of Basel, in Schaffhausen, and in Thurgau.

4. The Courts of Law.—The State Council must see that the functions of the tribunals are properly exercised, and the Grand Council appoints the judicial officials for four years. There are permanent tribunals for civil and criminal cases, and juries for the latter.

The Cantons thus possess legislative, executive, and judicial powers, and they constitute their own public services, the expenses of which they meet by levying the necessary local taxes.

CHAPTER X

THE organization of the courts of law and of the procedure in civil and criminal matters varies in the several Cantons, which are sovereign as regards them, except where from time to time the general Federal law has superseded the particular cantonal law. The civil codes in the French Cantons, except Geneva, are framed upon the basis of the *Code Napoléon*, with modifications. The German Cantons have codes differing considerably from each other and mostly original. Uri, Appenzell Inner-Rhoden, and urban Basel have only very ancient and insufficient codes, and in the first two there exist, side by side with the code, customary laws and usages to which, though unwritten, the courts give effect ; while in the last-named State the ancient Roman law supplements the deficiencies of the code much as our own common law is prayed in aid in cases where the existing statute law is silent or inadequate. It would be impossible within the limits of this work to give an insight into the intricacies of each cantonal system, and we will therefore confine ourselves to one, taking as an example that of the Canton of Vaud.

Justice is administered by the following courts:—

(*a*) For the whole Canton, by the cantonal Tribunal

and the *Juge d'Instruction* (for criminal investigations).

(*b*) In each of the nineteen districts, by the District Court (*Tribunal de District*).

(*c*) In each of the sixty *Cercles* into which the Canton is divided, by a magistrate called *Juge de Paix*.

Each municipality has also power to impose fines for petty offences in violation of police regulations.

1. The cantonal Tribunal consists of nine judges, elected every four years by the Grand Council or legislative authority of the Canton. They are almost without exception chosen from amongst members of the legal profession, and are re-eligible for election on the expiration of their original term of office.

This Tribunal is the supreme court of judicature in the Canton for all questions regarding the application of the cantonal laws; it has, however, no original jurisdiction in these cases, but only acts as an appellate court for the purpose of reviewing judgments of the inferior cantonal tribunals.

In criminal affairs a division of the Court, consisting of three judges, forms the *Cour de Cassation pénale* for appeals from the *Tribunaux Criminels*, or district Criminal Courts.

Another Chamber of three judges, under the name of *Tribunal d'Accusation*, performs functions very analogous to those of the Grand Jury in England.

2. *Juge d'Instruction.*— This magistrate has the superintendence of criminal affairs prior to the indictment; he either instructs the *Juge de Paix* or himself orders all the necessary measures for tracing and arresting offenders.

Every month he sends up to the public prosecutor (*Procureur-général*) the list of all criminal cases in course of investigation in the Canton.

3. District Courts (*Tribunaux de District*).—A District Court consists of a president and four judges, appointed by the cantonal Tribunal for a term of four years. As long as they remain in office, the members of the Court, if they happen to be advocates, have to renounce the practice of their profession.

President of the Court.—As a judge sitting alone the president has jurisdiction both in civil and criminal matters; he further makes interlocutory orders in the suits brought before him or before the District Court, thus deciding, subject to appeal, all incidental questions.

Sitting alone, he decides questions involving the presumption of life in the case of persons who have been absent for more than six years from the Canton, the emancipation of minors,[1] and the registration of donations *inter vivos*; he hears all petitions presented by heirs claiming the *beneficium inventarii* before accepting a succession;[2] he entertains all petitions relating to

---

[1] The cantonal and Federal legislation provides that minors over eighteen may be relieved from guardianship, and thenceforth considered of age, as regards the municipal law.

[2] *Beneficium inventarii.* The charges and claims upon the estate of a deceased person may exceed the assets. When the succession has once been accepted by the heirs, they become liable, on their own personal property, for the total amount of the debts. It may therefore be a matter of no small importance to them, before accepting the succession, to ascertain the real state of things. This is done in the following manner:— They apply to the competent court of law, which appoints a guardian or trustee to the estate, and issues a summons to all creditors to deposit their claims in the clerk's office, within a period varying from fifty to a hundred days. This summons is inserted at intervals in the official Gazette, with a notice that all claims (except those relating to mortgages) which shall not have been filed in the clerk's office before the expiration of the term will be dismissed. The exact situation of the estate being thus ascertained, the heirs are allowed a further term of six weeks to decide whether they will accept the succession or not. If they accept,

bankruptcy or filed by the wife of an insolvent husband
for the recovery, management, and control of her own
personal property and other matters.

The president further tries and decides all suits
where the amount in dispute is between £4 and
£20.

In criminal matters his jurisdiction extends over
offences punishable by a maximum of ten days' imprisonment, £20 fine, or an official and public rebuke.

The Court.—The District Court sits as a civil tribunal,
a criminal court, and a police court.

As a civil tribunal, its jurisdiction extends to all suits
where the claim amounts to £20 or more in value (those
which are carried directly to the cantonal Tribunal being
excepted); it decides every dispute in connection with
real estate ; and finally all suits concerning the civil
status of persons, divorce, etc.

The law on marriage and divorce being a Federal
law, it would, strictly speaking, have been more logical
to carry all actions to which its application might give
rise before the cantonal Tribunal and thence upon
appeal to the Federal Tribunal, but when the law was
under discussion, the Grand Council, looking at the
question of expense, on the one hand, and, on the
other, considering that a judge living in the neighbourhood of the parties was more likely to be better qualified
to decide upon such matters than an utter stranger,
totally unacquainted with the circumstances of the
litigants, gave the preference to an entirely opposite
course.   The jurisdiction of the District Court is maintained as it existed prior to the introduction of the

they assume the liability of the debts, only those being admitted which
appear in the *inventory* taken of those filed as aforesaid.   If the heirs
refuse to accept the succession, the estate is wound up in the interest of
the creditors under the control and supervision of the Court.

Federal law, and the appeal passing over the cantonal Tribunal now goes direct to the Federal Tribunal.

This is a most striking instance of the manifold complications which are continually arising owing to the co-existence of Federal and cantonal laws on matters closely connected.

The grounds upon which a divorce may be granted are determined by the Federal law, but the consequences of the divorce as regards the settlement of all financial questions, alimony, education, and care and maintenance of the children, are governed by the cantonal law exclusively. It therefore follows that, in so far as the divorce alone is concerned, the final decision upon appeal rests with the Federal Tribunal, whereas for all accessory matters, such as those specified above, the highest jurisdiction belongs to the cantonal Tribunal.

An action for divorce which is brought as a whole before the inferior court may therefore, if the parties are not satisfied with the decision, branch off upon appeal into two perfectly distinct suits.

For the trial of criminal cases the Court is formed by the president and two of the four judges. There is also a jury of nine persons.

The jury list is prepared in the following manner :—

Once in every four years, the electors of each township forming part of the district meet together in the month of November and elect the jurymen in the proportion of one to each hundred inhabitants, fractions of over fifty inhabitants counting for a hundred. There are a number of exemptions, and citizens of over sixty years of age, or whose names stood on the last list, as well as such as are disabled by sickness or permanent infirmity, may, upon application, have their names struck off the list.

As soon as the president of the Court receives information that a criminal case is about to come on, he appoints a day for the impanelling of the jury, and gives notice of it to the public prosecutor, to the witnesses for the prosecution, to the accused, and to his counsel.

On the appointed day the president causes numbers corresponding to the names of those jurymen who stand on the general list to be cast into a ballot-box, and with the assistance of the clerk of the Court, in the presence of the parties interested, he draws thirty-one numbers from the ballot-box ; a list comprising thirty-one names is thus made ; a journal of the proceedings is kept, and a copy of the same is forwarded to the public prosecutor and to the accused. Within the three following days the president strikes out nine names from the list and chooses two substitutes from the rest ; notice is given to the accused, to whom an equal term of three days is granted for proceeding in the same way ; there thus remain nine jurymen. If the accused are several in number, they, or rather their respective advocates, act in concert ; but if they are unable to agree, they refer to the president of the Court, who has again to resort to the ballot-box.

The jurymen elect their own foreman.

A peculiarity of the law worthy of notice lies in the provision that when the accused pleads guilty, the jury may be dispensed with at the trial, provided he files a petition to this effect in the office of the clerk of the Court.

The summons served upon each member of the jury mentions neither the name of the accused nor the crime for which he is indicted.

4. *Juge de Paix* and Court of the *Justice de Paix.*

(*a*) *Juge de Paix.*—The official obligations of this

magistrate are numerous; he is brought into constant contact with the public, and should possess not only a practical knowledge of the law but also tact and discrimination.   A thorough *Juge de Paix* acquires great influence, and for this reason, in spite of the insufficiency of the salary, whenever a vacancy occurs the candidates for office are numerous.

Before any civil suit is allowed by law to go before the Court for judgment, the would-be litigants are bound to put in an appearance before the *Juge de Paix*, whose mission it is to endeavour to reconcile the parties, and if he is a man of energy and tact, success very often attends his efforts, especially in the more remote parts of the Canton.

In his capacity of judge, he decides finally and without appeal all suits the subject matter of which is under £4 in value.

He further settles summarily all disputes as to wages within the above limit between masters and their servants, artisans, or workmen.

All disputes between travellers and hotel or boarding-house keepers.

All disputes between travellers and carriers as to loss of or damage to luggage.

All disputes between public porters or cabmen and those who hire their services.

The *Juge de Paix* presides at the proving of wills, he orders the acceptance or repudiation of successions where the heirs have not claimed the *beneficium inventarii*, and the delivery of the estate to the heirs alike under a testamentary or an intestate succession.

He may be further called upon from time to time to interfere in family dissensions of an acute character.

In criminal matters his functions are analogous to

those of the *Juge d'Instruction*, whose subordinate, however, he is. Finally, he passes sentence on certain classes of minor offenders.

The multiplicity of the avocations of the *Juges de Paix* explains the reason for their being comparatively numerous in so small a country as the Canton of Vaud.

(*b*) Court of the *Justice de Paix*.—This is a peculiar institution. Though a court of law, no suit can be brought before it; it has the supervision and control of guardians and looks after the interests of minors and of those persons who from mental infirmity are unable to manage their own affairs. Its action is of great importance, though in a limited sphere; it takes, in a great measure, the same position with regard to wards as the *Conseils de famille* provided for by the French code. It consists of four assessors, and is presided over by the *Juge de Paix*.

The mode of proceeding in civil cases is governed by the *Code de procédure civile*, adopted on the 25th November 1869, and subsequently modified by several distinct legislative enactments, introducing sundry amendments tending all more or less to simplify procedure and diminish costs.

In all civil actions, proceedings are instituted by the issue of a summons on behalf of the plaintiff, citing the defendant to appear before the competent judge.

This summons, signed, sealed, and delivered by the judge, is notified by the *huissier* (usher) of the Court to the defendant, who is thus officially informed of the nature of the claim brought against him.

On the appointed day the litigants appear before the judge, who, after giving them a hearing, endeavours to induce them to arrive at an understanding. They must attend personally or by proxy, and no professional advocates are at this stage allowed to appear on their behalf. If the attempt fails, as it very often does, the judge certifies in writing to that effect, and the suit enters into a new phase, and can only then be said to have really commenced as a contentious matter.

Within the sixty days following the plaintiff files his statement of claim in the office of the clerk of the Court. This petition embodies—

1. A statement of all the facts connected with the case which may tend to substantiate his claim.
2. A discussion of the law bearing on the facts described.
3. The conclusions—viz. the distinct enunciation of the claim, the acknowledgment of which is required from the Court.

Taking, for instance, the simplest form of claim, that for payment of goods sold and delivered by a tradesman to a customer, the conclusions would be framed in the following terms: "May the Court be pleased to decide with grant of costs that N. N. is A. B.'s debtor in the sum of —— for goods sold and delivered, bearing interest at the rate of five per cent per annum from the day of the date of the summons."

A copy of this statement of claim is served upon the defendant, together with a notice delivered by the Court that, within the term of (usually) twenty days, the defendant must file his statement of defence drawn up in the same form as that of the plaintiff's demand.

In his answer the defendant either admits or denies the statements made on the other side.

All uncontradicted facts are considered as proved by the defendant's admission, and it is not necessary subsequently to confirm them by means of oral or documentary evidence. The statements which are denied have to be substantiated at a later stage of the proceedings. Having thus disposed of his adversary's facts, the defendant enumerates those which he considers likely to justify his resistance to the original claim or to substantiate any counter-claim which he may desire to introduce.

The answer further contains a discussion and refutation of the plaintiff's arguments, and finally states the defendant's conclusions.

A copy is served upon the plaintiff, and as no reply in writing is allowed by the law, the parties can only await the day appointed by the president for the preliminary oral proceedings in order to determine the facts still in dispute, and to settle in what manner the requisite evidence shall be procured.

All these preliminary proceedings take place in the presence and under the direction of the president of the Court sitting alone, with the assistance of the clerk who keeps the minute-book or journal (*procès-verbal*) of the Court.

At this hearing before the president advocates are not only allowed to appear, but their presence is considered necessary.

The plaintiff, not being permitted to file a reply in writing to the defendant's statement of defence, deals at once, before the president, with the defendant's statements.

Both parties are now allowed to supplement their original statements by the introduction of others. The disputed facts on both sides remain to be proved, and each party gives notice of the manner in which he intends submitting evidence, whether documentary or oral.

All these matters having been duly specified and settled, the Court meets on the day appointed for the trial. The president conducts the examination of the parties and witnesses, and the advocates are allowed to put supplementary questions, but any attempt at brow-beating would immediately call for the president's interference and be put a stop to. Speaking generally, less license is allowed to the cross-examining advocate than is the case in England.

After the evidence has been heard, each advocate argues his case, the proceedings in public are then closed, and the Court retires to deliberate. The president recalls in succession each material fact as to which oral evidence has been given, and the members of the Court give their opinions separately. Each then votes as to whether the alleged fact may be considered as proved or not.

The conflicting conclusions are read to the Court, the arguments discussed by counsel in their pleadings are examined, and the Court decides.

Full liberty is granted to the Court to allow less than was claimed, but it has no power to grant more, however justified such a decision might be in equity.

The costs are either entirely or partially payable by the losing side, in the discretion of the Court.

The procedure in a civil suit before the *Juge de Paix* pursues the same general lines, but is necessarily of a somewhat more summary character.

Appeals to the higher Court are made in the form of a petition (*recours*) filed in the office of the clerk of the District Court ; from there it is forwarded to the cantonal Tribunal with a copy of the decision, journal of proceedings, and all other documents.

The appeal has for its object either the annulment

of the decision as embodying violations of the positive text of the law, or the reconsideration of the decision on the ground of a mistaken interpretation of the law as applied to the circumstances of the case.

On the appointed day counsel on both sides argue the case, and the members of the Court discuss the question, *coram publico*, in the presence of the parties. If the decision is annulled, the Court orders the transfer of the suit to a neighbouring district Court for a fresh trial. If the appeal is for reconsideration, the Court either revises, varies, or confirms the decision.

Witnesses never appear before the cantonal Tribunal, and, according to the law of procedure, there is no appeal from findings of fact by the Court below.

The suit which has passed through all the degrees of jurisdiction may still be reopened if, within the year following the final decision, the defeated party discovers a deed or document, the exhibition of which in due time or place must have ensured success; or if the other party, or one of the witnesses, has subsequently been tried and condemned for perjury committed in the course of the case; or if a document mentioned in the decision as having formed a material ground of the Court's opinion is proved in a criminal court to be a forgery.

The decision as to whether the suit may or may not be reopened rests with the cantonal Tribunal; if a re-hearing is granted, the parties find themselves re-placed in the position they occupied before proceedings were originally instituted.

In criminal matters the indictment is first read, then the president examines the accused, after which the members of the jury, the counsel for the prosecution (*substitut du Procureur-général*), the counsel for the complainant (if any), and the counsel for the accused examine him in their turn; the witnesses are thereupon called successively to give their evidence, after which the counsel for the complainant and the counsel for the prosecution address the Court, and finally the counsel for the accused is allowed the last word.

The president then announces the questions he proposes to leave to the jury; the parties are allowed to challenge these questions, the final decision resting in all cases with the Court. The president having put the questions as finally settled by the Court to the jury, the latter body retire to consider their verdict; if they cannot agree, a minority of four in favour of the accused is sufficient to secure his acquittal. The verdict once given, the jury's mission is at an end, and the members are dismissed by the president; if the verdict is favourable, the Court orders the immediate release of the accused; if unfavourable, the counsel are successively heard as regards the penalty applicable, and the Court decides.

The accused is allowed, provided he do so within three days from the date of his sentence, to appeal to the *Cour de Cassation pénale.*

Before this Court, as in civil matters before the cantonal Tribunal, witnesses are not admitted, the findings of the jury as to the facts being final and conclusive.

If the sentence be reversed and the decision annulled for irregularity in the proceedings, the case is referred to another criminal court, where a new jury is impanelled and a fresh trial takes place.

If the decision be merely reconsidered, this affects the penalty only, which may be inflicted in a more severe form or brought down to a lower scale.

Any convicted person has always this right of appeal for a revision of the proceedings or sentence on his original trial, and it is granted under conditions very much the same as those mentioned as prevailing under analogous circumstances in civil matters.

The law, it may be remarked, takes care to ensure citizens against the possibility of arbitrary arrest; no one may be arrested on mere suspicion of crime, or unless actually caught *flagrante delicto*, without a warrant from a competent magistrate; any person who is arrested must be examined by the judge within twenty-four hours, and as soon as the preliminary investigation has come to a close, the magistrate, before sending his report to the *Tribunal d'Accusation*, provides for the appointment of a counsel for the defence, under whose advice further inquiries are to be made whenever he considers it advisable in his client's interest.

It is probably known that in Switzerland there are no *avoués*, as in France, but only *avocats*, who act at the same time as advocates and solicitors. Each Canton lays down its own rules with respect to the practice of the legal profession; but when an advocate has passed certain technical examinations, the Federal Constitution grants to him the right to practise in all parts of Switzerland. The chief function of notaries is to draw up documents, to administer oaths, and to witness signatures. In some Cantons the same person can be both advocate and notary. Both are in general permitted to practise, after having obtained certificates that they have passed an examination before a cantonal committee. In case of misconduct, the offender is punished by the highest tribunal of his Canton.

A few words may be added respecting the gaols. They do not exist in all Cantons, so that convicts from one Canton have sometimes to be received in gaols of another. It has several times been proposed to establish a Federal gaol for dangerous criminals, or for vicious youths, but without success.

Solitary confinement is sometimes resorted to, generally during the early period of imprisonment, or by way of punishment. There are no treadmills, and corporal punishment has been abolished by the Federal Constitution. In some prisons wine and tobacco are interdicted; in others the prisoners are allowed to buy these luxuries.

Convicts who behave themselves well are promoted from one class to a higher, and enjoy some small privileges; and after serving two-thirds of their term, if over a year, they may be conditionally released. They then, until the expiration of their original term of imprisonment, remain under the supervision of the police, and may, without previous notice, upon a mere order of the cantonal department of justice, and for the smallest breach of good conduct, be sent to prison to serve out the remainder of their full term, the intermediate time spent out of gaol being in such cases counted for nothing. This privilege is never granted to any one who has been twice convicted.

CHAPTER XI

THE ARMY

FROM her position, the military importance of Switzerland is out of all proportion to the extent of her territory or the strength of her army. It has been pointed out by a recent military writer that a power which was master of Switzerland could debouch on the theatre of operations of the Rhone, Saône, Po, or Danube. From Geneva an army could march on Lyons, from Basel it could gain the valley of the Saône by Belfort, from Constance the Danube could be reached; Italy could be invaded, and the lines of defence of that country against France and Austria turned. In consequence of the peculiar position of Switzerland it was fully recognized by the powers at the Congress of Vienna that the general interest of Europe required that she should be constituted an independent and neutral State, sufficiently strong to ensure her neutrality being respected. The Act, signed at Paris on the 20th November 1815, whereby her perpetual neutrality and the inviolability of her territory were guaranteed, has already been recorded in Chapter I.

The Swiss have for ages been renowned for their sterling military qualities; in more recent times these have been principally displayed in the pay of other nations or in the personal service of foreign potentates. The Pope's Bodyguard was originally composed entirely of young Swiss, whose love of an active military career led them to take the field in a neighbouring country. The great stone lion carved by Thorvaldsen at Luzern was erected to the memory of the 786 officers and soldiers of the Swiss Guard who fell in the defence of the Tuilleries in 1792. At the time of the Peninsular War and at Waterloo, Swiss legions were raised by the British Government, and again in 1855 during the invasion of the Crimea. On this last occasion the British-Swiss Legion was composed of two light infantry regiments. They embarked at Dover for Smyrna, where they remained for about a year, and in June 1856 landed at Portsmouth *en route* for Shorncliffe, where they were disbanded. The articles of capitulation for forming foreign legions provided that "the bounty of £6 shall be payable by Her Majesty's Government in cash, and necessaries to each recruit finally approved." The recruiting officers abroad who held "Letters of Service" received £975 for every hundred men, out of which sum the expenses incurred in levying, maintaining, and forwarding the recruits to the established depots at Heligoland or Shorncliffe were defrayed. The officers and men were required to take the oath of allegiance to the Queen; they were subject to the same regulations as British troops, and were on the same footing as regiments of the line in respect of pay, supply of clothing, and appointments. As we shall presently see, the recruiting within the limits of the Confederation of Swiss citizens for service in the army of a foreign State was expressly forbidden by the Swiss Constitution; the men were therefore enrolled secretly and then marched across the frontier to a subsidiary depot at

Schlettstadt, in Alsace.   Colonel C. S. Dickson was Staff Commandant of the British-Swiss Legion during the Crimean War, and the names of the Swiss officers who served under him are to be found in our Army List for 1856-57.

Upon all the many occasions when Swiss have gone abroad for foreign service, the rank and file have always stipulated that their immediate leaders must be chosen from amongst their own countrymen.   In past times treaties which went by the name of military capitulations were often concluded between foreign governments and one or more Cantons.   These mercenary services were not infrequently secured by the representatives of foreign powers by means of bribery and intrigue, and there were occasions too when Swiss were found fighting against each other in the ranks of opposing armies.   The consequences were injurious to the morals of the people, and the Constitution of 1848 forbade the conclusion of any fresh treaties of this nature.   In 1849 there still remained one such Convention in force between several Cantons and the King of Naples.   But the Swiss troops having contributed to defeat the revolution, great indignation arose in Switzerland, they were recalled to their native country, and the last of these military capitulations came to an end.

The army is organized on what has been called the "voluntary-compulsory" system, to which the Swiss of their own free will resigned themselves in order to maintain the independence of their country; and it is interesting to note that they were the first nation in Europe to introduce a scheme of universal liability to military service.   This was naturally the result of the oppression to which the men of the primitive Cantons of Uri, Schwyz, and Unterwalden were subjected by

Austria and her bailiffs, rendering it absolutely necessary that every able-bodied man should be familiar with the use of arms. As the Confederation grew in power and extent through the admission of Luzern, Zürich, Bern, and other States, what between the number of foreign enemies who threatened its existence and their domestic broils, the Swiss were obliged for centuries to remain almost continually under arms; and hence they were trained from an early age in the use of the sword, the pike, and the cross-bow. The neighbouring powers on the other hand, distrusting their own people, reserved the use of arms for the high-born, and for mercenaries or serfs of the crown who were immediately disbanded on the conclusion of a war. It can therefore easily be conceived that the independent Swiss soldiers who from their youth fought for liberty in a mountainous country, where every inch of ground was familiar to them, were more than a match for these half-trained men led by haughty nobles who looked down upon them with contempt.

The great military systems of many European countries did not emanate from the nations themselves, but were forced upon them by aggressive military governments, and were the result of long-continued wars. In Switzerland the army is an essentially citizen force, one which is thoroughly representative of the nation; its ranks are not recruited (as in England) from what is practically one class, but are composed of all sorts and conditions of the people, from the lawyer to the artisan, and from the man of property to the labourer. The Swiss army may be compared in many respects to our militia and volunteer force, but the qualifications of each man in his civil capacity are utilized to a far greater extent. Thus, when he takes service under the flag of

the Confederation, the civil engineer becomes a military
engineer, a civil veterinary surgeon is put into the
cavalry or artillery, and a butcher or a baker would
be drafted into the commissariat department.   In the
administration of this citizen army we see not only the
most typical advantages, but also the drawbacks and
imperfections of that peculiar form of military organization.   It is a striking example of an army in which the
chief aim of those who in this country advocate " short
service" has been successfully attained—namely, the
existence of a large reserve of trained soldiers.   The
motto of our volunteers, " Defence not Defiance," might
well be adopted by the Swiss troops, for they are essentially a force of militia intended for defensive purposes
and to secure the neutrality of the country—an army
framed upon principles of the strictest economy, as may
be seen from the following table, which shows approxi-
mately the annual cost per man in the principal armies
in Europe :—

		£	s.	d.
Great Britain	.	£64	10	4
Spain	.	56	2	4
Austro-Hungary	. .	52	12	0
France	. .	46	13	6
Germany	.	46	0	0
Denmark	.	45	0	0
Italy		43	18	0
Belgium	.	40	10	0
Holland	.	31	0	0
Russia	.	22	16	0
Switzerland	. .	7	0	0

The Swiss army is absolutely complete in every
detail ; the medical, commissariat, and veterinary departments are thoroughly organized ; there is the proper

proportion of cavalry, artillery, engineers, and transport; the battalions are kept up to their full strength and all in readiness for service. In fact, all the adjuncts for making an army a mobile factor in the field are, with the Swiss system of administration, complete and in thorough working order. We, on the other hand, have a regular army, composed of close upon 200,000 men and 330,000 militiamen and volunteers, which has not been inaptly called " a conglomerated mass of unconnected atoms." In the opinion of many of our distinguished military men our enormous force of auxiliary troops could not be maintained in the field for three days; they are without the right proportion of artillery, almost destitute of cavalry, and without the nucleus of those departments by which alone an army can be maintained effective. It is a subject for reflection to us, a great and powerful nation, that a little country, not possessing a tenth part of our wealth, can put into and maintain effectively in the field between 150,000 and 200,000 men, a feat which we, in spite of our enormous budget, are incapable of achieving.

The last occasion when the Federal troops were mobilized for active service was in 1871, when Bourbaki's army was driven into Swiss territory. Misgivings arose in the mind of the nation as to the soundness of its military system, and it became evident that many radical changes must be made in the organization of the army. Consequently in 1874 a bill was passed in the Federal Assembly upon which the military system of the present day is founded.

The double sovereignty existing in Switzerland is noticeable in everything relating to the army. All laws which affect its organization emanate from the Confederation, but the duty of executing these laws is vested in the cantonal authorities, who take the necessary steps to prevent persons evading their obligations to service, and are responsible for the recruiting and maintenance of a certain military force proportionate to the area and population of each Canton. The nomination of the officers of the cantonal troops to the rank of *Commandant de Bataillon* is vested in the authorities in each Canton ; the officers must, however, have satisfied the Federal military authorities as to their capacity and fitness for the rank to which it is proposed to appoint them. Officers of higher rank than *Commandant de Bataillon* hold their commissions from the Federal Council. The infantry, field artillery, cavalry, and certain other troops are recruited by the Cantons and are termed cantonal troops. The engineers, guides, sanitary and administrative troops, and the army train are recruited by the Confederation, and these are called Federal troops. Arms are supplied by the Confederation, but the equipments and uniforms are furnished by the Cantons, for which they are subsequently reimbursed by the Confederation. As far as is consistent with military considerations, men belonging to the same Canton are enrolled in the same corps ; this is known as the *système territorial*. By an ordinance of the Federal Council in 1875, the country is divided into eight territorial divisions, each of which furnishes one complete infantry division.

In 1848, when the first Federal Constitution was discussed in the Assembly, it was proposed that the Confederation should be charged with the entire military administration. The proposal was rejected, the majority being unwilling that the powers of the Cantons should be diminished. In 1874 a reaction took place, with the result that the most important powers were vested in the Confederation. Within the last few months significant signs of a further reaction have shown themselves. The Canton of Bern proposed to transfer to the Federal Council all the privileges of military control which were vested in it by the revised Constitution of 1874. The question of the complete unification of the military administration has been recently mooted in the Grand Councils of Luzern and Schaffhausen. The complete centralization of the entire military organization has been recently discussed in the National Council, who, however, thought it undesirable to make any change in the existing system at a time when, owing to the troubled state of Europe, the country might be called upon at any moment to mobilize its army. The arguments which would be brought against this measure in the event of its being subjected to the Referendum would doubtless be that it was an attempt to establish a permanent army, and would increase the charges for military service, as well as being an encroachment upon the sovereignty of the Cantons. It should also be borne in mind that the Cantons cannot absolutely resign their military powers to the Confederation without a revision of the Constitution.

The 18th Article of the Constitution sets forth that every Swiss is bound to perform military service; all the brothers in a family are compelled to serve, and even supporters of families are not exempted. There are, however, certain officials, of whom the following may be given as examples, who are exempted from military service during the time they are in office : members of the Federal Council and certain officials of the Federal Tribunal, workmen employed in the government arsenals, directors and warders of prisons, attendants in public hospitals, post and telegraph employés, and ecclesiastics who do not act as army chaplains. Apart from these, every Swiss, whether he resides in the Confederation or not, who does not perform military service is subject to an annual tax in lieu thereof. Foreign residents who are settled in Switzerland are also liable, unless they belong to a country where the Swiss are exempt from service or from any similar tax in lieu thereof. During the year 1886 the budget of the Confederation showed that the sum derived from this source reached nearly £106,800, and the following year it amounted to £98,800. This money is shared proportionately between the Confederation and the Cantons. A Swiss waiter or clerk in London must pay for his exemption. In the case of Swiss citizens resident abroad some Cantons commission the consular representative of the Confederation to collect the money, while in others a note is made every year of the amount due, which is claimed when the Swiss returns home. As this tax is almost peculiar to Switzerland, it may be well to give some details regarding it. It consists of a personal charge of six francs (about four shillings and tenpence), and a supplementary charge in proportion to the income, but in no case is the sum total for which one individual is liable to exceed 3000 francs (£120). It is dispensed with in such cases as the following: those who have been disabled during military service, paupers, those who from physical or mental infirmities are unable to support their families, and Swiss who reside abroad and are already forced to pay a tax of exemption in the country of their residence.

The military forces of Switzerland are divided into three distinct classes—the Élite or active army, in which all citizens are liable to serve from the age of 20 to 32;

the Landwehr or first reserve, composed of men from the age of 32 to 44 ; and the Landsturm, consisting of men from 17 to 50 not incorporated in the Élite or Landwehr. This last reserve cannot, as a rule, be called upon for service beyond the frontier. In 1887 a bill was passed in the Federal Assembly by which the Landsturm, in the event of their being called out, were placed on the same footing with reference to the rights of combatants as the Élite or the Landwehr, a privilege which they did not previously possess.

The entire strength of the Swiss army is 202,479, without including the Landsturm, which is not yet completely organized for defensive purposes.

The army is composed of :—

	Élite.	Landwehr.	Total.
Corps d'État Major	42	16	58
Infantry	77,198	77,158	154,356
Cavalry	3,412	3,396	6,808
Artillery	14,519	7,920	22,439
Engineers	4,901	4,882	9,783
Sanitary Corps	4,534	3,056	7,590
Administration	634	530	1,164
Officiers Judiciaires [1]	28	16	44
Chaplains	80	64	144
Secrétaires d'État Major	77	16	93
Total	105,425	97,054	202,479

The number of recruits examined in 1886 was 30,323, and this roughly represents the number of young men who become liable to serve every year.

The enormous disproportion of cavalry to infantry is

---

[1] These officers are almost peculiar to the Swiss army ; according to their respective rank they either preside at court-martials or exercise the functions of public prosecutor for grave military offences.

owing to the fact that in Switzerland the former would hardly ever be required except for reconnoitring or vedette duties. It is doubtful, in such an enclosed country, whether a large force of cavalry would be of much utility. Moreover, it should be understood that the requirements of Swiss strategy would necessitate a defensive campaign only, in which the military operations of the troops would be confined to their own difficult country and narrow valleys.

The 8th Article of the Constitution states that the Confederation has the sole right to declare war, to make peace, and to conclude alliances and treaties. The executive power is exercised by the Federal military department. In order to facilitate the discharge of its duties, this department has at its disposal twelve heads of the various branches of the service. The Federal Council selects the officers for the general staff, or État Major, constituted in time of peace, which according to the military organization consists of 3 colonels, 16 lieutenant-colonels or majors, and 35 captains. The chief of the general staff (which may be said to correspond to the headquarters staff of the British army and the fixed staff of districts, *e.g.* Aldershot) is nominated for three years; the appointment may, however, be renewed. The Bureau d'État Major at Bern is divided into two distinct sections — the general section, which is immediately under the chief of the Corps d'État Major, and the railway section, consisting of 19 officers of various ranks. Since 1879 the Federal military department has been continuously under the direction of Colonel Hertenstein, president of the Confederation in 1888, until his lamented death on the 27th November of the latter year. Switzerland has lost in him an able and distinguished administrator. In the event of a war the

Federal Assembly nominates a general, who takes command till the troops are disbanded. The only general officer at present in the Swiss service is General Herzog, who commanded the troops in 1871 when Bourbaki's army crossed the frontier, and who still retains the higher rank, although doing the duties of a colonel. In order to qualify for an appointment on the general staff an officer must pass a ten weeks' course of instruction, and there is an additional course of six weeks for captains and majors who have successfully passed through the first one. There is no permanent college for officers of the general staff, such as the Staff College in this country. In Switzerland military instruction for officers as well as men takes a temporary form, and consists of courses held at regular intervals, which all are obliged to attend; in fact, the system of instruction forms one of the most remarkable characteristics of the Swiss military organization. In order to ensure a perfect uniformity in the instruction of the army, a permanent corps of 187 instructors of various grades, and representing all the arms of the service, is maintained. The members of the Instructional Corps are in fact almost the only permanently paid officers of the Swiss army.

The raw recruits are sent direct to one of the *Écoles des Recrues*, which are held at the following places :—

Infantry	I. Division,	Lausanne.
,,	II. ,,	Colombier.
,,	III. ,,	Bern.
,,	IV. ,,	Luzern.
,,	V. ,,	Aarau and Liestal.
,,	VI. ,,	Zürich.
,,	VII. ,,	St. Gallen.
,,	VIII. ,,	Coire and Bellinzona.

Cavalry	.	.	Bern, Zürich, and Aarau.
Artillery	.	.	Thun, Zürich, Frauenfeld, and Biere.
Engineers	.	.	Brugg and Liestal.

The recruits are kept at one of these establishments for periods ranging from forty-five to eighty days, after which they are drafted into the different arms of the service, and (with the exception of the cavalry, who turn out annually) the several branches of the service are called out once in every two years for a course of training (*cours de répétition*). Under the present system the Swiss infantry soldier has the following five periods of training during the ten years he remains in the Élite :—

1st year,	45	days as a recruit.
3rd ,,	16	,,	trained soldier.
5th ,,	16	,,	,,
7th ,,	16	,,	,,
9th ,,	16	,,	,,
Total	109	

The standard of height which is required of the recruits is 5 feet $1\frac{1}{2}$ inches. The chest measurement should be at least equal to one half the height, and in no case less than $31\frac{1}{2}$ inches. The average height of the men of the age of $19\frac{1}{4}$ in the Swiss army is 5 feet 4 inches. Men not having attained the height of 5 feet $1\frac{1}{2}$ inches on completing their twentieth year are definitively exempted from service, unless they are specially fitted by profession or business for service in the administrative troops, or as drummers, trumpeters, armourers, or other military handicraftsmen, in which case they may be recruited to serve in these capacities if their height is not less than 5 feet $\frac{5}{8}$ of an inch. We may mention that the minimum height for British recruits is 5 feet 5 inches, and the minimum chest measurement 33 inches. Every Swiss recruit is required to pass an *examen pédagogique*, which is conducted by an *expert pédagogique*, who is a member of the *commission de recrutement*. This enables the authorities to ascertain the degree of instruction attained by the youth of the country, and also assists them in appointing the recruits to the different arms. The examination consists of arithmetic, geography, and Swiss history, and no better proof could be given of the high standard of education in Switzerland than the fact that in 1885 there were only 0·3 per cent of the recruits found to be illiterate. Such recruits as do not come up to the minimum educational standard are required to undergo instruction at the recruits' school, and the odium attendant upon this is found to exercise a marked beneficial effect on the education of the peasantry.

Previous to the commencement of his military service the Swiss recruit has undergone a considerable amount of training. The word "raw," at any rate in the sense we use it in speaking of a squad of our recruits whilst learning the goose-step, could never be applied to a young Swiss who had just joined his regiment. The playground of the village school was his first barrack-yard, where he learnt gymnastics, the manual exercise, and the elements of company drill; so that on the day he receives his *livret de service* he has a far better knowledge of the rudiments of soldiering than the average British recruit. The *Tir fédéral*, so liberally encouraged by Government and the many cantonal and communal shooting societies, have, by making rifle shooting a national pastime, contributed their share towards raising the standard of marksmanship in the Swiss army. On fête-days one may see men in all the different grades in the service, from the newly joined recruit to the major of his battalion, standing together in the Schützengraben of the Commune, and there voluntarily spending the holiday afternoons in perfecting themselves in the use of the rifle. There is much of the "sportsman-soldier," if we may use the expression, about the Swiss marksman; his skill is by no means solely acquired during drill hours or at the regimental butts. The system of rifle meetings is, moreover, utilized for purposes of musketry instruction; thus each Swiss soldier is compelled to fire thirty rounds annually; if he does not do this at a cantonal rifle meeting, he is compelled to attend a three days' course under military supervision.

The officers of the cantonal troops are nominated by the Grand Council, or other corresponding authority in each Canton, upon the recommendation of the military cantonal director, after having successfully passed through the necessary schools of instruction. Promotion from lieutenant to first lieutenant takes place according to seniority; but the next steps, from first lieutenant to captain, and captain to major, are given on a consideration of the officer's general fitness and aptitude, without regard to his seniority. In the infantry a candidate for the rank of first lieutenant must be recommended by the captain of his company; but officers who desire to be promoted to the ranks of captain and major must be recommended by the officers commanding the regiment and the battalion. With the exception of those belonging to the corps of instruction, the general staff, and a few of the other officials, Swiss officers only receive pay during the short period they are called out for training.

Roughly speaking, taking an average case, the Swiss infantry soldier must spend a total period of 350 or 360 days in a school and in undergoing other courses of instruction before he receives a captain's commission, which may be said to be after a period of some eight years' service. It will therefore be seen that a captain in the Swiss army undergoes a very much smaller amount of training than an officer of the same rank in our militia, who has gone out annually with his regiment during a similar number of years. One of the greatest defects in a citizen army, perhaps the weakest point in its organization, is the difficulty of providing properly trained and thoroughly qualified officers. The greater the intelligence of the rank and file, the more severely are the capabilities of those who hold commissions put to the test ; moreover, as the periods of training are necessarily so short, it is absolutely requisite that the officers should be thoroughly acquainted with their duties, in order to make the greatest possible use of the time during which the men are under instruction. None are better aware of this defect in their military system than the Swiss themselves, and none are more ready to acknowledge it. Year after year, in the official report presented by the military department to the Federal Assembly, there is a wail as to the difficulty of obtaining really competent and suitable officers. Thus in the report for 1886 we find the following remark on the army : " Our population is simply not rich enough or strong enough in men for raising the number of really good officers which our military organization at present requires."

The Swiss soldier only receives pay during active service, or during his various courses of training. The pay of the commander-in-chief in time of war would only be £2 a day, while that of a private soldier would be eighty centimes. Neither officers nor men receive pensions at the termination of their service, unless they have been disabled by wounds or sickness resulting from military duties. If a soldier is killed in battle, or dies in consequence of wounds or disease contracted in the Federal service, his family have a right to an indemnity provided it can be proved that the deceased was dependent for his maintenance on his own exertions. No member of the Federal army can, as such, wear any decoration or accept any title granted by a foreign government.

. Although the cavalry have a yearly training in place of a biennial one as in the infantry, it may be said to be the most popular branch of the service, probably on account of the very generous inducements held out to the recruits by Government. The method of providing cavalry remounts is peculiar to Switzerland, and as it may throw some light on the same difficult question which is at present being widely discussed in England, the following sketch of the system pursued may be of interest.

The cavalry horses are generally obtained in Hungary and Germany, and are purchased by a remount committee consisting of the chief instructor of cavalry, two veterinary surgeons, and another selected officer. The horses are generally four-year-olds, the maximum price given for them being £60. After purchase they are sent for four months to the government depots at Zürich, Aarau, and Bern, where they are handed over to rough-riders and broken both as saddle and draught horses, and when ready are sold to such cavalry recruits as may require them. Those recruits of each yearly draft who elect to join the cavalry do so voluntarily in the first instance, but having selected that branch of the service they are compelled to provide themselves with horses, and if on joining their regiment they are unable to present themselves with a suitable and properly trained horse, they are assigned, under conditions we shall proceed to detail, one of the remount horses already alluded to. The conditions regarding the sale of trained horses to cavalry regiments are to be found in a regulation of the 19th January 1883. The auction is so arranged that, at whatever price the animal is knocked down, one half is paid by the State and the other by the recruit. One-tenth of the share he has paid is refunded to him at the end of each year's service, so that after ten trainings the horse becomes his personal property. During these years of service the horse is considered as being always at the disposal of the State, although in reality it is only required during the yearly days of drill and training, and at all other times it is kept by its part-owner, at his own cost, and he is held responsible for its care and good condition. In the event of any injury happening to the horse, the cause is at once investigated by a government board, who adjudicate whether the damage was occasioned by carelessness or culpable negligence, or whether it could be ascribed to pure accident and ordinary fair usage. In the former case a trooper is fined or forfeits the balance of his purchase-money, which is held by the State, and he is also compelled to provide himself with another horse. This system, although only recently made universal in Switzerland, is found to answer admirably. It is, of course, to every man's interest that his horse should be well taken care of, because, as already stated, it becomes his own property after he has completed his term of service in the Élite. Mounted officers of every branch of the service are bound to provide their own horses. Draught horses, including those required for field artillery, are hired in time of peace, and in time of war all the horses in the country are at the disposal of the Confederation. In the event of mobilization being imminent, the *Piket-Stellung*, as it is called, can be declared by the Federal authorities, the result of which is that throughout the whole country no horse can change hands. An examination of all the horses would then at once take place, and those found to be unfit for military purposes might be sold by their owners. The purchasers would probably be for the most part those whose horses had been claimed for service by the Government. The Swiss Government has upon its lists a sufficient supply of horses to complete the mobilization of the eight divisions of the Élite.

The fusiliers of the Élite and some of the younger classes of the Landwehr are armed with the Vetterli rifle, a weapon with a calibre of 10·4 millimetres and a magazine capable of containing eleven cartridges. It cannot, however, now be considered to be in the first rank of repeating weapons. Practically there is only one small-arms ammunition used throughout the three branches of the service. The armament of the Landsturm is not yet completed, but whatever weapons they may bring into the field, whether belonging to the men themselves or to the State, will be of the same calibre as the Vetterli. The introduction of a repeating rifle of 7·5 millimetres is under consideration.

With regard to the fortifications of the country, it is only necessary to state that there exist old works, which are acknowledged to be but of little value, at Luziensteig (Grisons), St. Maurice (Valais), and Aarberg (Bern).

The important works for the defence of the St. Gothard tunnel at Airolo will, however, when completed, be of considerable strategical importance with regard to operations on the Italian side.

Any one who knows Switzerland must have observed the extreme attention paid to the minutest detail in every department of government. This particular trait of the Swiss character is displayed in a marked degree in all the arrangements connected with the mobilization of the troops. In 1871, when the military organization was in a far inferior condition compared with what it now is, over 19,000 men were brought from every quarter of the country to watch the Franco-Swiss frontier, and it may safely be predicted that, owing to the experience then gained and to the development in recent years of the Swiss railway system, a concentration of the forces of the country in any desired direction could now be made with far greater facility than was the case at the time of the Franco-German war.

The Swiss soldier keeps his entire kit, his rifle, knapsack, and cloak, in his own home, and every man takes an honest pride in having each article in good condition and in readiness for inspection at any moment. Partly from curiosity, and partly with the view of testing this frequently repeated statement, we once visited a couple of châlets and asked their owners to allow us to see their Vetterli rifle, uniform, and accoutrements. Without a moment's delay they were in both cases produced, and we found all in first-rate condition. The inspection of arms, held annually in each district, is conducted with much strictness. Should the smallest spot of rust be found on the bore of a rifle by the inspecting officer, the weapon is at once sent to a gunsmith, by whom it is cleaned at the owner's expense. To be obliged to return from the inspection without a rifle is considered by the Swiss soldier as a very grave disgrace. He is certain to have to bear not only the taunts of his companions but the jeers of all the village lads.

When the Swiss soldier crosses his threshold for service he may be said to be in full marching order. So complete are all the arrangements that he has not even to apply for a railway warrant, but steps into the train at the nearest station. In the event of the troops being mobilized the railways would be entirely at the disposal of Government, which already has the control of the whole of the postal telegraphic system. Like the "Fiery Cross" in olden time, the wires would spread the news far and wide to every Canton in the Confederation and summon each citizen soldier, from the peasant in the remotest valley to his wealthier fellow-countryman in the plains, to hasten and rally round one another for the defence of the land they love so well.

General Trochu once said that "the spirit of an army is the spirit of the nation from which that army springs." These words have been amply confirmed as regards the Swiss soldier by a British officer of distinction, who had exceptional opportunities of seeing and of judging the performances of the Swiss soldier in the field. Speaking of recent divisional manœuvres he remarks as follows : "There is a thoroughly practical tone about the whole of the Swiss military arrangements. With little to catch the eye in the outward appearance of the Swiss troops, there is nevertheless to a soldier's instinct that which is more to the point than the pomp and glitter of many other armies, viz. a quiet determination to do their military service, a duty which they owe their country no less than themselves. This quiet feeling of patriotism is very visible in the countenances of the men, and I several times felt as I watched them that they could be trusted in a crisis or in a moment of danger. A soldier's instinct it is to know this, and I find it difficult to account for, but I have never known the instinct fail."

CHAPTER XII

CHRISTIANITY penetrated into Helvetia almost at the same time as into the country of the Gauls; and, as in England, its first authentic mention occurs in connection with the Roman soldier. From Lyons and Vienne in Dauphiné it extended up the valley of the Rhone as far as the Lake of Geneva; from Milan it was brought over to what is now the Valais. In the third century several small communities seem to have been established in different parts of the country,[1] and their existence in the fourth century is attested by Christian emblems upon tombs and monuments. In Helvetia, as elsewhere, there were persecutions of the new faith. Notwithstanding the authority of Eusebius, it has been long believed[2] that the Theban legion, consisting of 6000 Christians, suffered martyrdom in the valley of the Pennine Alps (Valais) during the reign and probably by the order of Maximian, to whom participation in the Empire had been given by Diocletian, that most cruel of persecutors. This massacre took place towards the end of the third or at the beginning of the fourth

---

[1] Amongst these places are those known by the modern names of Geneva, Avenches, Augst, Nyon, and Sion.

[2] See footnote in the sixteenth chapter of Gibbon's *Decline and Fall of the Roman Empire.*

century. There is a building at Sion erected in 377 by
Pontius, the governor or prætor of the district, on
which a well-known Christian monogram has been
carved, with an inscription stating that Pontius, in-
spired by piety, had rebuilt the temple to be more
beautiful than it was previously, and praying that the
Republic might always possess such men.[1]

After the downfall of the Roman Empire, many of
the little bands of Christian worshippers were not dis-
persed, but increased in numbers under the rule of the
Alemanni, the Burgundians, and the Franks. It is
true that in certain districts the cause of Christianity
suffered, and, like intellectual progress of every kind,
seemed as if it was destined to expand no further. In
some places the new faith altogether disappeared, and
the paganism which had apparently been extinguished
made fresh progress. Hence the mission established by
the Irish in central and eastern Switzerland at the
beginning of the seventh century has been considered
by many to be a new evangelization of the country.
"Patrick, the first missionary of Ireland, had not been
half a century dead," wrote the late Mr. J. R. Green in
his *Short History of the English People,* "when Irish
Christianity flung itself with a fiery zeal into battle
with the mass of heathenism which was rolling in upon
the Christian world." One of the first of these early
missionaries was Columban,[2] who had been trained under
the Abbot Comgall in the monastery of Bangor near
the modern Belfast, and who went to France with his
pupil Gall, a man possessed of less daring than himself,
but who could preach not only in German but in Latin.[3]

---

[1] Daguet's *Histoire de la Confédération Suisse*, seventh edition, pp. 36-38.
[2] Not to be confounded with St. Columba, who in 546, when forty-two
years of age, left Ireland and founded the monastery of Iona.
[3] Montalembert's *Monks of the West*, vol. ii.

After remaining for a short time at the court of King Childebert, they continued their journey eastwards in order to spread Christianity in the Helvetian and Rhætian districts. Their fervour in burning a temple and throwing away the sacrifices offered to heathen divinities nearly cost them their lives. Columban proceeded to Italy and founded the monastery of Bobbio, where the last years of his life were spent; Gall remained, and about the year 610 built a hermit's cell on the banks of the Siller, and took up his abode in it. Near this spot there arose in 720 the monastic settlement and the town called after this early missionary to the Swiss, who is often spoken of as the "Apostle of Switzerland." About the same period the great religious houses of Einsiedeln, Dissentis, and Pfäfers were founded. But of all these, the monastery of St. Gallen may be considered to have been the most important, and during the reign of the Frankish kings it became one of the greatest centres of learning in their vast kingdom. The Hospice on the Great St. Bernard was only founded in 962 by the Savoyard Bernard de Monthon.

During the centuries which preceded the Reformation, the Church life and the relations between the clergy and laity in Switzerland were similar to those which existed in Italy and Germany during the same period. It was, too, a precisely similar incident which at length impelled Luther in Germany and Zwingli in Switzerland to strike the first blows in the great religious struggle, viz. the scandalous conduct of a seller of indulgences and the evils which arose from their sale.

The first religious Reformer to arise in Switzerland was Ulrich Zwingli, born in 1484 at Wildhaus, in the Canton of St. Gallen. In the years 1512-15 he served

during the campaign in Lombardy against the French
as army chaplain, and was granted for his service a
pension from the Pope, which was, however, withdrawn
in 1517. Two years later he became pastor of the
Grossmünster at Zürich. On many points he was at
one with Luther and the other German Reformers, but
as regards liturgical matters he carried out his reform
more in accordance with the teaching of the Bible; he
also rejected the doctrine of the real presence in the
Lord's Supper. In order if possible to put an end to
these differences, Philip, Landgrave of Hesse, arranged
for a conference at Marburg between the German and
Swiss Reformers, but, after a discussion which lasted
three days, it dissolved without any satisfactory result.
Zwingli was, however, more a social and political reformer than a theologian, more soldier than priest. Thus
he desired to abolish the subsidies which were paid by
foreign potentates to the officials in certain Cantons for
the purpose of furthering their interests with the cantonal governments. He also endeavoured to organize
a "confessional alliance," to include not only foreign
cities, but even some of the great neighbouring powers,
a proposal which was strenuously opposed by the majority of the Cantons as tending, if successful, to lessen
the importance of the Confederation. In order to obtain
these objects Zwingli twice took up arms against his
fellow-countrymen, but without calculating the powerful
opposition he soon encountered. He did not perceive
that this arose from the mass of the people (especially
those in the Forest Cantons), but thought that it existed
only among the official classes, whose influence and position would be undermined in the event of his reforms
being carried out. His career ended in 1531, at the
second battle of Kappel, where he and many of his

companions were killed.[1] In recent years the people of Zürich have erected a statue to the Reformer whose name they hold in such proud remembrance. Zwingli is represented with a sword in one hand and a Bible in the other; he stands looking in the direction of Einsiedeln, where for some time he had officiated as preacher.

It was in 1528 that the great separation took place between the Reformers and the Catholics in Switzerland; it coincided on the whole with municipal and cantonal boundaries, and with the divisions formed by differences of language and race. It is not proposed to trace the reasons why one Canton declared itself Protestant while the one next to it sided with the Catholics. Suffice it to say that, in some instances, the cause which led to the change originated in the influence exercised by the nobility, in others the change was impelled by coercion on the part of a powerful majority. Such, for example, was the case in Bern, where the Oberländer were compelled to embrace the new faith by troops sent for the purpose by the cantonal government. It was, however, in the cities and towns that the Reformed doctrines spread most rapidly; in the Forest Cantons, on the contrary, the whole people remained stanch to their old creed, and have so continued up to the present day. In towns and thickly populated districts scandals were often caused by the illiterate portion of the clergy. These were of very rare occurrence in the rural districts of Switzerland, where there was little to distract the parish priest from looking after the well-being of his flock, and where in consequence he was generally beloved and respected.

After the death of Zwingli, the work he had commenced in Zürich was carried on by his former pupil

[1] See Chapter I.

Heinrich Bullinger, a man endowed with untiring energy
and activity, and remarkable for his great powers of
organization.   He succeeded in forming a union between the different branches of the Reformed Church,
not only in Switzerland, but in other countries; and
refugees from England, France, Germany, Italy, Hungary, and Poland, came to Zürich, not only to seek his
advice and counsel, but to obtain shelter and means of
support.   During the Catholic reaction under Queen
Mary, many Englishmen availed themselves of the
hospitality so generously proffered by the Zürichers.
The Reformed Church both in England and Scotland
watched the religious movement in Switzerland with
particular interest, and during this period a friendly
intercourse was kept up between Zürich and England.[1]
The unfortunate Lady Jane Grey used to correspond
with Bullinger, and some of her letters are now preserved in the Public Library at Zürich.   At this period
young men from there were frequently sent to Oxford,
and Englishmen came to that city to complete their
education.[2]   Among the refugees from the persecutions
in the time of Queen Mary were three young Englishmen who afterwards became bishops—John Parkhurst,
Bishop of Norwich; John Jewel, Bishop of Salisbury;
and Robert Horne, Bishop of Winchester.   They resided during their stay in Zürich in the Chorherrenstube
attached to the Münster.   On returning to England upon
the accession of Queen Elizabeth to the throne, they
sent a sum of money with the request that their hosts

[1] See original letters relative to the English Reformation, chiefly
from the Archives of Zürich, published by the Parker Society, 1846-47.

[2] They belonged to the more advanced school of Reformers, and on
returning home they were active in their opposition to the continued use
of the surplice in the Church of England, and to the attitude of kneeling
at Holy Communion.

would purchase some memento, not only as a small expression of gratitude for the hearty welcome they had received, but in token of the cordial relations which had always existed between them. Three silver cups were accordingly made, bearing respectively the dates 1563, 1564, and 1565. It may be mentioned that in 1887, at the celebration of the Queen's Jubilee, they were lent by the authorities to Her Majesty's Consul, and were used by the British subjects assembled at the Consulate on that occasion—a graceful compliment on the part of the Zürichers, which was fully appreciated by our countrymen.

The progress of the Reformation in western Switzerland was closely associated with the name of William Farel, a French refugee from the persecution of Francis I., who was sent in 1518 by the Bernese Government to propagate the Reformed faith in the Pays de Vaud, and later in Geneva. Farel was more successful as a preacher than as an organizer, still he played a prominent part in the Reformation. There were two events which hastened its progress in this part of the country, viz. the conquest of the Pays de Vaud by Bern, with the subsequent abolition of the Bishopric of Lausanne, and the arrival at Geneva of John Calvin. While travelling from Savoy to Basel he was, much against his will, detained " in the name of God " by Farel, who persuaded him to remain at Geneva and assist him in his imperilled work. Calvin proposed to establish a Theocracy on the frontier of France, Italy, and Switzerland, which would become for each of these countries a sort of " religious headquarters," if we may use the term. The town of Geneva was to be the capital of an international alliance, instead of the chief town of a small semi-independent State. This change could not, however, be effected without the help of the refugees, who came flocking in from every quarter, adding a distinctly new and important element to the population. In spite of almost insurmountable difficulties and fierce opposition on the part of some of the old Genevese families, Calvin and his party gained the day, and succeeded in founding a state of things which remained firmly established for more than 200 years.

We have already referred to the friendly intercourse which existed between the inhabitants of Zürich and the refugees from the persecution of Mary in England ; a close relationship was soon formed between Calvin and Beza[1] and the Reformers in Scotland, amongst whom the name of John Knox is especially associated with Geneva. The Churches of Calvin and Knox possessed many characteristics in common, and, to quote the words of the late Professor Dr. Vögelin, "each had an inflexible belief in the letter of Christianity, an exclusive orthodoxy, and an inexorable spirit of persecution." The burning by Calvin's orders of the Spaniard Socinian Servede, commonly known by his Latinized name of Servetus, was only equalled by the murder of Archbishop Sharp at St. Andrews. Apart from the Calvinistic doctrines which Knox infused into his Church there remain at the present time in Scotland many memorials of his stay in Switzerland — the "Geneva gown" is still worn in Presbyterian pulpits, and many of the Psalm tunes which are sung were introduced by him into his Psalter.[2]

---

[1] Properly De Bèze, originally from Burgundy. He became Calvin's ablest coadjutor.

[2] The *Book of Common Order* was written by John Knox at Geneva. (See M'Crie's *Life of John Knox*, vol. ii. 1818.) The wide-spread objection in Scotland to the use of written prayers first became prominent after the death of Knox ; an attempt is now being made to re-introduce this prayer-book into the services of the Church of Scotland.

We will now proceed to trace the gradual progress of religious liberty in Switzerland, beginning from the time of Zwingli and Calvin, when the principle of freedom of worship was admitted, though it was not till long afterwards that it was really secured. During the sixteenth century, when the country was particularly torn by religious dissensions and strife, treaties were concluded by the contending parties at four different times, the above principle being more or less defined in each. These treaties have been termed national peaces (Landfrieden).[1]

The first, which prevented open hostilities, was signed at Steinhausen (Zug) on the 25th June 1529, and contained a declaration that no one must be constrained in the matter of faith, or persecuted for his belief. The five Catholic Cantons of Luzern, Uri, Schwyz, Unterwalden, and Zug were to be free to preserve their belief. For what were denominated the common bailiwicks,[2] administered alternately by Protestant and Catholic bailiffs who represented the sovereign Cantons to which these districts were subject, it was provided that the majority in each place should decide whether it would "keep the Mass or accept the word of God," and that where the Mass had been abolished and the images burnt, nothing should be altered, but where the Mass and other ceremonies still existed, no *preacher* should be installed, *unless he was recognized by the majority*, and as to any alteration by the parishioners, the will of the majority should prevail; lastly, no member adhering to either communion could cause a citizen of the other to be seized or punished by reason of his faith.

---

[1] See Dubs, *Das Oeffentliche Recht der Schweizerischen Eidgenossenschaft*, second part.

[2] Districts which became subject to members of the League after the conquest of Aargau in 1415.

This treaty brought no peace. Many Protestants considered that not enough had been conceded to their side, whilst a great number of Catholics were of opinion that too much had been granted to their religious opponents.

Civil strife again ensued, and the defeat of the Zürich Protestants at Kappel in that Canton in 1531 with the death of Zwingli led to the second national peace, which was signed at Deinikon (Zug) on the 16th November in the same year, and which, whilst guaranteeing to Zürich its religious faith, prohibited that State from interfering in the affairs of the four Forest Cantons or of Zug. The alternative was also granted to the common bailiwicks to retain the right to preach (Protestantism) or to re-establish Mass (Catholicism), upon the principle of *parity*, as it was later termed.

The Catholics now rapidly recovered from the blow they had sustained from so many Cantons having embraced the Reformed doctrines. They regained much of their lost ground, especially in the subject territories, such as Thurgau and Ticino, and also in those Cantons where the adherents of the two communions were more or less equally divided. But of far greater importance than the outward restoration of the Church, then gradually taking place, was its inward regeneration. This, however, was accomplished more slowly, owing to the jealousy displayed by the Catholic Cantons regarding their sovereign rights, and from their great reluctance to adopt the laws proclaimed by the Council of Trent. There were three events of importance to the Catholics in Switzerland which helped to establish a connecting link between them and Rome. These were—the aggressive policy of St. Charles Borromeo, the establishment of a papal nunciature, and the arrival of the Jesuits and

Capucines. Both the latter events were effected by the influence of Borromeo. He was Archbishop of Milan, and his efforts for the restoration of Catholicism and the extirpation of heresy in the Italian bailiwicks of Ticino, and in the Valteline, a subject province of the Grisons, were attended with success. The foundation by him in 1570 of the Helvetic College, an establishment which still exists at Milan for training Swiss students of theology, proved one of the most effective means for diffusing throughout the Confederation the doctrines of the new and stricter school of Catholics. We are reminded of the great zeal and activity displayed by Borromeo as a political organizer by the union called the Borromean or Golden League, which took place in 1586, whereby the seven Catholic Cantons entered into a defensive bond. From this union many religious alliances were formed, perhaps one of the most important being that concluded in 1587 with King Philip II of Spain (also Lord of Milan), by which his assistance was secured in the event of a religious war.

Many years did not elapse before the burning hatred and political jealousy which at that time existed in Switzerland between Protestants and Catholics broke out afresh. Without entering into details of what happened in the first half of the seventeenth century, we may pass on to the third national peace, which was concluded at Baden in Aargau on the 23d January 1656, after the defeat of Bernese troops, mostly from that territory and Vaud, by Catholic Confederates at the first battle of Villmergen in Aargau. The principle was now admitted that where the common bailiwicks were concerned, any doubt as to whether a particular matter belonged to Federal law, especially in religious questions, should be decided by tribunals composed of an equal number of

Catholics and Protestants.   It was also decreed that
every inhabitant should be allowed to live in peace with
regard to his faith.   This was a decided step towards
individual religious liberty.

Still, as there was no umpire in these tribunals, the
Catholic arbitrators were apt to give one judgment and
the Protestant another, so that no definite result was
obtained.

In the next century the religious strife continued,
and after the defeat of the Catholics at the second battle
of Villmergen on the 25th July 1712, the fourth national
peace was concluded on the following 11th August at
Aarau (Aargau).   The principle was thereby established
that in the common bailiwicks each communion should
be treated upon the footing of parity.   There were a
number of other provisions, and amongst them it was
laid down that the adherents of one faith should not be
bound to contribute to maintain the worship of the
other.   The object clearly was to draw a broad line of
separation between the two faiths, and to grant equal
independent rights to both.   This arrangement produced a long period of lull in religious disputes, and a
strong desire for tolerance sprang up and soon spread
over the entire Confederation.   The invasion by the
French in 1798 helped greatly to unite the ranks of the
contending parties, and the clergy and laity of both
communions succeeded in mutually burying some of
their old controversies.   Catholics and Protestants alike
were but too willing to join hand in hand in self-preser-
vation and in opposing the ideas spread by the French
Revolution.

During the Helvetic Republic (1798-1803) the exercise of all faiths was permitted, provided that they did
not trouble public order and did not claim any sover-

eignty or privilege. The different communions were placed under the supervision of the police, who had the right to be made acquainted with the doctrines which each professed.

Again, in the Act of Mediation of 1803, it was declared that the Catholic and Reformed communions had full and entire liberty to perform worship in the respective places where their faith was professed.

In the Pact of 1815 religious questions were not mentioned, except in an Article which guaranteed the existence of convents and chapters, and the preservation of their property. The old bailiwicks were now merged in different Cantons, and it seemed to be considered that matters of faith had fallen exclusively under cantonal sovereignty, and were no longer within the domain of the Confederation. The consequence was the reappearance of the Jesuits, and in the new Cantons the majority showed an evident tendency to encroach upon the religious liberty of the minority.

Shortly after the Restoration which succeeded the fall of Napoleon, a dispute arose in the Catholic Church in Switzerland, originating with admirers of the policy of Joseph II of Austria. The most ardent supporter of these views was Ignatz Heinrich von Wessenberg, Bishop Coadjutor of Constance. As the Catholics were unable to check his zeal in propagating what they were so strongly opposed to, they adopted the somewhat high-handed measure of separating the rest of German Switzerland from the See of Constance, thereby limiting the sphere in which the bishop could exercise his influence. A national episcopate having long been promised by the Pope, the Sees of St. Gallen and the Grisons were joined into one, and the other German Cantons were united with the newly-formed diocese of Basel, the seat of the episcopate being at Solothurn.

The circumstances which led to the Sonderbund war in 1847 have been already related in Chapter I. When it had come to an end, and the Federal Constitution of 1848 had been accepted by the Swiss people, the Jesuits and affiliated societies were interdicted throughout the Confederation, whilst free exercise of religious worship was guaranteed to both Catholic and Reformed faiths. At the same time the Cantons and the Confederation were permitted to take any measures considered necessary for the maintenance of public order and peace between the communions.

By one stipulation, freedom of worship was limited to the two recognized Christian communions, and there was no mention of individual religious liberty. This brings us to the amended Constitution of 1874.

By this Constitution liberty of conscience and belief is declared to be inviolable. The free exercise of worship is guaranteed, within the limits compatible with public order and decency, and the Cantons and the Confederation can take the necessary measures for the maintenance of public order and peace between members of different religious communities, as well as against the encroachments of ecclesiastical authorities upon the rights of citizens and the State. Disputes respecting public or private law, which are caused by the creation of religious communities or by schism amongst existing ones, can be brought by way of appeal before the competent Federal authorities. No bishopric can be established upon Swiss territory without the approbation of the Confederation.

The order of Jesuits, and societies affiliated thereto, cannot be received in any part of Switzerland, and all active participation in religious or educational questions is forbidden to their members. This interdiction can be extended, by a Federal resolution, to other religious orders whose action is considered to be dangerous to the State, or disturbs peace between the communions. It is also forbidden to found new convents or religious orders, or to re-establish those which have been suppressed.

As elsewhere stated, the population of Switzerland amounts to nearly three millions, and of these there are now about 1,725,000 Protestants, and about 1,190,000 Catholics, the remainder belonging to various religious sects or to none at all—over eight thousand being Jews. A considerable majority of Swiss professing the Reformed or Protestant faith is to be found in Zürich, Bern, Glarus, Basel, Schaffhausen, Appenzell Ausser-Rhoden, and Neuchâtel. In the three primitive Cantons, and in Appenzell Inner-Rhoden, Ticino, and the Valais, almost all are Catholics. There are small minorities of Protestants in Luzern, Zug, Freiburg, and Solothurn. The Grisons, St. Gallen, Aargau, Thurgau, and Geneva all contain a large number of adherents of each faith.

During the early part of the present century a religious revival commenced in the Canton of Vaud, which spread among the followers of the Reformed Church in French Switzerland, and may be compared in some respects to the evangelical movement in the Church of England so closely associated with the name of Simeon. Some years later the preaching of the brothers Haldane at Geneva led to the formation of an evangelical body called the " Église Libre," whose members severed their connection with the National Church. The movement spread to Vaud and Neuchâtel, and in both these Cantons offshoots of the Reformed Church sprang into existence. It is curious to note that in each of the three instances the supporters of the *Église Libre* left the National Church for dissimilar reasons. In Geneva the differences of opinion were upon questions of theology. In Vaud the separation took place on account of interference in ecclesiastical matters on the part of the cantonal government, which, upon one occasion, ordered all the pastors of the National Church to read a civil decree from their pulpits on Sunday. In Neuchâtel the dispute arose partly from political reasons and partly on theological grounds. None of these Churches received any support from the State, and, with the exception of a foreign mission which they recently founded and jointly support abroad, their organization is entirely separate.[1] In the German Protestant part of Switzerland there are various evangelical societies whose views upon religious matters correspond in some respects with those held by the members of the *Église Libre*; they do not, however, possess the same complete organization, and may be likened generally to the Congregationalists in England. There are but few in German Switzerland compared with the French portion of the country, which contains Baptists and Methodists of different shades of opinion, and a great variety of other sects.

Until the time of the Vatican Council in 1870, the Roman Catholics, in Switzerland as elsewhere, unlike the Protestants, were an entirely united body; but the opinion of those who disapproved of the declaration of infallibility as an innovation, and who in consequence called themselves Old Catholics, gave rise to a move-

---

[1] A close relationship has always existed between these bodies and the members of the Free Church of Scotland, who, in 1843, some years after the formation of *Églises Libres* in Switzerland, seceded by the movement known as the Disruption from the Church of Scotland on account of the interference of the Crown in ecclesiastical matters.

ment which, as is well known, has attracted a good deal
of interest in England, and the visit in 1887 of two
English bishops to various communities of that sect upon
the Continent has once more brought the question of
intercommunion between it and the Church of England
into some prominence. The bishops went into Switzerland as far as Olten (Solothurn), where they were met
by Bishop Herzog of Bern and other Swiss who profess
the Old Catholic or, as it is frequently called in their
country, the Christian Catholic faith.

A number of communities of this sect exist in various
Cantons, and their proceedings with reference to some
edifices originally devoted solely to the celebration of
the rites of the Romish Church have certainly been the
subject of much adverse comment, even among Swiss
Protestants. The following facts, which are of common
notoriety in Bern, show how they obtained the right to
worship in the Roman Catholic church in that city.

It was only after the Canton of Bern had been
united to the diocese of Basel, and the city itself had
become the residence of some five thousand Roman
Catholics, as well as of the Federal authorities and the
diplomatic body, that steps were taken for the erection
of a church for the Roman Catholics, who had previously
worshipped in the Reformed French church. The project was encouraged by the Bernese authorities, and
through the strenuous efforts of the curé it was
accomplished in the face of great difficulties.

The building was commenced in 1859, and completed
in 1865. The cost amounted to upwards of £24,000,
of which sum the Confederation gave £2000, while the
Bernese government sold the site for the small sum, rela-
tively to its value, of £600. The residue was collected
from Roman Catholics in Switzerland and other countries,

such as Austria, France, Germany, and Italy. The Pope subscribed £13,600; the imperial family of Austria, the Emperor Napoleon III, and the Kings of Sardinia, Naples, and Bavaria each contributed various amounts; and a further sum, subscribed partly by the Bernese government and partly by collections from Roman Catholics, was expended in a presbytery and schools.

There can be no doubt that these foreign sovereigns were especially actuated by the desire of assuring to their representatives and countrymen residing in Bern the exercise of their religion in a building exclusively dedicated to the Roman Catholic worship. Similarly the Federal and cantonal authorities were doubtless moved to give aid in order to secure to the Roman Catholic members of the two Federal Chambers, as well as to civil and military officers of the Confederation, belonging to the same communion and forced by their duties to reside in Bern, the opportunity of worshipping in an appropriate building devoted to the sole exercise of their faith.

At the time of its foundation the affairs of the Roman Catholic Church, which was then one of the State Churches of the Canton, were regulated by an ordinance of 1823, by the terms of which the nomination of the curé was vested in the Bernese government. The temporal and financial business was managed by a parish Council selected by the Bernese government from among the Roman Catholic notables. This Council had no cognizance of questions of a spiritual nature, such as the superintendence of the religious services, of religious instruction, or of the uses to which the church might be put, all of which, as in other Roman Catholic communities all the world over, were reserved to the curé under the direction of his ecclesiastical superiors.

But, on the 18th January 1874, a new Bernese law was passed with reference to the organization of religious worship. It had been preceded by an ordinance, dated the 24th October 1873, for the reorganization of the Roman Catholic parish of Bern, and was followed by a regulation for the said parish, and it introduced a different order of things, by giving to the parish Council extended powers in ecclesiastical matters. This body was thenceforward chosen by the general vote of the whole parish Assembly, and became competent to direct the manner of religious services, the observance of Sundays and holy days, the instruction of the young, the maintenance of decency and morality in the parish, and, in particular and without previous consultation with the curé, the uses to which the sacred edifice might be applied. The result was that the custody of the keys was transferred from the curé to the Council, who became competent to admit anybody at will to officiate and preach in the church.

The first consequence of this legislation was to create a parish Council or Vestry composed exclusively of "Old Catholics," and this result was attributed to two circumstances : (1) many Roman Catholics considered it right to abstain from voting under the new legislation ; (2) those only who paid direct taxes had the right to vote, so that the poorer class of Swiss worshippers and all foreigners were excluded.

A feeling of hostility now arose between the curé and the new Vestry. The hands of the latter were strengthened by the establishment at the University of Bern of a theological faculty of Old Catholics, whose professors declared their intention of claiming a participation in the church at once. Matters came to a crisis in February 1875. The parish Council began by demanding the surrender to the Old Catholics either of the church itself or of the crypt, and proposing as an alternative that certain hours should be set apart for the service of the two faiths. Both of these proposals having been rejected by the curé, the Council passed a resolution on the 4th February authorizing the Old Catholic professors to officiate in the church at any hours which should not interfere with the curé. This resolution was also resisted by the latter, and he refused to surrender a duplicate set of the keys of the church. The Bernese government were then appealed to, and finally, on the 22d February, the prefect of Bern placed the curé under temporary arrest, his house was searched, and the keys were taken away. An offer by the prefect to leave him one set of keys was refused by the curé. It was thus that this church, like others in the Canton, came into the hands of the small community of Old Catholics. The Roman Catholic services are again held in the French Protestant church.

It may naturally be asked why the Roman Catholics objected to share the church with the Old Catholics. The answer is very simple: the Pope will not allow them to do so. He declares that the Old Catholics are apostates, and he forbids his faithful adherents to use any church in common with them, as being a place profaned by sacrilegious worship. He allows them, in case of need, to worship in a Protestant church, because in his eyes religious services celebrated there are not necessarily connected with the accomplishment of a sacrilege. Protestants do not say mass, and do not seek to sow dissension in the very pale of the Church at the head of which the Pope reigns. All this is of course well known to the Old Catholics, so that any offer on their part to share the church in Bern with Roman

Catholics would seem to be at least a work of super-erogation. The *legal* right of the former to worship in that church is of course not disputed.

Notwithstanding the broad principles laid down in the Constitution with reference to religious liberty, the supposed requirements of public safety are interpreted in such a fashion as sometimes to lead to interference with its exercise to an extent unknown in England, or generally among English-speaking people. Each Canton possesses vast discretionary powers by which it can interfere with the services of any body of worshippers whose proceedings can be considered as tending to endanger public peace or security, and if we are to accept the views expressed by the Jesuits or by Mormons and Salvationists who have recently been expelled from Swiss territory, the law by which the authorities are enabled to take action is occasionally interpreted in its widest sense. In certain Cantons no religious pro-cessions are permitted to take place in the public streets, nor can the Roman Catholic clergy wear their ecclesi-astical costume, and there are towns where the street preacher who attempted to address a crowd of idlers on a Sunday evening would run a very fair chance of being interrupted by the police.

In England, on the other hand, we have seen, marching through the streets of Cambridge, under-graduates wearing their academic gowns over the red jerseys of the Salvation Army, and accompanying on brass instruments the melodies sung by their companions as they perambulated the principal thoroughfares.

Again, during a mission held in the spring of 1885, the choir and clergy of St. Thomas's Church (arrayed in their surplices, holding lighted candles in their hands, and headed by the sacristan bearing the cross) might have been seen threading their way through the crowd of omnibuses and hansoms in Regent Street, chanting litanies as they walked slowly along, and halting at intervals in order that one of their number might deliver a short address. But perhaps the best instance which could be given of the great religious freedom in England is that of the procession of Catholics which makes its way every year to the shrine of the Confessor in Westminster Abbey.

There is no one religious organization for the whole Confederation, the ecclesiastical system differing in each Canton. There is no chaplain in the Federal Palace at Bern, nor are the meetings of the two Chambers opened with prayer as are those of our own Houses of Lords and Commons. The people in every Canton decide what form of religion they shall adopt, and whether it be Catholic or Protestant it becomes, properly speaking, the established Church of the Canton, the term "National Church" being only applied to Reformed communions in Protestant Cantons. The majority of citizens can dispose of the Church funds belonging to the Canton. These are derived from a variety of sources. In some Cantons the National Church is supported by a special tax, which, however, is not levied on those who do not belong to that body. In others the cost of maintaining public worship is defrayed entirely by the State, out of Church property which has been appropriated for that purpose, a guarantee having been given that in future the Church would be supported out of the cantonal chest. Then, again, there are Cantons where a considerable amount of Church property still exists from which the requisite funds are supplied. No attempt will be here made to describe the various systems adopted by all the twenty-

two Cantons, but in order to give some general idea of
the organization of the National Reformed Church we
shall take as an example that of Vaud, the largest of the
Protestant French Cantons.   It contains a population of
247,500 souls, all of whom are Protestants of various
denominations, except 15,000 Roman Catholics, chiefly
resident in five parishes in the district of Echallens, and
about 300 Jews.

The ecclesiastical law of the Canton is dated May
19, 1863, and the following are some of its provisions.

By Article 3 the State guarantees to the Church all
liberty compatible with constitutional order; it maintains
the establishments required for preparing candidates for
the ministry, and provides for the support of the pastors.
By Article 4 the Church, under the supreme supervision
of the State, participates in its own administration by
means of representatives chosen from among its members,
in conformity with the ecclesiastical laws and regulations.
By Article 5 religious instruction, ceremonies, the choice
of books for the services in church, and, in general, all
spiritual matters, are regulated by the representatives of
the Church, subject to the sanction of the State.

There are four distinct bodies which take part in the
administration of the affairs of the National Church :—

1. The Parish Assembly.
2. The Parish Council.[1]
3. The Ecclesiastical District Council.
4. The Synod.

(1) The parish Assembly consists of all males who
have attained their twenty-first year, being members of
the National Church, in the enjoyment of their civic
rights, and domiciled in the parish for at least three

---

[1] In Vaud the parishes are grouped in eight ecclesiastical districts.

months previously. Among other duties it elects the members of the parish Council, nominates candidates for the office of pastor, and votes upon questions laid before it by the cantonal Grand Council. Eight days' notice of the meetings of the Assembly must be given by the pastor, who makes the announcement from his pulpit.

(2) Each parish Council is composed of the pastor or pastors who officiate in the parish, and from four to fourteen councillors according to the population and the number of Communes in the parish. They are nominated for three years and are re-eligible. They must be members of the Assembly and possess votes, must have attained their twenty-sixth year, and been previously domiciled for at least one year in the parish. Within fifteen days after their election they are publicly installed in their new office in church after morning service. The chief duties of the members of the Councils consist in furthering everything which tends to the advancement of religion and morality, and in relieving the sick and poor in the parish. They choose delegates to represent them at the district Council, to which body they make proposals and suggestions regarding matters affecting the Church, and they are present at the installation of pastors and at the admission of those who are about to be confirmed. Minutes of all their deliberations are preserved in the parochial archives.

(3) In each ecclesiastical district there is a district Council with its headquarters in the principal town. It is composed of delegates from the parish Councils, the number of laymen being always double the number of pastors. They are appointed for three years, and are re-eligible. The district Councils meet annually for two days at most in ordinary session, but the sittings

may be prolonged by authorization of the State Council or executive of the Canton. Each district Council can be convoked in extraordinary session upon the demand or by authorization of the State Council. The latter has the right of sending a delegate to represent it at all the assemblies of the former. The work of the district Councils principally consists in selecting deputies for the Synod, in inspecting the parishes, and in the supervision of the pastors and the parish Councils. They receive annual reports from these bodies regarding questions as to the maintenance of public worship and the religious wants of the parish. They discuss these reports, and decide upon the measures to be adopted. The deputations sent by the district Councils to the Synod are chosen by ballot, and each consists of three pastors and six laymen who are members of the particular Council.

(4) The Synod is composed of the delegates from the district Councils, professors of theology in the Canton, and three delegates chosen by the State Council. Its meetings are held annually in some one of the principal towns, which is always selected the previous year; its deliberations last for three days at most, but, as in the case of the district Councils, they may be prolonged by authorization of the State Council, which at the conclusion of the proceedings receives a copy of the minutes. There can also be extraordinary meetings. The Synod devotes its attention to all that concerns the welfare of the National Church. It also provides general regulations as to the celebration of religious festivals, the books to be used at divine worship, matters regarding religious instruction, discipline, the ordination of pastors, and the inspection of parishes.

The Synod, when not in session, is represented by a synodal commission, composed of the president of the Synod and six members chosen for three years by ballot. Of these seven members three must be pastors and four laymen. It may be described as the executive of the Synod; the members prepare whatever is to be brought before the larger body, and see that its decisions are faithfully carried out.

No one can become a pastor of the National Church of Vaud until he has attained his twenty-fourth year. He must either possess a degree from the Academy of Lausanne or pass the examination required by the *commission de consécration*, which meets once a year and consists of fifteen members, of whom four are delegates from the State Council, eight are sent by the Synod (four at least being pastors), the remaining three being professors of theology, chosen by that faculty. Ordinations take place in church, the prefect administers an oath to the candidate, who then swears allegiance to the Constitution of Vaud, promising to maintain and defend the liberty and independence of the Canton, and to do everything in his power for its advancement and prosperity. He then swears that he will faithfully endeavour to fulfil the solemn duties now imposed upon him, and that he will preach the Word of God in all its purity. After this oath is taken the ordination proceeds.

Upon a vacancy taking place in a parish, the cantonal department of public instruction is immediately informed thereof by the parish Council, and an intimation of the fact is made in the *Feuille des avis officiels*, together with a request that applicants for the appointment will send in their names to the department within a fortnight. The list is then forwarded to the parish

Council where the vacancy has occurred, and that body calls a meeting of the Assembly to select by ballot the names of two candidates. These are then submitted to the State Council, which nominates one of them to the vacant post.

CHAPTER XIII

The 27th Article of the Federal Constitution declares
that primary education is to be provided by the Cantons.
It is obligatory, and, in the public schools, gratuitous.
It must be sufficient, but it is exclusively under the
direction of the civil authority. The privilege of attending the public schools is secured to adherents of every
communion without their having in any way to suffer
as regards liberty of conscience or belief, and the Confederation must take the necessary measures against
Cantons who do not fulfil their obligations in this
respect.

Although it has been thus provided that the Confederation should exercise a certain control over the
Cantons in this matter, all attempts to define such control
have, up to the present day, failed, and all the details of
school administration, organization, and inspection are still
in the hands of the educational department in each Canton.
How this power of control should be put in force has for
many years been a thorny question which has never yet
received a satisfactory solution. In 1882 the Federal
Council laid before the Chambers certain proposals with
a view to an inquiry which would have been intrusted
to the Statistical Bureau for the purpose of showing

what Cantons did not fulfil their duties regarding the supervision of their educational organization, and also what measures were still necessary for the fulfilment and execution of Article 27. The National Council went much further than the Federal Council, as it passed a resolution on the 28th April charging that body, by the department of the interior, not only to make the necessary inquiries and report upon the best means for insuring the complete execution of the above-mentioned Article, but also to see whether it might not be possible to legislate upon the matter ; with this end in view it was proposed that instead of a mere clerk in the Statistical Bureau, a functionary having the title of Secretary of public instruction should be appointed. In the June session of the same year the Council of the States adopted the resolution, though only by a small majority. It was an open secret that the head of the Federal department of the interior favoured the conclusions of the Assembly. The Radical party desired that all religious societies should be excluded from participation in the conduct of primary schools, and that religious teaching of a dogmatic nature should, as being perplexing to children, be banished from among the subjects taught. The opposite party, which of course included the Catholics and Conservatives, declared that the aim of the Radicals was to "banish God from the schools"— an expression so frequently used by the former, that it may almost be said to have become their battle-cry.

The Conservatives and Catholics, who, as we have already pointed out in another portion of this work, are always the stanch supporters of cantonal sovereignty, also maintained that the appointment of a new Federal functionary would be the thin end of the wedge, and would probably be followed by a Federal law depriving

the Cantons of all initiative in the matter of education, and thus encroaching gravely upon their cantonal rights. The Catholics especially were up in arms, and they were by no means alone, for the extraordinary number of 180,995 citizens demanded that the resolution should be subjected to the Referendum. The popular vote was taken on the 26th November 1882, and the measure was rejected by the large majority of 146,129. Protestant as well as Catholic Cantons reversed the fiat of the Federal Assembly, and the only Cantons in which the Ayes prevailed were urban Basel, Thurgau, and Neuchâtel. This result may be considered to have settled the question for the present, the people having so decisively shown their will in opposition to their representatives. The majority wished to preserve Christian education for the young, and also to retain for each Canton sovereign authority over its schools. It is true that during the extraordinary session of March 1888 the subject was again broached, and the following motion of Herr Schäppi was discussed in the National Council :—
"The Federal Council is invited to examine whether, from the experience and proofs hitherto obtained, the school system of all the Cantons corresponds with the provisions of Article 27 of the Federal Constitution, and to present a report on the results of this inquiry." Herr Schäppi declared himself to be a partisan of instruction under Federal control, and in favour of a uniform series of Federal manuals to be used in all the various cantonal schools. The motion was, however, ultimately withdrawn.

We must confess that it appears difficult to instruct all children after the same pattern in a country with so diversified a surface and containing three distinct nationalities, with their respective languages of French, German, and Italian, not to mention Romansch. In the mountainous regions, during winter, the children can hardly be expected to attend school regularly, although the parents are no doubt technically liable to fines if they do not. In the industrial and rich centres all the conditions of life are entirely different, the schools are always within reach, intellectual life is more developed, and there is more time and taste for instruction. The laws affecting education vary in every Canton, each having its own system, but all are based on the broad principle that every citizen is bound towards the State to utilize on behalf of his children those means of instruction which are afforded at the public expense. Previous to the Constitution of 1874, when primary education first became compulsory throughout the Confederation, the national machinery for placing a career of some kind within the reach of every boy or girl was in certain Cantons even more obviously defective than in England before the Education Act of 1870. The schools were chiefly supported by the different religious denominations, by charitable societies, and by benevolent individuals. There was no systematic scheme of teaching; nothing which would justify the boast which can now be made in England as well as in Switzerland, that the son of the poorest peasant has the means at his disposal by which he may rise to the highest position in the government. During the old regime it depended entirely on the caprice of a child's parents, or the amount of authority they were able to exercise over him, whether he was placed in a school, or took the trouble to attend it. Catholics and Protestants of all denominations alike framed their scheme of instruction with the idea, in the first place, that it should serve as a means of instilling their individual beliefs and opinions into the minds of their pupils, and the notion of

giving them a suitable preparation to enable them to
fill in after years an honourable and useful place in
their State was but a secondary consideration.

The clause in the Constitution which made primary
education compulsory was universally popular in all
the Cantons.   The authors of Article 27 seem to
have had none of those misgivings and forebodings
which were frequently expressed in England previous
to 1870, when many members of Parliament declared
that any such measure was calculated to interfere with
the liberty of the subject, and ominously predicted that
it would produce a national commotion not much less
dangerous than that which attended a poll-tax.   "With
the matter of education," wrote Mr. (now Sir) Horace
Rumbold, when Secretary of Legation at Bern, "the
Swiss people manifest a veritable passion, and it is a
thing worthy of sincere admiration, though but natural
perhaps in the land that gave birth to Rousseau, Pesta-
lozzi, Fellenberg, and others, to note what heavy self-
imposed pecuniary sacrifices they cheerfully make to
the cause.   The public foundations, the private gifts,
the State contributions devoted to education by this
otherwise thrifty, close-fisted race, may be truly said to
be noble in the extreme."

A Swiss citizen takes an honest pride in his school,
and everything connected with it.   The school-house in
any town or village, from the capital of the Canton to
the most remote hamlet, is certain to attract the notice
of a stranger as one of the most solid and commodious
buildings in the place.   No site, however costly, would
be looked upon as thrown away by being used for a
school-house, provided there were good reasons for believing that particular spot to be the healthiest, the
most central, and generally the most suitable position

that could be found in the district. We may mention two instances of this—one in Zürich, where a school was built at a cost of £43,000 on the Linthescher-Platz, one of the chief open spaces of the city ; the other in Bern, where a couple of houses in the more modern part of the Rue fédérale were purchased for the purpose of being converted into a girls' school. No subjects take up a larger share of the attention of the communal or cantonal authorities than those which relate to the schools under their supervision. It is difficult for an Englishman, who seldom takes up a local newspaper without seeing some case brought before the magistrates in which a parent is prosecuted by the School Board for refusing to send his child to school or for non-payment of fees, to understand the eager and deep-rooted enthusiasm with which a Swiss, be he young or old, regards the educational system of his country. Throughout his whole life, from the day he enters it as a junior scholar till he becomes a man and has to bear his part in its administration, school is in one way or other always being brought before him. In almost every town and village the primary schools are attended by the children of the rich and poor alike without distinction ; in Switzerland there is no class of vagrant or destitute children which the ordinary school system fails to reach, and the visitor may see, side by side, an orphan who is fed and clothed by the Commune and the son of a well-to-do tradesman or professional man receiving the same instruction, each being under precisely the same discipline. In Zürich, where primary instruction in private establishments is permitted, about 97·5 of the children of all classes attend the public primary schools. In fact the educational system of Switzerland has become one of the great means of cementing together the different classes and sections of the community, and of tightening those bonds which hold the Confederation so firmly together. It will therefore be easily understood that the Swiss parent looks upon the school-house, not merely as the place where his children are educated and fitted for making their way in the world, but as a political nursery where many of those doctrines cherished by the stanch republican are developed and fostered among the younger generation.

The Swiss have shown even a greater spirit of religious toleration in all that concerns their educational system than they have done in ecclesiastical matters. This, as Sir Horace Rumbold remarked in his report of 1868 already quoted, "is one of the most creditable features of their educational system, and appears the more striking that the country is nearly equally divided[1] between Roman Catholics and Protestants, so mixed in some Cantons as to be barely distinguishable, so sharply divided in others as to have preserved intact the most marked characteristics of either creed, and all, barely twenty years ago, engaged in the bitterest civil strife."

In those Cantons where the population is mostly composed of Protestants or Catholics, the religious instruction in the primary schools is always given on fixed days at stated hours, so that every facility for absenting themselves may be afforded to children whose parents wish them only to receive secular instruction. The real religious training of the young is left to the clergy, and takes the form of preparation for confirmation. We give the general plan followed regarding religious instruction in the primary schools of Vaud,

---

[1] There are at present about 1,190,000 Catholics to 1,725,000 Protestants. See page 176.

Geneva, Neuchâtel, and Luzern, not only as examples of the various methods in vogue, but also to illustrate the vast amount of divergence existing amongst the various Cantons in nearly every detail of organization :—

Vaud.—Religion is taught mainly from a historical point of view.

Geneva.—No religious instruction is at any time given in the public schools themselves, and the actual school-houses are at no time permitted to be used for the purpose. On the other hand, the State gives a yearly subvention to a *consistoire*, or body of pastors and curés, to whom parents can, at their discretion, send the children for instruction.

Neuchâtel.—There is no system of religious instruction, but the school-houses are permitted to be used for the purpose by suitable persons at convenient hours.

Luzern.—The religious instruction of the young is left entirely to the Roman Catholic clergy.

Mixed schools (*paritätische Schulen*) exist in many of the Cantons where the population is composed both of Protestants and Catholics, and are attended by children belonging to either communion. These schools cannot be called secular. In Bern, for example, elementary religious instruction is given in the simple truths common to all Christians, and in readings from the Bible. In a Canton like Zürich, where the Protestants are largely in the majority, a Roman Catholic child generally receives this instruction with his Protestant school-fellows till he has reached his tenth or eleventh year, when his special preparation for confirmation usually commences. This system of mixed schools appears to work well even in Cantons like St. Gallen, where the Roman Catholics are to the Protestants in the proportion of five to three, and where, during the years preceding the Sonderbund War, violent feuds prevailed on the subject of religion and education. If the Catholic or Protestant minority in a Canton find themselves strong enough to do so, they not infrequently establish schools exclusively for the children of their own adherents, as, for instance, in the case of the Protestants of Morat, who have built several schools, and also at Carouge, in the Canton of Geneva, where there is a Roman Catholic school which may be described as being strictly denominational.

We have already stated that primary education is compulsory by law. The obligation goes thus far: all parents are bound to give their children instruction at least equal to that afforded in the public primary schools. With the solitary exception of the Canton of Solothurn, where all children must receive their instruction in the public schools, parents are at liberty to teach their children at home or have them educated in private establishments. The State interferes only in the case of a child not receiving the minimum of education decreed by legislation, and by means of fine and imprisonment it can enforce very severe punishments on those who violate or infringe the law in this respect. The obdurate father who persists in refusing to allow his child to attend school, and who neglects to teach it at home, may indeed, according to the letter of the law, even run the risk of seeing it committed to the custody of others.

Thus far we have attempted to sketch the broad principles upon which the general scheme of popular instruction is based; we shall now endeavour to convey some idea of the educational machinery of the country by describing the system at present existing in Zürich.

We are led to select this as the particular Canton in which to investigate the subject by the fact that the city of Zürich is one of the greatest scholastic centres, not only in Europe, but in the whole world. The superiority of this State over other Cantons in all matters relating to education is perhaps the only concession which the entire Confederation would be willing to make to any single Canton. By far the largest portion of the cantonal budget is devoted to schools, the annual cost of each scholar in an elementary school being no less than £2 : 4s., a sum far exceeding the corresponding charge in other Cantons. The healthiest and most commanding position in the town belonged to the municipal authorities, who, instead of building residences for the wealthier citizens and thereby increasing the wealth of the corporation, used the ground for erecting the Polytechnic school, the University, and the various departments connected with them. It is impossible to walk through the streets and see at every turn substantially built schools, and all the many other evidences of the flourishing scholastic life which exists there, without realizing that everything connected with the well-being and education of their children becomes a matter of first importance with the people of Zürich. We purposely arranged our visit at a time when examinations were being conducted, and we noticed that there was nothing theatrical about the performance of the pupils ; they appeared to be perfectly unconscious of the presence of the crowd of friends and parents in the room, who were taking the liveliest interest in the day's proceedings. The desks and school furniture were of the newest and most approved pattern. The corridors were large and airy, and though the season of the year necessitated the heating of the building, we everywhere found the ventilation to be admirable. The museums and laboratories are a notable feature of the Zürich schools; these are very complete collections of botanical, geological, zoological, and anatomical specimens, all carefully labelled and arranged, as well as excellent chemical and physical apparatus. The museum of the Linthescher-Platz School was specially referred to by the Royal Commission on Technical Instruction in 1886 as "a type of what such a school museum should be." The specimens are generally collected and arranged by the teachers.

In Zürich, as indeed throughout the whole of Switzerland, the supervision and organization of all educational matters—primary, secondary, as well as technical—are under the control of the head of the educational department of the Canton. It should, however, be remembered that this functionary exercises no jurisdiction over the Polytechnic school at Zürich, which is under the authority of the Federal government. His salary is generally in proportion to the wealth of the Canton; in Zürich it amounts to £200 per annum.

In the majority of Cantons regularly-paid inspectors are appointed by the educational department, and are generally chosen among schoolmasters or those of the clergy whose pastoral duties are sufficiently light to permit of their devoting a certain amount of time to the supervision of the schools in their neighbourhood. In Zürich, on the other hand, the inspection is voluntarily conducted by members of the district School Boards, composed chiefly of professional men, pastors, or persons of influence, who are elected for a period of three years by all the citizens in the district. These Boards form the executive machinery of the corresponding departments of the cantonal governments, and the duties of the members chiefly consist in seeing that all cantonal laws are faithfully enforced by the communal authorities.   They decide on all questions regarding the course of the studies to be pursued in the schools, the books to be used, etc., and in general act as a final tribunal of appeal in any controversies that may arise between the teachers and the local authorities.   The schools are always open to any member of the Commune, as well as to the inspectors, who rarely give the teachers notice of their approaching visit.   Women are not eligible for election as school inspectors.

In every Commune there is a school Commission whose duties may be said to correspond with those performed by members of the School Board in an English village.   The members of the Commission are elected by the communal Assembly from among their own body, and also from the communal Council.   They form practically the executive of the district School Board, who on their part (as we have already stated) carry out the instructions of the cantonal government. They are responsible for providing sufficient school accommodation for the children of the Commune, and they see that the buildings are kept in repair.   One of their number must visit each school at least twice every year, and satisfy himself that any suggestions made by the inspector have been duly acted upon.   Poor children are supplied gratuitously with books, at the discretion of the Commission, and at their recommendation a poor scholar who shows marked ability and diligence is provided by the district Board with the means of continuing his studies in the higher schools.   They deal with parents who neglect to send their children regularly to school, and have the power of expelling a scholar.

In Zürich all children who have been dismissed from a primary school are compelled by a law recently passed to receive private instruction, either at the expense of their parents or, in the case of the poor, at the cost of the State. Corporal punishment is forbidden in the majority of the Cantons. The Commune provides the site for the school buildings. These are erected partly at the expense of the Commune and partly by the Canton, which grants subsidies varying from five to fifty per cent according to its wealth. The Commune provides light and fuel and keeps the building in repair; for more costly alterations, however, the Canton also provides subsidies. The most minute regulations are laid down by each Canton regarding the construction of school buildings, as, for instance, that the windows must face the east or south-east, and that the benches must be so arranged that the light falls upon the pupil's left hand.

The teachers, who are drawn from the same class as in England, are elected by the communal Assembly for a period of six years. In some Cantons the appointment must be made subject to the approval of the State educational department. In Zürich the minimum salary of a teacher in a primary school is £48, and in a secondary school £72 per annum, half of which is paid by the Canton and half by the Commune, which also provides a free house and garden and fuel. The Canton gives an additional £4 for every four years' service up to £16. In this Canton, teachers, after thirty years' service, receive a pension of not less than one half of their salary at the time they retire. There is no pupil-teacher system in any part of Switzerland, and in a school with several teachers there is no headmaster, all having the same equal authority. The Canton leaves each Commune to decide whether male or female teachers shall be employed in the primary schools, which are attended alike by boys and girls. In some Cantons the local *patois* is used in instructing the very youngest pupils. All teachers are trained for a period of four years in one of the cantonal preceptors' colleges, which they usually enter at the age of fifteen, after having passed a satisfactory examination in the subjects taught in the third year's course of the secondary schools.

In towns, children from four to five years of age are usually sent to the Kindergarten schools, conducted according to Froebel's system. The attendance is optional, they have no State endowment, and are conducted by private individuals. Children between the ages of six and fourteen are compelled by law to attend school, and must remain in a primary school until the age of twelve, when they may either be sent to a secondary one, or, subject to the prescribed attendance at a supplementary one, may enter into practical life. By the Federal Factory Act of the 23d March 1877, no child can be employed in a mill or public workshop till he has attained the age of fifteen. In rural districts the holidays are fixed with due reference to the harvest and the vintage, and to the tourist season. Throughout the whole year they extend over some eight or ten weeks.

The supplementary schools are intended for the benefit of children who are required by their parents to assist in work at home. The course of instruction extends over four years, but those who have remained in them for two years (until the age of fourteen) are absolved from further compulsory attendance. Supplementary schools are held on two mornings of the week,

the chief aim of the teacher being to try and help the
scholars to retain what they have already learned in the
primary schools.

The chief educational institutions in the town of
Zürich may be classed as follows :—

   Compulsory—Primary Schools.
       Supplementary Schools.
    Optional—Secondary Schools.
       Gymnasium or High School.
       Technical School.
       Polytechnic.
       University.

The course in the secondary schools is three years
for boys and four for girls. In Zürich these are not
"mixed." In those set apart for girls all the subjects,
with the exception of needlework, are taught by male
teachers. The gymnasium or high school is usually
entered by boys on leaving the primary school; the
course is six and a half years, and is preparatory for
the University. Pupils who obtain a "certificate"
during the sixth year of the gymnasium curriculum are
enabled to enter the University or the Polytechnic without an entrance examination. The technical school
follows on the secondary school, and prepares pupils for
the Polytechnic or for direct entrance into trade.

The following list will convey some idea of the vast
educational resources in Zürich. Some of the establishments are founded or endowed by the State :—

High-Class Ladies' College.
Training School for Female Teachers.
Veterinary College.
Agricultural School.
Art Training School at the Technical Museum.

> Academy for Music.
> School for Silk-Weaving.
> Training Schools for the Kindergarten System.
> School of Industry and School for Artisans.
> Kaufmännischer Verein : Commercial Courses and
>   Instruction in Languages.

In 1882, during the period of commercial and industrial depression which followed so closely upon those years of exceptional prosperity between 1860 and 1874, the Federal Assembly unanimously requested the Federal Council to inquire into the state of trade and industry in the Confederation. An inquiry was accordingly set on foot through the medium of the Federal department of commerce and agriculture, and the result clearly showed that there was a strong feeling throughout the country that the system of technical education should be developed and improved. A desire was also manifested that collections of industrial models should be formed in various centres. It was also suggested that in mountain districts a large industry might gradually be developed by the manufacture of children's toys, and that in those parts of the country where osiers could be cultivated, establishments for learning basket-making might advantageously be started. The Federal Council, after due consideration, decided that the best way of effecting the desired object with reference to technical education would be to grant subsidies to the existing technical schools, as well as to others which might be established, and this system was adopted by a Federal resolution which was passed by the Chambers in 1884. In that year a subsidy of £4000 was voted by them, and it was expected that the annual sum required would not exceed £6000 ; but in 1886 the subsidy already exceeded £8200, and in 1887 it amounted to over £9200.

It is perhaps needless for us to state that in Switzerland there is no national scheme of art or technical instruction such as exists in this country in connection with South Kensington. Provided certain duly specified subjects are studied, the Federal authorities do not interfere in any way with the methods of instruction followed in the different schools they subsidize. As in the case of primary instruction, all matters of detail are left to the Cantons. In fact, the only educational establishment within the limits of the Confederation which can be said to be under the control of the Federal authorities is (as already stated) the Polytechnic at Zürich. This is undoubtedly the most remarkable educational institution in the whole of Switzerland. In England it would probably be called a technical university. It was founded by the Confederation in 1854. About that time a great impulse was given to engineering and manufactures by the extension of the railway system and the establishment of factories throughout Europe. A demand at once arose for highly-skilled labour owing to the widespread introduction of steam, and consequently schools were created in various parts of Europe, in which the necessary scientific training, with its practical applications, could be imparted so as to enable workmen to compete with trained English artisans. This institution comprises seven distinct schools, with courses varying from two and a half to three and a half years, viz. :—

1. Architectural.
2. Civil Engineering.
3. Mechanical Engineering.

4. Chemical Technology (including Pharmacy).
5. Agriculture and Farming.
6. Normal School.
7. Philosophical and Political Science.

To give some idea of the completeness and extent of the Polytechnic school, we may mention that there are two hundred distinct courses of lectures given during the year by forty-five professors and thirteen assistants. The total annual expenditure is a little under £20,000. It is attended by some eight hundred students, who each pay £8 to £10 per annum for a complete course of instruction in the school to which they belong.

Among the more important technical schools in Switzerland we may cite the Teknikum at Winterthur, the school of art and the school of silk - weaving at Zürich (already mentioned), and the school of art at Geneva. Foremost among the horological schools is that of Geneva, the first founded in the Confederation, having been established in 1824; since then similar schools have been built in the Canton of Neuchâtel at La Chaux-de-Fonds and Le Locle, which are the principal centres of watch-making in the Jura, and at Neuchâtel and Fleurier; also at St. Imier and Biel in the Canton of Bern. In the latter Canton there are two schools of wood - carving, one at Meyringen and the other at Brienz, the former being in every respect vastly superior to the latter.

Great attention is devoted to the various agricultural schools in Switzerland. We have already alluded to the agricultural department in the Polytechnic at Zürich, which, along with the school of agricultural chemistry attached to it, is attended by those who wish to study the higher branches of the subjects taught there. Not only practical but theoretical instruction is given in the farm schools at Strickhof (Zürich), and the Rütte (Bern), which also has a dairy school. During the winter months purely theoretical schools are held at Lausanne, at Sursee (Luzern), and at Brugg (Aargau). There is an institution for experimental vine-growing at Lausanne, a school of gardening at Geneva, and dairy schools at Sornthal (St. Gallen), and Treyvaux (Freiburg). From time to time lectures and short courses of instruction are given in different parts of the country on horticulture and viniculture, fodder-growing, cattle-breeding, etc., by which some knowledge of the theory and technical details of agricultural science is given, with the view of awakening a spirit of enterprise in the more remote districts of the country. We may mention that a most interesting report on technical instruction in Switzerland has recently been written by M. Henri Loumyer, Secretary of the Belgian Legation at Bern.

The Swiss universities resemble the German and Scotch more closely than they do the English, as there are no colleges or halls of residence, and the teaching is professorial rather than tutorial.

There are four universities — Basel, Bern, Zürich, where the lectures are given in German, and Geneva, which is chiefly attended by students from the French-speaking Cantons. These universities contain the four faculties—theology, medicine, philosophy, and law. There is an academy at Lausanne and one at Neuchâtel, but these institutions do not comprise the four faculties. All efforts to establish one large Federal university have as yet been unsuccessful, the university authorities being unable to decide which city should have preference over the others. The Swiss universities are attended by about 2200 students, among whom are some 500 foreigners divided among the four faculties as follows : 212 are studying medicine, 197 philosophy, 43 theology, and 40 jurisprudence. The matriculated students, Swiss and foreign together, give a preponderance to the faculty of medicine, which counts 749 adherents ; philosophy is studied by 515, law by 301, and theology by 219. The non-matriculated students, " hearers " as they are called, are about 400 in number; nearly one half (183) attend lectures at Geneva. At the University of Zürich there are 60 female students, 40 of whom attend the medical faculty.

The excellence of the educational system in Switzerland can best be judged by its results. That " every child in the entire Confederation who is not mentally incapacitated is able to read and write " is no mere idle boast on the part of the Swiss, but a well-authenticated fact. Some years ago a member of the Geneva section of the Swiss Statistical Society, wishing to test a system of instruction to be applied to adults, was at great trouble to find a person wholly incapable of reading and writing. After much difficulty he succeeded in securing his man, who, however, upon inquiry proved to be no citizen of the Swiss Republic, but a Savoyard. We have already spoken of the large sums of money so ungrudgingly spent upon school buildings and educational purposes in every Canton. A candidate for some public appointment not infrequently urges his claim for election by promising to cut down the expenditure in the departments over which he hopes to have the control, but no one ever dreams of trying to gain the goodwill of his electors by suggesting that there should be any diminution made in the sums devoted to public instruction.

The poor value the right which their children

possess to be educated at the cost of the State as one of the most treasured privileges conferred upon them by their Constitution, and the rich on their part look upon popular education as one of the surest and best means of preserving the tranquillity and prosperity of the Confederation, where the government is practically in the hands of the masses.

This latter view of the subject was happily expressed by a wealthy Bernese patrician as follows: "It is for our advantage to educate our masters."

CHAPTER XIV

THE total area of Switzerland is 15,964[1] square miles,
or less than one half that of Ireland, and of this nearly
one third is unproductive. There is no other country in
the world where, crowded into so small a space, we find
such enormous variations in the elevation and form of
its surface, so great a variety in the composition and
condition of the soil, or such great changes in the tem-
perature and the strength and distribution of atmo-
spheric resistance. If we were to start from the lowest
level on the southern slope of the Alps, say about 650
feet, where the lemon, the almond, and the fig ripen in
the open air, and were thence to ascend to an elevation
of some 9500 feet, where every vestige even of the most
primitive artificial cultivation ceases, we might trace
nearly every species of vegetable growth known in
Europe. Those who have crossed one of the Alpine
highways between Italy and Switzerland must have
noticed the continual change taking place in their sur-
roundings, as the diligence toiled slowly up the steep
and winding road. They will doubtless recall the vineyards which were passed during the first stage of the

---

[1] The figures upon which this chapter is based have been furnished
to us by Herr Schneebeli, of the School of Agriculture, Zürich.

day's journey, then the rich productive patches of soil, the green pasturage, and the thick forests ; higher up the gnarled roots of the pines and the wide stretches of stunted furze, till at length the increasing keenness of the mountain air reminded them that they were approaching the great snow peaks.

In order to give some idea of the vegetation of Switzerland, as well as of its relative distribution, we shall divide that country into three parts, according to their respective elevations.

1. *The Lowland District*, reaching from 646 feet, the lowest level in the Confederation, to an elevation of 2625 feet, includes the country extending from south-west to north-east, from the Lake of Geneva to the Lake of Constance, through which the line of railway between Geneva, Bern, Olten, Zürich, and Romanshorn passes. This district also includes the warmest and most sheltered part of the whole of Switzerland, which lies on the banks of Lakes Lugano and Maggiore, and on the southern side of those great Alps which completely protect it from the cold northerly winds. The sunny slopes on the lower ground are generally planted with vines, which flourish in the north of Switzerland at a height of 1640 feet, and in the south at 1970 feet. In the well-watered valleys and on the shady slopes are some of the richest meadows in the country, the upper part of these slopes, which are unsuited for cultivation, being generally covered with forests. This is the great fruit-growing district, the trees being planted in the pasture land.

2. *The Mountain District*, extending from 2625 to 4265 feet above the sea-level. It includes the greater portion of the Jura range, as well as the entire lower Alpine region. Grain and potatoes are here chiefly cultivated. The grass slopes are used alternately as

meadows and for pasturage; the former produce most abundant crops of hay. The oak, the plane, and the beech flourish towards the upper boundary of the district. Orchards are rarely planted above 3600 feet.

3. *The Alpine District*, extending between 4265 and 7550 feet, where artificial cultivation practically ceases. This may be subdivided into a *Lower* (reaching to 5900 feet) and an *Upper District*. When the former is not planted with forests it is used for pasture, and as it is comparatively easily reached from the valley, milch cows are nearly always brought there to graze, hence the name Kuhalp. Small patches of grain and potatoes are raised, the former growing at a height of 5250 feet and the latter up to 4920 feet. Groups of châlets which are inhabited all the year round are only found on the lower confines of the district, those higher up being used temporarily during the pasturing season, which usually lasts for about ten or twelve weeks. The deciduous trees gradually disappear, their place being taken by conifers. In the *Upper District* the pasturing season lasts only from four to six weeks. The steep grass slopes, often difficult to reach, are generally used for feeding young cattle, sheep, or goats, from which their name Schafalpen is derived. The forests seldom extend as high up, though single firs and larches may be seen at a height of 6562 feet, while the ground which is not used for pasturage is generally covered with a low shrub growth of fir and Alpenrosen.

The total area of land under cultivation in Switzerland is 5,378,122 acres, of which 1,715,781 acres, or 31·9 per cent, are meadow land, and 1,962,656 acres, or 36·5 per cent, are pure pasturage. The arable land covers an area of 1,533,093, or 28·5 per cent of the whole; vineyards, 87,714 acres, or 1·6 per cent; while the ground devoted entirely to gardening purposes may be estimated at about 78,870 acres, or 1·5 per cent.

From what we have said it will be seen that cattle-breeding, growing grass, and fodder are by far the most important branches of agriculture in Switzerland. Throughout the whole of the country both soil and climate are extremely favourable for these purposes.

The Swiss possess two excellent breeds of cattle, the *Parti-coloured* and the *Brown*, the differences prevailing in each being mainly in point of size and greater or less degrees of fineness. The first-mentioned breed is supposed by some to have been brought by the Germanic tribes from the northern part of Europe, and is seen at its best in the valleys of the Simme, Saane (or Sarine), and Kander, in the Gruyère and Bulle districts, and generally over the western and northern parts of Switzerland. The cattle belonging to this race are large and amongst the heaviest in Europe; their ground colour is white, and it is marked with dun, reddish-yellow, or black. The milk afforded from the cows of the *Parti-coloured* race is admirably adapted for making cheese and butter. The breed as a rule is easily fattened, and, owing to its strength and size, is suited for draught purposes.

The *Brown* race consists of the heavy Schwyz breed, the medium-sized breed from Unterwalden and part of the eastern Cantons, and the smaller mountain breed. It has been called the " turf-breed " (Torf-Kuh), and is considered to be more ancient than the parti-coloured races. Its headquarters are in Schwyz, Zug, Luzern, and Zürich, thence eastward and southward.

There is a breed in the Valais known as the Hérens, which is considered by many to be a separate and primitive race. These animals, having short stout bodies, are admirably suited for the steepest and most inaccessible pasturage, where a heavier breed could not possibly be kept, and which are therefore usually overrun by herds of goats. They are readily fattened, the quality of their meat is greatly prized by butchers, and they are renowned for their enormous powers of draught.

During recent years strenuous efforts have been made, not only by the Federal government but by various agricultural societies, to improve the home breeds. On this subject a vast difference of opinion seems to exist, many high authorities on agricultural matters having considerable doubt as to whether the importation of foreign bulls is really the best method of attaining this object. Mr. Conway Thornton, when a secretary to H.M.'s Legation at Bern, pointed out in his interesting report on cattle-breeding in Switzerland (from which we have largely borrowed) that, bearing in mind the extremes of heat and cold the cattle have to endure, the rough weather to which they are so often exposed in the Alpine districts, and the steep, almost inaccessible position of the slopes where they often graze, it is obvious that if the necessary qualities are brought out by careful selection in breeding, native stock will be more likely to adapt itself to such unfavourable conditions than any imported breed. In 1880 a great impulse was given to the careful breeding of cattle in Switzerland by the establishment of four herd-books.[1]

The following table on the subject of cattle-breeding is based upon the agricultural statistics for the year 1886.

---

[1] A number of interesting articles relating to cattle-breeding in Switzerland appeared in the *Field* during 1881.

Description.	Cows and Oxen.	Horses.	Pigs.	Sheep.	Goats.	Total.
Number of head .	1,212,538	103,410	394,917	341,804	416,323	...
Value . . .	£14,429,200	£2,097,160	£837,240	£273,440	£299,760	£17,936,800
Percentage of each species on total value . .	80·4	11·7	4·7	1·5	1·7	100
Number of head per acre of cultivated land .	·0226	·0195	·0733	·0636	·0774	...
Gross annual yield	£11,409,680	£2,802,160	£1,012,610	£121,000	£338,610	£15,684,120
Percentage of each species on total yield . .	72·7	17·8	6·5	0·8	2·2	100

These figures show that there are a far greater
number of cows and oxen in Switzerland than any other
kind of cattle. The use of cattle for draught has a very
considerable effect on the aggregate profits from keeping
them. The gross receipts from cattle (excluding manure)
are :—

For Milk . . .	£6,970,528	6	5
,, Slaughter . .	2,151,030	0	0
,, Draught . .	1,312,128	0	0
,, Cattle and Meat exported	975,993	19	2
Total . .	£11,409,680	5	7

The average amount of milk produced every year
is 332,305,292 gallons, of which 319,482,548 gallons
are cows' milk, and 12,822,744 from goats. About
141,513,174 gallons are consumed by the population,
36,792,113 are used for feeding calves and pigs, and
about 6,000,000 are employed in the manufacture of
condensed milk and infants' food. One half of the
remainder of the milk is made into butter and the other
half into cheese, the chief article of agricultural export
in Switzerland. There are no fewer than 5500 cheese-

making establishments in the Confederation; in 1886, 12,967 tons were exported amounting in value to £1,451,220. Nearly 285 tons of butter are annually exported, by far the greatest quantity being sent to Paris and London.

In thus describing the pasture-farming of Switzerland, it has been unnecessary to say anything about the system of land tenure prevailing in the Alpine districts. The pasturage is owned by the different Communes and townships,[1] but the manner in which the soil is appropriated has a very decided influence upon the cultivation. The 5,378,122 acres which, as we have already pointed out, are devoted to agriculture in Switzerland are divided among 258,639 proprietors, the average size of the farms throughout the whole country being thus not more than 20·75 acres. From these figures it will be seen that by far the largest portion of the ground under cultivation is composed of small or medium-sized farms. As only a comparatively small portion of the soil can be said to be highly productive, the country is unable to support its population, and large quantities of agricultural produce have annually to be imported. These consist chiefly of grain, wheat, and flour, and amounted in 1885 to £5,247,345, and in 1886 to £6,140,361, being respectively £1 : 16 : 5 and £2 : 1 : 7 per head of the population.

The question of rent is in Switzerland an unimportant one, as it is rare to find a farm which is not worked by the owners. It must, however, be borne in mind that in very many cases the land is heavily mortgaged, a state of affairs which is inevitable in a country where there is such a continual subdivision of property. In the Bernese Oberland the subdivision of the land is

---

[1] In the lowland districts the land belongs almost entirely to private owners.

carried on to a greater extent than in any other part of
Switzerland.   While residing at Bern we once heard of
a case where a cherry-tree was found to belong to no
fewer than seven different proprietors.   This system is
the great foe to agricultural enterprise, and one of the
causes of the constant emigration taking place from the
pastoral districts.   Another drawback is the extreme
difficulty which may occur in securing unanimity among
different small proprietors, when a work such as making
a road is contemplated.   The consent of all the proprietors whose land might be affected has in certain Cantons
to be obtained ; a small number can therefore obstruct
altogether by putting one difficulty after another in the
way of a project which would be advantageous to the
majority of their neighbours.   In many Cantons, however, laws have been passed by which questions of this
kind are decided by a simple majority.   In the case of
works of public importance, destined to benefit the State
or the Communes, it has long been a fixed principle
throughout the whole of the Confederation that the
interests of the individual must give way to that of the
community.

Many of the holdings, especially in the Alpine
districts, are reduced to such a small area that they
barely suffice to support a single family, so that the
further subdivision of the land in these localities may
practically be said to be impossible.   In Aargau, Thurgau, and certain other Cantons, the Government has
tried to solve this difficult problem of preserving a just
balance between undue accumulation of land on the one
hand, and infinitesimal subdivision on the other, and
laws have been passed fixing the limit to the subdivision of the land at a minimum ranging from 5000
to 20,000 square feet.

Still, numberless advantages accrue from the system, and it helps to maintain a spirit of independence and self-reliance among the population. The peasant proprietor who cultivates his own land feels that he has a direct interest in the State, and it would indeed be difficult to find in Europe a more industrious and contented people on the whole than are the Swiss.

Throughout the Confederation the whole of the land is freehold, and the cost of transfer, which varies in each Canton, is extremely moderate—indeed there is probably no country whose laws afford equal facilities for the purchase and transfer of land, which has in consequence become extremely valuable and is much sought after.

There is no Federal land code, and each Canton possesses the power of framing its own laws relating to the tenure of land. Although these laws vary very considerably in detail, their general tendency undoubtedly is to discourage centralization or the accumulation of landed property by a few individuals. The following particulars on the subject with reference to the Canton of Bern are taken from a report on land tenure written in 1881 by the late Mr. Francis Carew while a secretary of H.M.'s Legation at Bern :—

"The sale of land in any part of the Canton is absolutely free and unrestricted, the only formality being a contract signed by both parties and then deposited at the cantonal registry office. The fee for this, the greater part of which reverts to the Canton (a small portion being, however, paid to the Commune), amounts to about 7 per 1000, which may be taken as a very fair average of the cost of the transfer of land throughout Switzerland. No official record is kept of leases, hence it is impossible to say with absolute accuracy how much of the land is occupied by tenant-farmers or cultivated by the proprietors themselves. The ordinary duration of an original lease is from five to ten years. Cases of sub-letting are very rare, and in the neighbourhood of Bern are practically unknown. As regards improvements effected on the property, it is customary for landlord and tenant to share the expense, although in the case of improvements of a more durable nature, as, for instance, the erection of new farm buildings or additions to old ones, the whole expense is frequently borne by the landlord. There is, however, no fixed rule on this point, which is entirely a matter of previous arrangement between landlord and tenant. The farmer is in no way bound to any particular rotation of crops; it is an important fact, worthy of notice, that an attempt to exhaust the soil unfairly is almost unknown. The out-going tenant is bound to hand the farm over to his successors in no worse condition than that in which he found it, and if the requisite amount of straw, manure, etc., is not forthcoming, he is bound to replace the deficiency.

" No agreement of any kind takes place between the out-going and in-coming tenant as to the goodwill of the farm, unexhausted improvements, etc. ; the landlord, who is certainly in a far better position than in many other European countries, arranges with both parties, and the result obtained is as a rule satisfactory. In the event of a property being sold, whether the tenant-farmer has notice to quit or not, the vendor and vendee arrange between themselves as to the amount of compensation to which the tenant is entitled, and an offer is made to the latter accordingly."

About one half of the arable land is sown in grain, the remainder being used for potatoes, turnips, clover, green maize, vetch, etc. The following table gives the

value of the various crops (exclusive of grass and clover)
which are yielded by the arable land :—

<pre>
From grain, 1,203,125 qrs. at £2 : 6 : 7
    per qr. £2,800,000
From vines, 25,068,780 gallons at 1/5½
    per gallon   1,823,200
From potatoes, 246,049 tons at 5/8
    per cwt.   1,400,000
From fruit, 9,625,000 bushels at 1/9
    per bushel   840,000
From industrial plants .   .   .   720,000
                                              ──────────
                                              £7,583,200
</pre>

If to this we add the profits derived from cattle
(after having deducted the labour value of horses
and oxen, which amounts to £12,589,600), we find
the aggregate product to be £20,172,800. About
£138,440,000 are sunk in land and farm buildings; the
cattle may be valued at a total of £18,185,160, and
agricultural instruments at £6,062,000 ; the annual cost
of working the farms is £13,336,400. Swiss agriculture
has therefore a working capital of £176,000,000.

Both the cantonal and Federal governments have
recently been called upon to determine the best means
of fostering and promoting the agricultural interests of
the country. Since 1883 an agricultural section has
existed in one of the Federal departments at Bern, and
nearly every Canton has framed laws which tend to the
advancement of agriculture.

During the years 1883-87 the grants made towards
this object have been £12,120 per annum. In 1888
the sums voted by the cantonal authorities amounted to
no less than £22,800, which, together with the Federal

subsidies, is spent in supporting the various schools of
agriculture, of viniculture, model farms, etc., to which
we refer in our chapter on education, as well as in giving
prizes at the exhibitions held in the different Cantons,
and in the purchase of valuable stock for breeding
purposes. These sums do not include the outlays which
have been made for the correction of water-courses or
for forestry, a subject to which we shall presently
allude.

In many of the Cantons agricultural and horti-
cultural societies have been founded, which display a
vast amount of activity and energy. The Swiss Central
Association is an important body, one of the chief aims
of which is to develop a widespread co-operative system
throughout the country, by which small farmers may not
only unite in purchasing implements, but in disposing
of their stock and the produce of their land, thus
transacting business under far more advantageous
circumstances than it would be possible for them to do
individually.

As already stated, about 1·6 of the soil under
cultivation in Switzerland is devoted to vineyards,
which flourish best on the slopes surrounding the Lakes
of Geneva, Neuchâtel, Biel, and Zürich, and in the
valleys of the larger rivers, and in certain plains in the
northern part of the country. The only Cantons
where the vine is not cultivated are Unterwalden and
Appenzell. Ticino possesses the greatest number of
vineyards, amounting to 32 square miles; Vaud comes
next with 21; the third being Zürich with 20 square
miles. The culture of the vine in Switzerland is carried
on at a greater elevation[1] than in any other part of

---

[1] See description of the lowland district at the commencement of
this chapter.

Europe with the exception of Savoy and the Alpes maritimes in the south of France. The chief aim of the vine-grower in Switzerland is to obtain the largest possible crop, and Herr Schneebeli has informed us of a perfectly well-authenticated instance where some two acres of ground yielded 6600 gallons of wine. If we take the yield of the vineyards at 440 gallons per acre we shall find that the average annual production of wine amounts to 31,266,400 gallons; the price is usually £1 : 4s. per 22 gallons, representing a total of £1,705,600. The wine produced is not sufficient for the wants of the population, and 15,400,000 gallons are annually imported, exceeding the exports by 11,000,000. The foreign wines are for the most part consumed by the tourists who come in such great numbers every season to the country.

The principal vines in Switzerland are the Clävner, White Traminer, the Rauching, and the Ebling. The Clävner is the plant from which the red wines of northern and eastern Switzerland, as well as of Neuchâtel, are almost without exception produced; it is only in Ticino and the southern valleys of the Grisons that red wines are made from any other grape. The White Traminer is cultivated almost exclusively in Vaud and Geneva; it is, however, grown to a certain extent on the shores of the Lakes of Neuchâtel and Biel, and is also to be found in the Valais and rural Basel. The Rauching is chiefly to be found on the shores of the Lake of Zürich and in the Simmenthal. The Ebling is principally to be met with in the Cantons of Schaff-hausen, Thurgau, and Basel, as well as in the district known as "the wine country," near Zürich. The last-named plant yields white wines. In addition to these vines there are others of more or less importance.

Valais and Ticino have different species peculiar to them and especially adapted to the soil; in the latter Canton about one third of the vines are the *vitis latrusca* or wild vine, which yields a poor crop. In the Valais the Arvine and Amique, which furnish excellent white wines, deserve especially to be mentioned. A delicate wine is made from the Riesling. The Rèze produces the "Vin du Glacier," so called from the fact of the inhabitants of the Val d'Aniviers storing the casks in their famous cellars in an elevated region.

The following are the best-known wines produced in the Cantons of Vaud, Valais, and Neuchâtel:—

Vaud.—La Côte, Lavaux, Dézalay, Montreux, Villeneuve, Yvorne.

Valais.—Dôle, Malmsey, Johannisberger, La Marque, Coquimper, Vin du Glacier, Fendant.

Neuchâtel.—Neuchâtel, St. Blaise, Cortaillod.

A great deal of red wine comes from various German Cantons, the best-known kinds being Hallauer from Schaffhausen, Neftenbacher from Zürich, and Goldwändler from Aargau. The monastery of Einsiedeln has a celebrated vineyard which produces the far-famed Leutschen wine.

Sparkling wine is made in the Cantons of Neuchâtel and Vaud; a dryer brand of the wine grown in the former Canton has begun to be imported into England.

As early as the commencement of the fourteenth century it became necessary to exercise a certain economy with regard to the consumption of wood in the more populous portions of Switzerland. In 1314 the authorities of Zürich forbade their foresters "to fell, float, or sell timber from the Sihl-

wold"; in 1339 we find Schwyz forbidding charcoal - burning in the neighbourhood of its principal
town, and in 1592 a decree was published in
Bern enjoining care and economy in the felling of
trees.[1]

The forest laws of the seventeenth century dealt
almost entirely with the maintenance and the protection
of timber, and it was not till 1702 that a Commission was
appointed in Zürich to discuss the best means for increasing and improving the forests. Some years later
the Physical Society of Zürich and the *Société économique* of Bern devoted their attention to these subjects,
with the result that the respective governments of these
Cantons passed revised decrees which contained the
most essential elements of forest legislation, and have
remained the groundwork of subsequent enactments.
The unsettled state of the Confederation at the beginning of the present century interrupted the development
of forestry, but upon the revival of general industry
in 1830 the matter was once more brought into
notice.

The whole question was some years afterwards taken
up by the Federal government as being one of importance to the Confederation, and in 1855 a school of
forestry was founded. At first the Cantons were
naturally disposed to look with suspicion on any legislation calculated to interfere with or encroach upon their
sovereign rights, and this was especially the case in
those districts where large tracts of forests were owned
by Communes and *bourgeoisies*. Great pains were
taken to enlighten these bodies as to what their true
interests really were, and no sooner did they fully realize

the importance of the subject it was intended to deal with than all dislike which had been expressed at the proposed legislation rapidly disappeared. Even in the most backward Cantons the great value of forests to the Confederation soon became apparent, not only from their relation to domestic economy, but as a support to the soil in precipitous places, and also from their connection with various meteorological phenomena. To these reasons was added the urgent consideration of the rapidly-increasing price of timber. It was probably the serious impression produced in Switzerland by the disastrous floods of 1868 which determined the insertion in the revised Federal Constitution of 1874 of the 24th Article, conferring upon the Confederation the right of supreme supervision with respect to dykes and to forests in mountainous regions, and of aiding in measures for confining torrents within proper channels and for replanting woods at their sources. A necessary result of the insertion of this clause was the creation of the posts of Inspector and Sub-Inspector of forests. The forest administration in the majority of Cantons is conducted by a department under the rule of a member of the executive government, assisted by the chief forester of the Canton. In Uri, Nidwald, Glarus, and Appenzell, however, it is confided to a committee chosen directly by the people.

In Switzerland the pay of the forest officials is by no means large. Cantonal forest inspectors receive £120 to £180 per annum, district foresters £88 to £112, and under-foresters are paid at the rate of about £48 a year. A house and garden or free lodgings are hardly ever included in this remuneration.

The following table shows how the total forest area
of Switzerland is distributed :—

	Acres.
State Forests	81,945
Communal Forests	1,299,075
Private Forests .	573,940
Total	1,954,960

CHAPTER XV

COMMERCE

THE following figures show the amount of the special
or non-transit trade of Switzerland during the years
1885-87 :—

	1885.	1886.	1887.
Imports	£30,218,082	£31,969,202	£33,481,396
Exports	26,398,573	26,696,945	26,843,705

To give some idea of the general (including transit)
trade of the country, about £12,000,000 must be added
to each of the above totals. When we compare these
figures with the statistics of other countries for the same
period, we find no State in Europe in which there is so
great a general trade per head of population. England
and Belgium come next; then follow France and Germany. The commerce of Italy (with a population
nearly ten times greater than Switzerland) does not
amount to more than double that of the Confederation,
and the difference between Austrian and Swiss commerce
is even still more remarkable. These facts are all the
more striking when we remember that Switzerland possesses none of the advantages in geographical situation,
or in its topographical features, which would enable us
to account for the remarkable extent and development
of the commerce of the country. It lies far removed

from the sea-coast, its surface is intersected by the ranges of the Alps and the Jura, and it does not possess a single coal-mine, canal, or navigable stream. The great amount of water power obtainable in many of the Cantons may to a certain degree be said to compensate for the lack of coal, and with the aid of this inexhaustible water supply several important branches of industry have been introduced and have rapidly developed. The admirably-organized railway and telegraph systems, as well as the post-roads in the lowland districts and upper valleys, have facilitated the intercourse with neighbouring countries, and the construction of the Gothard and Arlberg lines has in recent years given a very perceptible impetus to commerce. These roads and railways have, as a rule, been built at an enormous cost; the Swiss, be he an Oberland farmer or a civil engineer, has constantly to struggle with the many difficulties occasioned by the rugged surface of his country. It is mainly from the fact of the soil being unable to support its own population that the inhabitants of the country have always been compelled to look in other directions for the purpose of gaining a livelihood. Up to the commencement of the present century the legions for foreign service (referred to in our chapter on the army) were often raised on the understanding that some commercial concessions would be granted by the power under whose flag the Swiss temporarily served. It was only after the capitulations came to an end that industrial pursuits attained a wider development, and gave promise of the important place they were destined so soon to fill in the Federal budget.

It is always difficult to explain fully the disproportion between the amount of imports and exports of any country. It must be remembered in the case of Switzerland that nearly the whole of the raw material, as well as the half-finished goods used by the manufacturers, require to be imported; and also that large quantities of articles of food of all kinds have to be brought into the country. An excess of imports may mean that the country has large investments abroad, or that many of its people are engaged in business in foreign parts, and send home a portion of their earnings year by year. This is certainly the case with Switzerland, which also receives large sums from the great army of tourists who year after year flock to the "Playground of Europe," and bring into the country a considerable amount of specie, which they spend there. It is only in recent years that the Federal authorities have done anything to prevent foreign competition; but they have at last been roused to impose in self-defence certain higher duties. Measures of this kind are considered simply as weapons to be used in extraordinary circumstances, such as if the commerce of the country became the object of undue restrictions on the part of a foreign State.[1]

It will easily be understood that the industries of Switzerland are largely affected by the protective policy so universally adopted by those neighbouring countries where at one time the best markets for Swiss goods were found. The manufacturers have now no other choice but to try and extend their trade to transmarine markets, where there is not only a vast amount of competition, but far more risk and uncertainty attending the

---

[1] By Article 34 of the Federal Customs Law of 1851 the Federal Council is authorized under extraordinary circumstances, and especially in time of scarcity, or when the commerce of the country becomes the object of undue restrictions on the part of a foreign State, to make any temporary changes in the tariff which may seem desirable, under reserve of the approval of the Federal Assembly in its next session.

sales than there would be in doing business in markets nearer home.

We shall now enumerate some of the principal imports, our figures being taken from the commercial statistics for 1886-87; whenever it has been found possible to do so, we have given after each amount the different sources of supply in the order of their relative importance. As may readily be supposed, by far the largest item, £9,200,000, representing one quarter of the total amount of the imports, is for articles of food of all kinds, in which sum may be included £280,000 for tobacco, which is the average amount annually sent from America.

Grain and flour	£3,600,000	Austria, Russia, Germany.
Cattle for slaughter	1,200,000	Austria, Germany.
Wine	1,000,000	France, Italy, Austria.
Sugar	600,000	Austria, Germany, Holland.
Coffee	480,000	America.
Fruit	240,000	Austria, Germany.
Poultry	200,000	France.
Eggs	160,000	Austria, Italy.

The imports of textile stuffs amount to £11,200,000, of which sum £4,200,000 is for raw material, £3,600,000 for half-made, and £3,400,000 for finished goods; woven textures, to be afterwards embroidered, or intended for dyeing, are included under this last head.

The most important are :—

	Total Import.	Raw Material.		Half-made Goods.	Finished Goods.
Silk	£6,000,000	£2,400,000 to	£2,600,000	£3,000,000	£400,000
Cotton	2,600,000	1,200,000 ,,	1,400,000	200,000	100,000
Woollen	2,200,000	400,000 ,,	600,000	200,000	1,600,000

Italy and France are the chief sources of supply for silk, Egypt and the United States of America for raw cotton, England sends the greater part of the manufactured cotton goods, wool is obtained chiefly in Germany, and linen goods to the amount of £400,000 are furnished by Belgium and France.

Among other more important articles of import we may mention the following, which are obtained chiefly from Germany :—

Chemicals for industrial purposes	£1,000,000
Leather and leather goods .	1,000,000
Hosiery and ready-made clothes .	1,000,000
Iron and ironware . .	920,000
Live animals . . .	800,000
Coal and coke . . .	720,000
Other metals and hardware, including machinery . .	600,000
Wood and furniture . .	480,000
Petroleum . . .	280,000

About £1,400,000 of gold and silver is brought every year into Switzerland.

In the following list we give some of the principal exports, by far the most important of them being the first named :—

Textile products . . .	£14,600,000
Watches, jewellery, etc. . .	3,200,000
Cheese and condensed milk .	2,000,000
Articles of food, wine and beer .	1,000,000
Machinery . . .	800,000
Gold and silver coins . .	800,000
Cattle	600,000
Hides, skins, and leather .	600,000
Dye-stuffs, wood, and furniture .	400,000
Minor industries, in which is included wood-carving . .	2,000,000

The value of the exports of the silk industry is £7,600,000, of which about £600,000 consist of articles of intermediate trade, £2,600,000 of half-made goods, and £4,400,000 of stuffs, ribbons, worked goods, and silk embroideries. Germany is by far the largest customer for the half-made goods. About £3,600,000 of finished goods go to England, France, and the United States of America. Embroideries to the value of £3,600,000 are annually exported, being sent chiefly to England and the United States. In this last sum are included the goods sent to the Arlberg and Swabian districts for finishing. Cotton yarns amount in the list of exports to £800,000, the largest quantity being sent to Germany, France, Austria, and Italy. Nearly £2,000,000 of cotton textures of all kinds are exported, £600,000 in white, and £1,200,000 in variegated colours and prints; the former are principally used by the Alsatian cotton printers, the best market for the latter being in the East, and in the southern countries of Europe. The woollen industry has recently attained considerable importance, the export of combed yarns to Germany and Austria being nearly £320,000. The export of watches seems, at least for the present, to be somewhat on the decrease; the greatest number are sent to England, the United States, Germany, Italy, Austria, France, and Russia. Cheese is sold chiefly to France, Italy, and Germany. England is the largest purchaser of condensed milk.

It would be impossible to give in detail particulars regarding all the industrial products of the country; the following table, based on statistics taken in 1886, will, however, serve to show the commercial relations of Switzerland with other nations:—

	Amount Imported.	Amount Exported.
Germany	£10,446,889	£6,394,259
France .	7,526,933	5,570,214
Italy .	4,758,296	2,324,684
Austria .	3,670,980	1,433,203
Great Britain .	1,824,208	4,161,326
United States .	851,774	3,507,506

The next table has also been compiled from the statistics for 1886, to show the aggregate of special trade between Switzerland and other countries :—

	Amount Imported.			Amount Exported.		
Europe	£30,271,350	10	5	£21,683,732	17	7
America .	986,220	0	10	3,986,328	10	5
Africa	373,306	2	5	207,266	0	10
Asia .	300,206	0	10	775,652	5	7
Australia .	38,119	13	7	43,965	19	2
	£31,969,202	8	1	£26,696,945	13	7

Every year slight variations occur in these figures owing to political changes in the relations between different countries, and various other causes by which commerce is affected throughout the world. In looking over the commercial statistics for past years, one cannot help noticing that while the amount of imports is always steadily increasing, the exports on the other hand almost invariably remain unaltered. This fact, when properly regarded, is far from being a sign of the absence of prosperity.

The silk industry is the oldest in Switzerland, and has existed there since the thirteenth century, the most important centre of raw silk manufacture being at

Zürich. Ticino is the only Canton where there are
filatures for reeling the cocoon into silk. Zürich and
Basel may be considered to be the headquarters of silk
waste spinning, the products being generally sent to the
silk looms on the Rhine. The large number of hands
employed in silk throwing, *i.e.* in uniting the threads
into yarn, have suffered much not only from foreign competition, but from the Federal Factory Act of 1877, which
forbids the employment of children under fifteen years
of age, a salutary enactment from which, in the long
run, Switzerland will certainly benefit. The Zürich
stuff-weaving and the Basel ribbon-weaving industries,
in which hand-looms in private houses still take an
important part, have sadly fallen off owing to the
introduction of steam in the large manufactories, and
although the products of both these industries have a
high reputation they are by no means in a prosperous
condition. The protective duties levied by the other
countries of continental Europe and by the United
States, together with the increased introduction of
machinery, and the preference which we are informed is
now being shown for woollen goods, have combined to
counteract the efforts constantly being made to foster
and extend these industries. In order to retain the
position they formerly held, the silk manufacturers
adopt every possible means of extending their business;
some of them have even been compelled to remove their
mills across the Swiss frontier and now carry on a
formidable competition with their own countrymen; as,
however, these manufacturers no doubt remit home part
of their profits, the loss to Switzerland on this score is
less than it might appear.

Owing to the introduction of machine spinning, the
present position of the cotton industry is in some

respects similar to that of the silk trade, notwithstanding its having attained very considerable importance at the beginning of this century. Twisting, spinning, and white goods weaving, especially in eastern and northern Switzerland, suffer from English competition and the protective duties of other countries. Cotton spinning is for the most part carried on for home consumption, white goods being woven for the printworks in Glarus and Alsace. Coloured goods weaving has also seen its best days; the Asiatic markets now open to the Swiss manufacturer are but a poor substitute for those which he has lost in Europe in consequence of the high tariffs. The largest market for this class of goods is found in the Balkan Peninsula in spite of Dutch competition, which is stated to be keenly felt.

Cotton printing, which is chiefly carried on in the Canton of Glarus, where it has been established since the middle of last century, is much handicapped by English competition in foreign markets, while the almost prohibitive duties recently imposed by Italy and Austria have tended still further to check its development. The Glarus printworks can now only obtain a market for certain goods, and owing to these unfavourable conditions for the production of coloured goods and prints, yarn and cloth dyeing naturally suffer also.

With the cotton industry is generally included that of embroidery, which has most unexpectedly increased during the last thirty years, although it has at the same time undergone a great variety of changes. Its head-quarters are at St. Gallen and in eastern Switzerland. Only the very finest work is now done by hand, as the machinery recently introduced has attained to a marvellous perfection; notwithstanding this, embroidery may still be considered as one of the home industries of Switzerland. It has suffered to so great an extent from excessive over-production that the manufacturers have in self-defence been compelled to organize among themselves a sort of trades-union; if they succeed in persuading their most formidable rivals in Saxony to come to a mutual understanding, there is every prospect of a prosperous future for one of the most beautiful and artistic industries in Switzerland.

The woollen and linen industries, at one period most prosperous, are no longer so important; and it is considered of the very greatest advantage to the manufacturers of both these classes of goods that the home markets from which they are driven by German competition should be secured to them by means of a moderate protective duty.

Straw-plaiting and elastic-weaving have recently made considerable progress, though China is a formidable rival in the former, and the latter industry suffers from over-production and the constantly-changing caprices of fashion.

Next in importance to the textile industries comes that of metal working, and under this head watchmaking undoubtedly holds the foremost place. Switzerland may be said to be the home of this industry; there are many districts throughout the country where families have for generations followed the various branches of the craft, and the schools of watchmaking (referred to in our chapter on education) are attended by pupils from every quarter of the world. The trade has been established in Geneva since 1587; it soon made common cause with the jewellers, thus laying the foundation of that intimate union between mechanical industry and art which has given to Geneva the reputation it now holds. Gradually the watchmaking industry spread to Vaud and Bern, and to Neuchâtel, owing, it is said, to the importation of an English watch into a remote village, when a young blacksmith, Daniel Jean Richard, examined it, and succeeded in constructing one in imitation.[1] Efforts are now being made to extend this industry into eastern Switzerland. In those districts where it has recently been introduced, machinery for the production of cheap watches for wholesale export has been fitted up, while in the localities where the trade has been carried on for a number of years, and where the workshops contain an elaborate and expensive plant, only the most costly articles are manufactured. The watchmaking industry has lately suffered much from American competition, as well as from the protective tariffs in foreign markets. Among the many improvements which the Geneva watch manufacture claim to have made, we may mention the " Keyless " or " Stem-winding " watch.

Closely allied to the watchmaking industry, and carried on in the same districts, is the manufacture of scientific instruments, jewellery, musical boxes, and elaborate mechanical toys. Geneva has always held the highest rank in the manufacture of musical boxes, and it is there that these instruments have undergone all their principal improvements, from the old-fashioned musical snuff-box which played only one tune, to the Orchestrion whose powerful tone may almost be compared to that of a small band. Nothing illustrates better how universally these instruments are known in every quarter of the globe than to see musical boxes which are adapted to play respectively only Chinese, Japanese, or Persian airs.

---

[1] See report on watchmaking in Switzerland by Mr. Conway Thornton, formerly a secretary to H.M.'s Legation at Bern (1884).

We have already alluded to the fact that the Swiss are obliged to import not only nearly the whole of their raw material but also half-finished goods. Notwithstanding this, the manufacture of machinery, which is principally carried on in north and central Switzerland, especially in Zürich and Winterthur, has attained to very considerable importance during the last thirty years, and in various branches may be said to have steadily held its ground against foreign competition. Of late years, however, Germany, Italy, and Austria have adopted protective measures in order to benefit their foundries and machine shops; the machine industries of Switzerland are consequently at present undergoing a somewhat severe and trying crisis, but Messrs. Escher Wyss and Co. of Zürich still hold their own in the contest.

It is said that previous to the passing of the Federal law, by which a monopoly in the manufacture and sale of spirituous liquors was granted to the Confederation, there were upwards of 20,000 distilleries in Switzerland; and of these no fewer than 12,000 were in the Canton of Bern. By far the larger number were small establishments consisting of a single still used by the villagers. An important branch of the spirit industry consists in the production of liqueurs, such as Absinthe, Vermuth, Gentian, and also Kirschwasser, the best quality of this last being made in the Cantons of Zug, Schwyz, and Bern. The total amount of spirit distilled in Switzerland in 1882 amounted to 1,540,700 gallons.

According to statistics published at the time of the Exhibition at Zürich in 1883, there were 423 breweries in the Confederation, the majority of which were said to be fitted with the most improved plant. Up to the year 1840 the consumption of beer was small, even in

the largest towns, but on account of the subsequent
increase in the price of wine the demand for malt liquor
gradually became greater. The brewer in Switzerland
labours under great disadvantages, as his barley, hops,
coal, and even most of his plant, have to be imported;
while, on the other hand, it is difficult for him to export
his produce owing to the high tariffs in the neighbouring countries. The amount of beer annually brewed
in Switzerland is 24,541,150 gallons; some 1,276,580
gallons are imported, of which 1,230,359 gallons come
from Germany. The export amounts to about 308,140
gallons, of which 220,100 are sent to France.[1]

Tobacco has been grown in Switzerland for many
years, chiefly in the Cantons of Vaud, Valais, Freiburg,
Bern, the Grisons, and Aargau. Since the increase in the
duty on imported tobacco leaves, it has also been cultivated in Thurgau and the rural district of Basel. The
quality of Swiss tobacco is by no means good, and
out of the 1378 tons annually grown in the Confederation, only a small quantity of leaves is exported. The
number of hands employed in cigar factories is about
15,000. The present position of the manufacturers is
most unsatisfactory; with a view of benefiting the
growers the import duty is low, while it is almost
impossible for them to export their goods, not only
from the high duties but on account of the monopolies
which exist in Italy, France, and Austria. The following
table shows the amount of tobacco imported and exported in 1887 :—

	Imports.	Exports.
Raw leaves .	4741 tons.	227 tons.
Cigars and cigarettes	118 ,,	328 ,,
Pipe, snuff, and chewing tobacco	39 ,,	74 ,,

[1] The subject of wine has already been treated in the preceding chapter.

The consumption of tobacco in Switzerland has been estimated at $12\frac{1}{2}$ lbs. per annum per head of the male adults in the population.

Of the remaining industries of the country we may enumerate the manufacture of cheese and condensed milk (both of which may perhaps be considered to come under the head of agriculture), stoneware, cement, chemicals, chocolate, and preserved fruits. At Thun and Geneva there are establishments where the so-called "artistic" pottery of these towns is produced, which is largely bought by the numerous tourists who pass through them.

Swiss wood-carvings are known all over the world, and their production affords employment to a very large number of persons in the Oberland. It must be remembered, however, that the manufacture of *parqueterie* floors and of furniture is financially of much more importance to the country. The industry of wood-carving was introduced into Switzerland some sixty or seventy years ago by a native of Brienz named Christian Fischer, who used to spend his spare time in making wooden egg - cups, napkin - rings, needle-cases, and similar trifling objects for sale. It occurred to him that the neighbourhood would be greatly benefited if the young men could be induced to employ a part of the long winter evenings in wood-carving. In order to carry out this scheme he started a night-school, an enterprise in which he was cordially encouraged and aided by two Oberländers, Christian Flenz and Peter Baumann, and thus was laid the foundation of an industry which now gives employment to between 5000 and 6000 persons. It was Fischer who first conceived the idea of making tiny models of Swiss châlets, which at once found a ready sale among the travellers who were then making the "grand tour" of

Europe. The next objects he selected as models were the flowers and creeping plants which adorn so many of the Oberländers' homes, and add such an infinite charm and beauty to these picturesque little dwellings. In the carving of flowers Peter Baumann soon attained the greatest artistic skill and proficiency, specimens of his work being even now much sought after as models by the younger generation in the craft. The old man is still alive, and although nearly ninety appears to have lost none of his skill. While these pages were in course of preparation we visited his workshop at Brienz, and found him just putting the finishing touches to a panel on which he had carved out of the solid wood a marvellously realistic bunch of roses. Pointing first to the fresh flowers which lay on his bench and then to his own work, he exclaimed with a tone of genuine satisfaction in his voice, " Jetzt, das ist ganz wie Natur." As we have stated in our chapter on education, schools of wood-carving have been established at Meyringen and Brienz, both being subsidized by the Confederation. Their management is to a great extent in the hands of local dealers, who are in many instances not only the largest but the most constant customers of the two establishments. The result naturally is that the attention both of masters and pupils is directed more to the manufacture of those bizarre objects, familiar to every one who has walked through the main streets of Interlaken, than to the production of works of real artistic value.

There is one class engaged in this industry who, although small in number, occupy in it a foremost place, the Führer Schnitzlers, "guide-carvers," if we may use the term—such men as Melchior Anderegg, his sons, the late Andreas Maurer, and the brothers Andreas and Hans

Jaun, who reside in the neighbourhood of Meyringen. From boyhood upwards they have all been keen sportsmen, and therefore (as may naturally be supposed) their special forte lies in carving birds and animals, and among them especially the chamois, the graceful forms of which few men have had better or more frequent opportunities of observing. Without any regular training they have mastered the technical difficulties of their craft, and they possess a remarkable power of imitating the subjects which are familiar to them. We may mention that a few years ago a statuette was sent to the Dudley Gallery by Melchior Anderegg, the figure being that of one of his old friends and employers, which he carved from a photograph. One cannot better characterize the work of such men than by saying that it is the embodiment of some of Mr. Ruskin's theories as to what the artist's aims ought to be.

CHAPTER XVI

SOCIALISTS AND ANARCHISTS

By Article 70 of the Federal Constitution of 1874 the Confederation has the right to send out of its territory foreigners who compromise the internal or external security of Switzerland.

The Federal Council decrees the expulsions as the executive of the Confederation and as a matter of administration, and they are carried out by the proper cantonal authorities. It acts by virtue of paragraphs 8, 9, and 10 of Article 102.

These are as follows :—

8. It (the Federal Council) watches over the interests of the Confederation abroad, especially as to the observance of its international relations, and it is, in general, charged with foreign relations.

9. It watches over the external security of Switzerland, and the maintenance of its independence and neutrality.

10. It watches over the internal security of the Confederation, and the maintenance of tranquillity and order.

In every case the Federal Council has absolute discretion, and is only subject to censure from the Federal Assembly if it is considered to have abused its power.

The question of the right of asylum has been at times a difficult one for Swiss statesmen, but the invariable principle that has guided them, even when there has been pressure from abroad, is stated to be that Switzerland, whilst maintaining that right in its integrity, cannot allow foreigners who have taken refuge upon her soil to abuse her hospitality by organizing conspiracies against foreign governments, still less to lay plans for the commission of crimes against individuals, or for injuring their property. Switzerland is a sacred soil for those who take refuge upon it in order to live peaceably, and who attempt nothing that threatens the security of the nation which affords them hospitality. But no leniency must be shown to those who act in a contrary manner, and they must be expelled in accordance with the Article in the Constitution.

In a case which will be mentioned later, Federal-Councillor Droz, speaking, on the 29th March 1888, in the National Council, made the following remarks :—

"One of the most precious rights of our sovereignty is the right of asylum. In all times we have liberally opened our house to political refugees, oftener not from sympathy for their persons or their doctrines, but from humanity. The result has frequently brought trouble upon us ; it is almost the sole point with respect to which, since 1815, we have had difficulties with our neighbours. But we have always firmly maintained our rights as a sovereign State, and we wish to continue to do so. Only, foreigners who come to our country on the plea of being political refugees or by virtue of treaties of establishment must allow that they contract duties towards us. They must not only respect our institutions, but conduct themselves towards other countries as we are bound to do ourselves. The feelings of bitterness which they may cherish against the authorities of their native land cannot in our eyes justify acts of hostility on their part originating in our territory. If we allow them to make use of the liberty of the press and the right of meeting guaranteed by the Constitution, it is on condition that they show themselves worthy of the same; otherwise it is our right and our duty to apply the laws of our country to them. Now these laws do not solely point to judicial proceedings; they also provide for the expulsion of foreigners who compromise the internal or external security of the Confederation."

There is no doubt that the doctrines of Socialism have been on the increase among workmen in Swiss cities and towns, and the progress of what is called "State Socialism" is evidenced by the increased liability imposed upon masters, manufacturers, and railway companies.

German Socialists are in considerable numbers in Switzerland, and their principal centre has long been at Zürich. In general they advocate the doctrines of the Social Democrats, have scarcely any contact with professed Anarchists, and are not enemies of the political institutions of Switzerland. Their object is rather to introduce the principle of State direction of labour than to attempt a political reorganization of the State. They are not plotters in the criminal sense of the word, and are for the most part travelling artisans, well-behaved, and industrious in their callings. Many have been unsuccessful in business at home, and some are deserters from the German army. They are in tolerably intimate relations with Swiss Socialists of the artisan class.

A few Russian Socialists are to be found at Zürich, but their principal centre is at Geneva, which contains only a small number of Germans of that type. In the beginning of 1888 there were in the latter town, according to a well-informed newspaper correspondent, some eighty-four Russian, Polish, and American students, and some twenty political refugees. The students are said generally not to pursue any active political object, whereas the refugees from Russia, whilst taking no serious part with reference to conspiracies in their native country, occupy themselves industriously in the propagation of their doctrines; and they possessed at the period above mentioned four small printing establishments, which represented different shades of opinion. The Poles have also one printing-office, which publishes Socialistic pamphlets, mostly translations from the German.

The Swiss Socialists are usually harmless workmen and artisans in cities and towns. They indulge in theories, but stop short of crime. They will assemble at cafés and develop their ideas over a glass of beer, but they will refuse to listen to those who advocate the use of explosive materials or the murder of individuals under the plea of the regeneration of society. For instance, in the early part of 1884 an Anarchist, said to be a Bohemian, came to Bern, and at a café openly favoured the doctrine of propagandism by crime, and the destruction of numbers of human beings through the action of dynamite, but he met with not the slightest encouragement from the Swiss Socialists who were present; and we have always believed that official action against men of this stamp would be applauded by the whole Swiss people, at least with but few exceptions.

Anarchists have also been found in Switzerland who are ready to commit any crime under the plea of forwarding social regeneration, and the most active among them have generally been foreigners. In 1884 there were several societies in different towns taking the name of *Freiheit* and connected with the famous Most. Many members were German or Austrian subjects, and some of these have been expelled from Swiss territory on non-political grounds.

The Federal Council, as has been explained to us

upon the best authority, looks upon a foreigner who has assassinated a police agent for denouncing him, or who has been implicated in robbery or murder with a view of obtaining funds for the Anarchist cause, not in the light of a political offender, who could consequently invoke the right of asylum accorded to that class in Switzerland, but as an ordinary malefactor, who can be proceeded against for having committed an offence at common law.[1] If he is convicted on this latter ground, he can be delivered up to the authorities of his native land upon a proper official demand being addressed to the Swiss Government by virtue of an extradition treaty existing between the two countries. If he objects to his extradition on the ground of the offence being political, he can appeal to the Federal Tribunal. If he is not extradited, he is expelled by virtue of Article 70 of the Constitution. Those who advocate insurrection against foreign governments, or regicide, come clearly within the scope of this article.

In 1879 a foreigner, who wrote articles in an Anarchist newspaper published in Switzerland called *L'Avant-Garde*, was found guilty of having publicly incited his readers to assassinate kings and magistrates of foreign States, and was expelled the country.

In the same year another foreigner was expelled, among other reasons, for having written an article in the *Tagwacht* signed with his initials, in which he reproached the German Socialist democracy for its patient and expectant attitude, recommended it to employ "energetic agitation," and to strike hard as "the sole means of settling the question." The consequent sacrifice of some thousands of men was declared by him to be a matter of indifference.

---

[1] *Délit de droit commun.*

There are also foreigners who have been expelled from Switzerland because, although not themselves guilty of direct participation in crimes committed by others, they are still so closely connected with the actual perpetrators as to be clearly chargeable with what amounts to moral complicity.

It is unnecessary here to recount in detail the action of Socialists and Anarchists in Switzerland during the last few years. In 1885 an important investigation was made concerning the doings of the latter, and some foreigners were again expelled.

On the 27th January 1888, during the discussion of a law proposed by the Imperial Government to the Reichstag at Berlin for rendering the measures against Socialism more severe, a Socialist deputy read a letter addressed by himself and one of his colleagues to the Zürich captain of police, as to two men of German origin stated to be instigators of anarchy in Switzerland in the pay of the Berlin police. The answer from the Zürich official was also read, in which he admitted the accuracy of the facts which had come to the knowledge of the two deputies.

The Federal Council, feeling that the time had now come for a better organization of the *police des étrangers,* or political police, sent a message to the Chambers on the 12th March, demanding a supplementary credit of £800 for this object, and giving in justification a detailed account of what had happened.[1]

The committee in each Chamber to whom the message was referred reported unanimously in favour of the grant, and on the 20th March M. Droz made the speech in the National Council of which we have given an extract above, and which dealt with the political

[1] Published in the *Feuille Fédérale Suisse* for 1888.

side of the question in a manner alike distinguished by frankness and eloquence. He spoke as head of the department for foreign affairs, being deputed to do so by his colleagues, all of whom were present with the exception of one who was indisposed. He did not disguise the feeling in the country when it was found that instigators of anarchy and disorder in Switzerland were salaried agents of the German police, although entirely unknown to the Minister of the Interior, and he animadverted upon the action of the Zürich official in returning an answer to the Socialist deputies as being a breach of administrative discipline. He mentioned that confidential communications had been exchanged respecting these matters with the German Legation verbally, as befitted friendly nations, and he concluded with the remarks quoted above respecting the right of asylum.

The speech was loudly applauded, and the grant was voted unanimously and without discussion. In the Council of the States, three days later, after another speech from M. Droz, the grant was adopted in a similar manner.

The principles upon which Switzerland acts with reference to the right of asylum have thus been plainly laid down by the Federal Council and accepted unanimously, without one word of discussion, by the two Chambers, representing respectively the whole Swiss people and the whole of the Cantons.

It was in accordance with these principles that the Federal Council, on the 18th April 1888, issued a decree ordering the expulsion from Swiss territory of four foreigners who were members of the German Socialist Committee at Zürich, and were engaged in the printing-office of the *Sozialdemokrat*.[1]

---

[1] Published in the *Feuille Fédérale Suisse* for 1888.

This newspaper had been for some time the organ of the German Socialists in Zürich. It was issued from a printing-office and bookseller's shop, which, though purporting to be Swiss and having a Swiss citizen as the nominal head, was in reality under the direction of the committee of German Socialists. Their object was to publish newspapers and pamphlets of a kind which would be prohibited in Germany, and then to have them imported clandestinely into that country. The *Social-demokrat* appears to have had few subscribers in Switzerland, and to have been almost exclusively destined for Germany, into which country from 10,000 to 12,000 copies were said to be secretly conveyed every week. It did not profess to preach anarchy, but it advocated social revolution, and it indulged in violent language against German institutions and authorities.

Another publication called *Der Rothe Teufel* had been printed at Zürich in the early part of 1887, containing articles in verse and in prose, with illustrations, of a hostile character towards the German imperial family and authorities. It was ultimately discovered that this print also was issued from the same office.

The Federal Council considered that these publications contained matter tending to compromise the good relations existing between Switzerland and her neighbour Germany, and that there had been an abuse of Swiss hospitality. It therefore decreed the expulsion of the four foreigners mostly concerned. The editor of the *Socialdemokrat*, being a Swiss, could not be included in the decree, which was duly carried out by the Zürich authorities.

CHAPTER XVII

FORMERLY the mode of execution in Switzerland was either by the guillotine, or by a short but very heavy two-handed sword, with which the prisoner was decapitated.

By the 65th Article of the Constitution of 1874, capital punishment was abolished, the provisions of the military criminal code being, however, reserved in time of war. Corporal punishments were also abolished.

Some years later the question was again agitated, and in 1879 the Federal Council sent a message to the two Chambers deprecating any revision of the above Article. Much discussion ensued, and much difference of opinion was manifested in the Chambers. Eventually they came to a compromise, the old Article was repealed, and the following short one adopted in its stead :—

Article 65.—"No sentence of death can be pronounced for a political offence. Corporal punishments are interdicted." This modification was accepted by the popular vote on the 18th May 1879 by 200,485 to 181,588.

There was no doubt a political principle at stake as well as the question of scaffold or no scaffold. The Cantons, as has been seen, are very jealous of any curtailment of their sovereignty, and inasmuch as the adoption of the revision of Article 65 reserved to them the alternative of re-establishing the penalty of death for non-political crimes or not, many electors in certain Cantons—as, for instance, Vaud—voted for the revision.

They thus seized upon the opportunity of limiting the competency of the Confederation in criminal matters, and thereby increased cantonal rights in this respect.

Zürich, the two half-Cantons of Basel, Ticino, Neuchâtel, and Geneva (all of which had abolished capital punishment before the new Federal Constitution came into force), and also Bern and Thurgau, voted against the revision. In Solothurn the votes were almost equally divided. The Catholic Cantons in general gave the greatest majorities in favour of the revision.

Since then Luzern, Uri, Schwyz, Upper Unterwalden (Obwald), Zug, Appenzell Inner-Rhoden, St. Gallen, and the Valais, representing 20 per cent of the Swiss population, have re-established capital punishment in their codes. But they have done so only in name, for no execution has taken place in any of these States since 1879.

Zürich had pronounced against the revision of Article 65 by 36,460 votes to 19,243.

But on the 2d October 1882, 11,999 electors of this Canton, moved by a series of brutal crimes, exercised their right of popular initiative by demanding that the question should be submitted to the people. The Grand Council, not being competent to modify the terms of the petition, referred it to the people, whilst advising its rejection. It was nevertheless adopted on the 27th May 1883 by 28,394 to 25,259. This vote, however, only related to the principle, and in order to give effect thereto, first the cantonal Constitution, and then the criminal code, would have to be revised.

The question of the revision of the Constitution was submitted to the people of Zürich on the 5th July 1885, the Grand Council proposing an article which in substance would have limited capital punishment to cases of murder. This course was followed, although the majority of the deputies were opposed to the people's decision in 1883, because constitutionally the Grand Council felt bound to make the proposal. The people rejected the article by 27,577 to 21,377, and since then capital punishment may be said to be virtually abolished in the Canton. It is indeed affirmed that the Grand Council, which possesses the right of pardon, would, even if sentence of death were passed, never allow an actual execution to take place again.

The rejection of the above Article seems to have been due in some measure to the decision of the Grand Council of Luzern, three weeks previously, in the case of a man who had been condemned to death for having, in complicity with his wife, beaten and tortured to death his little daughter of five. This sentence the Grand Council, by 95 to 35, commuted to imprisonment for life, with five years' cellular seclusion.

The late Herr von Segesser, the president, then a man of sixty-eight, chief of the Clerical party and commanding much influence in the Canton, made an eloquent speech in favour of the commutation of the sentence. He argued that the criminal was dead to society, that he must be left to divine justice and allowed time to repent. He concluded by saying that he himself had reached that age when, any day, he might be called to another life, and that he did not wish to appear before the Eternal Judge with his hands soiled by blood.

Only one other sentence of death has been pronounced in Switzerland since the amended Article 65 came into force, and that was in St. Gallen upon a woman guilty of infanticide, and in her case the sentence was commuted by the Grand Council of the Canton.

From what has been recorded above, it seems clearly to result that, although there are moments when public opinion gets excited after the commission of a series of brutal crimes, there is a widespread feeling in Switzerland against capital punishment, which, if in theory it may still be said to exist in certain Cantons, is yet virtually abolished throughout the land.

It may be added that in all but one of the eight Cantons in which the penalty of death has been re-established, even if an execution took place, it would be carried out privately.

Opinions differ as to the reason why the guillotine has become almost an impossibility in Switzerland. According to a writer in the *Gazette de Lausanne* of July 7, 1887, it was not to be attributed to any softening of manners, nor to any progress in civilization among the masses, nor to a change produced among the people with reference to the justness and fitness of capital punishment. He considered that this shrinking from the application of a law felt to be just is rather to be ascribed to a lack of physical courage, and to a physical dread of the horror of the scaffold.

On the other hand, a Swiss from one of the German-speaking Cantons has stated to us that this was not at all the opinion of people in his part of the country. His view is the following: "The educated and enlightened classes of the country consider that society can exist without the barbarous, useless, and demoralizing penalty of death. Without speaking of the horror of the execution of innocent persons, against which possibility no legal precautions will ever be found sufficient, the value of human life must of necessity be lowered in the eyes of the more ignorant criminal classes, if the State takes the life of a citizen at a public or private execution. The Swiss people look to the better education of the masses, and not to capital punishment, as the best safe-guard for society."

CHAPTER XVIII

INTERNATIONAL UNIONS

THE establishment of various international unions, having their seat at Bern, on the soil of neutral Switzerland, is a matter which well deserves the consideration of thoughtful men, as tending to bind nations closer together, and thus working in the direction of peace. The fact, too, that Switzerland has been chosen as the home of these unions is one which will gradually give to her a peculiar position of honour and usefulness in the world.

A report upon this subject by Mr. Conway Thornton will be found in one of the Blue Books presented to Parliament in 1885,[1] and is well worth perusal.

The following particulars, gleaned almost entirely from this report, will be sufficient for our present purpose.

In 1863, as is well known, a private committee, the members of which belonged to different nationalities, assembled at Geneva, and drew up a plan for the protection of the wounded in battle. They then requested the Federal Council, as the central government of the country in which they had held their sittings, to propose

---

[1] Commercial, No. 26 (1885). Reports from Her Majesty's Diplomatic and Consular Officers abroad on subjects of commercial and general interest. Part IV.

to the other governments that a diplomatic conference
should be held in Switzerland in order to discuss this
humane and important question. The Federal Council
accepted the task, and the consequence was that delegates from many powers were sent to Geneva, where the
memorable Convention of the 22d August 1864 was
signed.

This Convention may fairly be looked upon as the
origin of the selection of Switzerland by the powers for
the natural seat of various international unions which
have since been founded.

In the course of 1865 the International Telegraph
Union came into existence upon the signature of the
Convention of Paris. Although this Union for a short
time dispensed with a central administration, and
although it was proposed at the Vienna Conference in
1868 that the administration should be a shifting one,
and should remain between the dates of each Conference
at the capital in which the last had assembled, it was
ultimately agreed that a permanent administration must
be established, and that the Swiss Confederation should
be requested to give it shelter. This point being
settled, the office of the International Telegraph Union,
the first of its kind, was established without further
delay at Bern.

In 1874 the International Postal Union was formed,
and a year later the central office of this Union was
also constituted at Bern. A member of the Swiss
Federal Council, Mr. Borel, who had already been president of the Confederation, accepted the directorship,
resigning his political office, and he has discharged his
new functions as head of what since 1878 has become
the " Universal " Postal Union with an ability which has
been acknowledged on all sides.

Passing mention may be made of two additional international conventions concluded in Switzerland, one against the phylloxera, and the other for the regulation of the transport of goods by railway. As to the former, a Convention was signed in 1878 at Bern, which was selected as the seat of future meetings. It requires no central administration. As to the latter, which is naturally confined to continental nations, after several conferences a Convention was signed in 1887 at Bern, where a central office will be established.

The International Union for the protection of industrial property was constituted by the Convention of Paris in 1884, after ten years of negotiation, and the result of conferences in 1884, 1885, and 1886 at Bern has been the formation of one more important International Union, that for the protection of literary and artistic property, which was secured by the signature of the Convention of Bern on the 9th September 1886. This Convention has been ratified by nine States, including Great Britain with the whole of her colonies.

The central office for these two Unions is also established at Bern.

The international offices above mentioned are practically the only ones in the world, for the Bureau du Mètre, established near Paris, which is the only institution in another country partaking of an international character, cannot be reckoned in the same category, and is, moreover, scientific and not commercial.

Mr. Thornton concludes his report with the following observations :—

" It is difficult, when passing through the quiet streets of Bern, to realize the importance of the operations which are being unobtrusively carried on, or the world-wide scope of the interests involved. Yet it cannot be doubted that these interests form a more effectual guarantee for the preservation of Switzerland as an independent State than any other that could be devised. This position she has gained by the study of the conveniences of mankind, or, in other words, by making herself useful to every one, while offending none. It may even be hoped that this spirit may in time extend itself to other nations with beneficial results to humanity at large. The confidence reposed by other countries in Switzerland, in the formation of these unions, tends to create a more unrestrained intercourse between them in matters of daily life, which can hardly fail to be productive of a progressively improving understanding among them all. Systems can now be compared, useful discoveries shared, and legislations simplified and assimilated. Through the possibility of obtaining accurate returns from all parts of the world, the science of statistics also will henceforward be capable of increasing development, and excellent results may be expected to flow therefrom. No one, finally, who has lived for even a few years in Switzerland, and has learnt to appreciate the practical good sense so largely prevailing in that energetic little country, will hesitate to rejoice at the destiny which now more than ever before seems assured to it, of retaining an honoured place among the nations."

CHAPTER XIX

IT has been suggested to us that it might be useful to
include in our work some comparison between the political institutions of Switzerland and the United States.
There are three principal points of resemblance with
respect to their Constitutions.

1. In each the Federal State has originated in the
desire of the separate States or Cantons to form one
solid League as regards other nations.[1]

2. In each the principle is proclaimed that the
independence of every component State or Canton is
only curtailed so far as is necessary for the existence
of the League, and its beneficent action in matters of
common concern.

3. In each there are two Chambers, one representing
the people, and the other the States or Cantons.

If we go on to compare the Constitutions of Switzerland and the United States, the first point which strikes
us is that whereas the latter is drawn up in terse but at
the same time comprehensive terms, the former contains
a vast number of elaborate Articles upon a variety of

---

[1] Originally the American States were not quite so unconnected with
each other as the cities in Switzerland which expanded into Cantons, but
the connection of the latter with the Empire must not be forgotten.

subjects. The reason would appear to be that the origin of the two Federations was radically different. In the United States, shortly after the revolution which turned thirteen British colonies into as many independent States, each with a Constitution of its own, certain Articles of Confederation establishing but an imperfect Union were first adopted. It was soon found necessary to replace these Articles by a more formal instrument, and this was effected by the Constitution drafted in 1787, which came into existence in 1789 and is substantially the organic law as it exists at the present day.

In Switzerland, on the contrary, the actual Constitution may be considered as the outcome of centuries. The League, increasing in size from time to time by the adhesion of fresh States, passed through a number of developments and various stages of foreign interference, until in 1848 the first purely Swiss Constitution obtained the assent of the people. Although its framers had studied that of the United States, the contrast between the two is very marked. The present Swiss Constitution gives to the Federal authorities power and supervision over a variety of special interests, and this system has worked well in a country of small extent. But in one so large as the United States, with such diversified and local aspects, a different system was required. The American Constitution, leaving much to be inferred from the rights deemed inherent in man and indefeasible, is confined chiefly to the enunciation of fundamental rules and general principles, and seeks to avoid as much as possible encroachments upon the domain of ordinary legislation. Concisely stated, the government of the Union is one of limited and enumerated powers, and any restrictions which it contains are imposed upon it and not upon the States, except where they are expressly mentioned. On the other hand, the restrictions abounding in the Swiss Constitution apply mostly to the Cantons through the direct and discretionary powers granted to the Confederation with respect to a vast field of legislation.

The Swiss Confederation can, in fact, stretch its arms out so as to embrace all the component parts of a compact little country, consisting of twenty-two Cantons, with rather less than three millions of inhabitants, whilst in the widely-extended Transatlantic Republic, reaching across the whole continent, the influence of the central government is in many matters but slightly perceptible. The thirteen States which began with about three millions have become thirty-eight with fully sixty millions of people, including the eight territories. Independent local governments, with full control over all domestic concerns, became indispensable, and it has been considered that each component part could in general manage those concerns with more intelligence and zeal than any distant governing body.

We will now proceed to notice some striking differences between the two Republics.

1. Revision of the Constitution.—In Switzerland the question of total or partial revision is submitted to the Referendum when one of the Chambers decrees it, but the other withholds its consent, or when it is demanded by fifty thousand vote-possessing citizens; and if the people accept the principle, the popular vote is again taken upon the particular measure which has been framed in consequence by the Federal Council and adopted by the Chambers.

In the United States the following is the process:—

"The Constitution makes provision for its own amendment. Two-thirds of both Houses of Congress may propose amendments, or, on the application of the legislatures of two-thirds of the States, may call a Convention for that purpose. Any amendment proposed by Congress, or by a Convention so called, is submitted to the States for ratification. If ratified by votes of the legislatures of three-fourths of the States, or by Conventions assembled in three-fourths of the States (according as Congress may direct), it becomes a part of the Constitution of the United States. But no amendment can be proposed which deprives a State, without its consent, of its equal representation in the Senate."[1]

2. Legislative authorities.—There are essential differences between the legislative assemblies of the two countries. The two Swiss Chambers are co-ordinate ; the American Senate possesses certain powers which do not belong to the House of Representatives. The Senate alone is entrusted with the ratification of treaties, and with the confirmation or rejection of the appointments made by the President (in each of which cases a two-thirds majority is required) ; it also tries United States officials who are impeached. The members of the American Senate are chosen by the legislatures of the respective States for a fixed term of six years ; those of the Swiss Council of the States serve for different periods, the duration of their functions being left entirely in the hands of each Canton. The same members can always be re-elected both to Congress and to the Swiss Chambers.

Again, the House of Representatives alone can present articles of impeachment, and all revenue bills must originate in it, but are subject to amendment by the Senate. The members of the former are elected

---

[1] See the excellent article in the *Nineteenth Century* for February 1888, by Mr. E. J. Phelps, late United States Minister in London.

for two years instead of three like the Swiss National Council, and each must inhabit the State from which he is chosen. This need not be the case in the National Council.

3. Executive authorities.—The President of the United States and the President of the Swiss Confederation cannot well be compared with each other. The former has extensive powers, whilst the particular functions of the latter are limited to certain formalities, all the other business of the executive being transacted by the members of the Federal Council, of which he is one.

The comparison, therefore, should rather be drawn between the American President and the Swiss Federal Council, as being the real executive authorities in the two countries respectively.

The American President is elected for four years, and is eligible for re-election. As a matter of fact no President so far has been re-elected more than once, and the general sentiment of the nation so much disapproves the idea of a third term of office that no out-going President has ever been nominated for one. The process of choosing a President has become a somewhat complicated matter. By the Constitution it was provided that each State should appoint a body of electors equal in number to the senators and representatives which are returned from it to Congress. The theory was that certain best men should have the privilege of selecting the best man for President. This was a decidedly conservative theory; but in practice the electors have now become simply the mouthpiece of the people's choice in each State. Each party in different States sends delegates to a Convention in some particular city. Names are submitted to the delegates, and one ballot succeeds another until some one obtains an absolute majority. He becomes the candidate of the party, whether on the Democratic, Republican, or other ticket. Each State then appoints its electors, who are expected to vote solid for one or other of the particular citizens chosen at the Conventions by representatives of the parties.

The Swiss Federal Council is elected by the Chambers for three years out of all citizens eligible for the National Council; its members can be, and are continually, re-elected.

In the United States the President is the nominee of one of the two great political parties, and his advent to power is marked by important and often very sweeping changes in the officials at home, and generally by a re-modelling of the diplomatic service abroad.

In Switzerland the whole of the members of the Federal Council are not the nominees of one political party, and the various officials keep their places for long and indefinite periods, whilst no one thinks of changing a single diplomatic representative upon a fresh election of the Council.

The American President has a suspensory veto upon all Acts passed by Congress. He cannot prorogue or dissolve either House, but he has great personal power. He is commander-in-chief of the army and navy; he signs treaties with foreign powers, chooses his own cabinet, and makes numerous other appointments; but they, as well as the treaties, are subject to the Senate's ratification already mentioned. He has also the right of pardon in the case of offences against Federal laws. He sends to Congress, upon its opening, a message relating to the condition of public affairs, and recommending any particular subjects to its attention.

Although the Cabinet, as in Switzerland, consists of seven members, this number rests upon no law, and is in the discretion of the President. Each superintends the work of a special department, and lays before the President reports and other business matters connected with it, for his examination. The latter deals authoritatively with whatever comes before him from each department, approving, disapproving, or altering as he pleases, and if he is dissatisfied with any member of his Cabinet he can, in the present state of the law, dismiss him, if he does not resign of his own accord.

The members of the Cabinet are not appointed for any fixed period; they have no influence at all outside of their own departments; they do not even speak in either branch of the legislature like the Swiss Federal Councillors, though there is no statute forbidding them to do so, as either House might allow any one of them to attend, if it desired to hear him. For the passage of any particular measure through Congress the services must be obtained of some Congressman who will consent to take charge of it. The United States Cabinet is thus simply a board of departments, wholly dependent upon the President.

The functions of the Swiss Federal Council have been explained in Chapter IV. Each member has an equal voice in the affairs which are within the competency of the whole body, every legislative measure must emanate from it for submission to the Chambers, and the measures which they adopt are promulgated by it when sanctioned, if need be, by the popular vote. Treaties concluded by the executive must be confirmed by the legislative authority.

There is no general Message presented by the Federal Council to the Chambers upon the opening of a session, but it is constantly addressing Messages to them upon a variety of matters for discussion and decision. It also presents to the Assembly an annual report of its proceedings.

The Swiss Federal Council may be termed, as already stated, an executive committee for the management of business, and the President of the year does not possess greater influence than any of his colleagues.

4. Judicial authorities.—In each country there is a supreme court of law.

In America the number of judges of this court is fixed by Congress, and at present they consist of a chief-justice and eight associated justices. The President appoints them, subject to confirmation by the Senate, and they hold office during good behaviour.

In Switzerland the Federal Assembly appoints the judges of the Federal Tribunal for six years; they are nine in number, and can be re-elected. The Assembly also appoints a president and a vice-president out of the nine every two years. There are also nine substitutes, similarly chosen for six years. The court seems to be rather in the nature of a body of arbitrators.

The attributions of the supreme court in the two countries differ materially, especially in the following important point.

Every judge of the Supreme Court of the United States is bound to treat as void all legislative Acts, whether proceeding from Congress or from the State legislatures, which are inconsistent with the Federal Constitution, or are in excess of the legislative powers which that Constitution confers. The Supreme Court only inquires into the validity of Acts of Congress for the purpose of determining a question brought before it in a legal proceeding.

The Federal Tribunal, on the contrary, cannot inquire into the constitutional character of a law or a resolution of a general nature which has been adopted by the Federal Assembly, any more than of a treaty ratified by that body. It is bound by the Constitution to accept those laws and resolutions, and to apply them to the cases submitted to its judgment.

The reason is clear. The measures which, after being framed by the Federal Council and adopted by the Federal Assembly, are accepted by the people, either tacitly or through the Referendum, thus obtain the sanction of the Swiss people. Hence the Federal Tribunal must bow to the decision of the people, and regard all such measures as constitutional and inviolable.

In the United States there is not only a Supreme Court, standing at the head of the whole Federal judiciary, but there are also such inferior courts as Congress may from time to time establish in the different States of the Union, and the judgments of the Supreme Court are executed by the officers of that judiciary without the aid of State officials.

In Switzerland there are no such subordinate courts, and the Federal Tribunal has no officers of its own to execute its judgments, so that both it and the Federal Council, which has to see to their execution, must rely upon cantonal officials to carry them out. Nor is there a hard and fast line fixed by the law, separating exactly the attributions of the Federal Tribunal as judicial authority, and the Federal Council and Federal Assembly as political authorities.

The following remarkable differences also exist in the two countries.

(*a*) There is no Article in the American, as in the Swiss, Constitution whereby the Federal power is called upon to guarantee each particular State Constitution, though it does guarantee a Republican form of government to every State.

(*b*) In America not only can the President exercise a suspensory veto upon all Acts of Congress, but the State governors, with the exception of four, have a veto upon the Acts of the State legislatures. There is no equivalent in Switzerland.

(*c*) Each American State possesses two Chambers. In the Swiss Cantons there are either Landsgemeinden or one-chambered legislatures with executive councils.

(*d*) In America the executive authority in each State is appointed by the popular vote. In Switzerland this is only the case in some Cantons.

(*e*) Another difference may be mentioned. If the post of Swiss President becomes vacant during the year, as by the death of Herr Hertenstein, it is not filled up for the remainder of the year, whereas in a similar case in America the Vice-President immediately becomes President for the residue of the term.

It is hardly necessary to remark that the system in our own constitutional country is widely different from that in either of the above two Republics. Still we may notice shortly the following points.

We have a Sovereign above all who, though seldom, at least in domestic affairs, exercising without the previous assent of Parliament those extensive powers which are by law the prerogative of the Crown, yet possesses a certain amount of political influence, and is continually performing political duties of a most serious nature.

The Cabinet consists of a number of individuals, all of whom have, in practice, their seats either in the House of Lords or in the House of Commons, though, according to Mr. Bagehot, they need not be exclusively chosen out of the members of the legislature. At their head is the Prime Minister, who is the embodiment of the whole in the sight of the Crown. The members of this Cabinet are generally taken entirely from one political party; coalition ministries are seldom formed, and are not likely to have a prolonged existence. As long as the members are generally agreed in their policy there is no change, but if any one or more should take a decidedly opposite view to the rest, he or they would find it necessary to resign. They are not elected, as in Switzerland, by the Parliament, but they are virtually a committee of Parliament; neither do they hold their offices for any fixed time. They can, with the assent of the Queen, cause the Parliament to be dissolved, and a fresh House of Commons to be elected, whereas the Swiss Federal Council, though created by the Federal Assembly, cannot dissolve it. They are not simple heads of departments as at Washington, but they administer, in their collective capacity, the affairs of our vast Empire in addition to their departmental duties, having, as has been well remarked, for the time being the confidence of that popular assembly, the House of Commons, which is itself the mirror and embodiment of the popular will.

If they lose that confidence they can either resign at once or appeal to the people. In the latter case the House of Commons is dissolved, and by the new elections the will of the constituencies is declared. If it is unfavourable to the existing Cabinet, the Prime Minister at once obtains an audience of the Sovereign and places his resignation and that of his colleagues in his or her hands. The Sovereign will doubtless consult the outgoing Premier as to the statesman who, in his opinion, should be sent for and entrusted with the formation of a new ministry, and he will probably name the leader of the Opposition to which he owes his defeat.

CHAPTER XX

THE limits of this volume prevent our treating many additional subjects. Among these is the important matter of the consumption of alcoholic liquors in Switzerland. This grave question has been taken up seriously of late years, and a Message from the Federal Council to the Federal Assembly in 1884 dealt exhaustively with it. The deleterious effect upon the population, more especially observable in certain districts, of the pernicious habit of imbibing at all hours drams of the poisonous *schnaps* produced in small private distilleries, and the increase of indigence and crime occasioned by habits of intemperance, called loudly for legislation. When the subject came on for discussion in the National Council in the spring session of 1885, some members insisted particularly upon the necessity of adopting measures for the solution of a serious social problem, and they approached the subject from a moral point of view. Others treated it rather in the light of a fiscal question, and the majority were in favour of abolishing the local duties levied in certain Cantons under the name of *ohmgeld* or *octroi*. Finally, a partial revision of the Constitution was adopted in 1885, and the bill subsequently framed for carrying out the same became law in 1887, being accepted by the popular vote in the great majority of the Cantons. It established a monopoly in the manufacture and sale of spirituous liquors by the Confederation. Whatever may be the general results of the new system, the hope is entertained that by the abolition of private distilleries a stop will be put to the consumption of poisonous *schnaps;* and the bulk of the expected surplus will be employed in indemnifying those Cantons where the local duties will shortly be all abolished.

Another matter which certainly deserves notice is the passing of a heavy progressive income-tax in the Canton of Vaud. A tax of this species already existed in various Cantons, but not to the same extent as that which came into operation in Vaud on the 1st January 1887. It cannot be doubted that the system of categories, at the high rate created by the new law, is calculated to press very materially upon the rich, and it was warmly advocated by the Radical party, who represented it to the country people as calculated to throw the cost of additional public burdens upon the wealthier class, and thus to diminish the amount of taxes to be paid by the poorer citizens. The Radical Government represented this progressive income-tax as a measure which would simply carry out the principle that in real as well as in personal property those who possess a superfluity should be taxed rather than those who have only a sufficiency. The Conservative minority declared that the result of the new law would be the departure of rich men from the Canton, of which there have already been instances, and the wholesale exoneration of the agriculturists, the heavier load of the common burden being cast upon the shoulders of the few, with utter indifference to any degree of just proportion.

We now pass on to some other subjects of interest, with which we will conclude our work.

It has been seen that the Swiss Confederation, commencing as a simple alliance for defensive purposes between three small communities in 1291, and increasing from time to time by the addition of neighbouring cities and territories till it embraced twenty-two Cantons, became, by the Constitution of 1848, a Federal State, and that, as such, it possesses a central power exercising supreme authority in all foreign relations, but having its sovereignty limited in internal matters so as to encroach as little as need be upon the independence and sovereignty of each particular Canton.

The nature and attributions of the Federal Council, or executive authority, are particularly worthy of attention, and Swiss statesmen appear, by its creation, to have gone far towards solving that important problem which has puzzled other democratic countries, viz. how to combine an efficient executive with democratic institutions. The members of the Federal Council do not all belong to one political party. It is true that when a vacancy occurs, as in the case of the late President Hertenstein in 1888, the new member is taken from the party then forming the majority in the Chambers, but still with such restrictions as are dictated by tradition and unwritten laws. In the case of Herr Hertenstein, a Züricher, he was replaced by Herr Hauser, a Zürich Democrat. The Assembly would doubtless only have selected a citizen of another Canton if no suitable candidate could have been found among the Zürichers belonging to the Left, as it has always been the custom for Zürich to be represented in the Federal Council. Herr Hauser being a moderate man, the Centre also adopted him as their candidate, the Right choosing a

Roman Catholic for theirs, as a protest against the total exclusion of their party from the executive.[1]

When a triennial election takes place, it is customary to leave the members of the Federal Council unmolested, if they have done their duty. Hence men like Herr Welti, Herr Hertenstein, and Herr Hammer have never been removed, although they owed their elections originally to the Centre, now reduced to a mere handful. This system has the evident advantage of great continuity in the executive government, whilst a sufficient change is introduced by the by-elections. The Federal Councillors are thus not changed *en bloc* upon every fluctuation of party feeling, and yet the body cannot be said to be really out of harmony with the Chambers. The people acquiesce in this arrangement, not only because they consider the members to be good men of business, but because they are conscious of possessing that powerful engine called the Referendum, whereby the ultimate fate of any law is wholly in their hands. It is, in fact, owing to the power of the popular vote that the Swiss are content to possess competent Federal administrators without particular reference to their politics.

With regard to religious matters, there certainly have been signs during the last years of a lull in the *Kulturkampf*, of which Switzerland has long been the theatre.

Upon the opening of the summer session of the Federal Assembly in 1886, Herr Zemp, an Ultramontane from Luzern, was elected vice-president of the National Council. No member of this extreme party had ever been thus chosen since the passing of the Constitution

---

[1] We have been informed that, upon a fresh vacancy, it is probable that a Roman Catholic of the Right may for the first time be chosen to be a member of the executive, after the clearly-expressed wish of that party to have a representative.

of 1848. He succeeded in due course to the presidency
of the Chamber, and it is a curious fact that in 1887
three Roman Catholics, all from the Canton of Luzern,
were at the same time presidents of the two Chambers
and the Federal Tribunal. This circumstance seems to
have led some foreigners to the conclusion that a reaction had come over Switzerland in a conservative sense,
but that was not at all the case. It could be quoted
as evidence that religious passions had become less
intense, otherwise Herr Zemp at least, respected as he
is, would most probably not have been elected to his
high office owing to his Ultramontane views.

As far as the Federal Council is concerned, they have
shown a manifest desire, whenever occasion has offered,
to labour in the interests of peace between the two great
religious bodies in Switzerland.

The material condition of the mass of the Swiss
people may on the whole be pronounced to be satisfactory. Still there is a strong tide of emigration among
the natives flowing every year, particularly to the
United States. The German Cantons supply the larger
contingents, the contributions from the French Cantons
being trifling in comparison. The number varies. In
1880 it exceeded 7000, in each of the two following
years it rose to nearly 11,000, and in 1883 it reached
12,758. Since then it has diminished considerably, and
in 1887 it had dropped to 7558, of whom 6448 went to the
United States. The emigrants are mostly from agricultural districts. From the Canton of Bern, where the
land is generally mortgaged, even for much more than
half its value, there is a constant stream of emigration.
With all their reputation for thriftiness, what with fêtes
and other amusements many Swiss peasants are apt to
spend more than they can afford. Debts are thus con-

tracted, and, as the family increases, these liabilities become greater, and are gradually consolidated into a mortgage. There is thenceforward a heavy interest to discharge, and finally, when it is found impossible to make both ends meet, everything is sold off, and the family leave, going mostly to Basel and thence by the weekly emigrant train to Hâvre, and from there by the corresponding steamer to New York, on their way to join relations or friends who have already followed a similar course. Their place is probably soon filled up from Germany.

There does not seem to be any marked hostility between rich and poor in Switzerland. The political equality of all citizens is cited as one reason, and inasmuch as property is more equally distributed than in many other countries, there is no display of great luxury, there are no magnates in the land, while charity is not wanting towards the poorer brethren on the part of those who are better off.

The officials, whether Federal or cantonal, are in general a laborious thrifty race, who are remunerated upon a low scale of salaries, and the cost of the central government is trifling compared with that in other countries.

Another matter which deserves attention is the recent organization of a Federation of Swiss working-men (Arbeiterbund). Delegates, consisting of both Catholics and Protestants, nearly 200 in number, from different industrial societies met at Aarau in April 1887, and they represented about 100,000 men of the labouring class. Their object was to found a Federation of all such societies with the view of raising the social and material condition of that class, without distinction of creed, and the Federal authorities have given a kind of semi-official character to the organization by agreeing to grant a certain salary to an Industrial Secretary appointed by the Federation. He is to be a kind of agent between the industrial classes and the Federal Government, his functions being confined to economic subjects, the domain of politics being strictly excluded.

In this way questions of wages, of compulsory insurance, and of the civil responsibility of masters can be examined and discussed with greater weight and calmness.

An important movement has been set on foot by the meeting at Bern, on the 21st October 1888, of fifty-seven delegates from different parts of the country, resulting in the fusion of two societies with the object of forming a fourth political party under the denomination of Social Democrats. This movement is in no sense international, and the party will be composed solely of Swiss citizens. Its general programme is stated to include the organization of democracy and a centralized State, the separation of Church and State, the nationalization of commerce and industry, and the equal division of the profits of labour among all. Such matters as the election of the Federal Council by the people, the suppression of the political police, compulsory insurance, the creation of a State bank for the monopoly of the issue of bank-notes, and the State purchase of railways figure in the special programme for 1888-89. It is too early to forecast the future of this new party. Its creation indicates, for the moment at least, a certain *scission* between different sections of working-men, and represents a tendency of a more socialistic character than the Grütliverein, which, it may be remembered, is an association of men of the labouring class. For the present the Grütliverein seems inclined to stand aloof from the new association. If the latter ever rise to the position of a permanent party, with representatives in the Federal Assembly, some members of the actual Radical majority will probably end by joining them, whilst others would be likely to move in an opposite direction towards the Centre.

Enough has been written in Chapter XI to show that Swiss soldiers still keep up their reputation at home, and the impression made upon foreign officers who have attended the autumn manœuvres has been decidedly favourable. In that chapter we have briefly noticed the late tendency towards a greater centralization of the army. This is becoming more and more apparent in military circles, both in the French and German Cantons. The different societies of officers throughout the land have, with scarcely any exception, now pronounced themselves in favour of complete centralization with regard to the organization and administration of the army, and of thus placing it entirely under Federal authority. The small share of activity left to the Cantons in military matters under the present Federal Constitution would thus be taken away, and the Cantons, as such, would have no more influence in them, especially as regards the appointment and promotion of officers, which has hitherto been to a certain extent in their domain. The supporters of the proposed centralization lay stress, among other arguments, upon the numerical differences existing between various divisions and subdivisions of the army. Some divisions and some regiments or battalions which ought to contain the same number of men vary greatly owing to the fact that the men of one Canton cannot be incorporated with those of another Canton.

The opposers of centralization, on the other hand,

contend that by a stricter application of the existing law, any improvements considered to be necessary may be carried out without having resort to so important a step as a revision of the Federal Constitution. They further oppose the movement on the ground that, in the present uncertain state of European politics, it would be unwise to undertake a modification of the military organization. War, they argue, might break out at any moment, and if the army were found at such a crisis in a state of transition from one system to another, it would be in a less efficient state for defending Swiss neutrality than it is at present with any deficiencies which may exist.

Without entering further into the question, one may point out that if, as is likely, it is soon brought before the Federal Assembly, the promoters of the centralization of the army will hardly be able to confine the discussion upon a matter involving a revision of the Constitution to it alone, and other parties will not lose the opportunity to bring forward motions proposing revision upon other matters as well, which will hardly fail to produce much political agitation. Still, the opinion of the great bulk of Swiss military men has been clearly pronounced in favour of absolute centralization.

Ninety-four delegates from different sections of the Federal Society of Officers met at Bern on the 4th November 1888, and after a prolonged discussion the following proposition was adopted, with only seven dissentients :—

" The transfer to the Confederation of all legislative and administrative attributions and competencies concerning the military organization of the country is an imperious necessity, in order that the defence of Switzerland may be insured by an army fit to take the field and ready to fight. The central committee of the Federal Society of Officers is requested to communicate to the members of the Federal authorities the resolution adopted by the Assembly of to-day, as well as the *procès verbal* of the deliberations and reports of the cantonal sections."

Switzerland, as a nation, has always been distinguished by a spirit of lofty patriotism, and by an intense love of independence, and in a speech delivered by Vice-President Hammer on the 5th April 1888, when a monument was inaugurated near Näfels in commemoration of the 500th anniversary of the victory of Swiss over Austrians, he described the present position of his native land in the following eloquent words :—

"Never has our country been so united. Never have its resources been more abundant, nor its military force more considerable and better organized. But at the same time never has Switzerland been so surrounded as to-day by colossal, powerful, and strongly-armed States. We remain here, a very small people, standing up in the midst of these great nations, if we may compare ourselves to them, but confiding in God and our own selves, with our eyes open. We live in good friendship with all our neighbours, and, in all human probability, we can hope that this will be the case in the future. Still, no nation can flatter itself that it will always remain free from trials. Whatever may come to pass, there will be found in us and in our sons the Swiss spirit, vigorous and resolute."

APPENDIX

SINCE the text of this volume has been in the hands of the printers, the Federal Statistical Bureau has published a statement of the provisional results of the census of December 1888. Some modifications may yet have to be made by the Bureau, but the numbers now given are sufficient for our present purpose.

The following table shows the population in each Canton as taken in the years 1870, 1880, and 1888, as well as the number of foreigners, Protestants, and Catholics at the date of the last census :—

	1870.	1880.	1888.	Foreigners.	Protestants.	Catholics.
Zürich	284,047	316,074	337,205	34,607	294,236	40,402
Bern .	501,501	530,411	536,182	15,552	468,096	68,226
Luzern	132,153	134,708	135,396	3,180	7,939	127,533
Uri .	16,095	23,744	17,313	576	378	16,892
Schwyz	47,733	51,109	50,363	1,677	1,097	49,289
Obwald	14,443	15,329	15,049	457	331	14,699
Nidwald .	11,701	11,979	12,558	618	126	12,397
Glarus	35,208	34,242	33,828	1,305	25,935	7,790
Zug .	20,925	22,829	23,013	886	1,394	21,696
Freiburg .	110,409	114,994	119,086	2,421	18,869	100,524
Solothurn .	74,608	80,362	85,783	2,619	21,898	63,539
Baselstadt .	47,040	64,207	73,754	25,601	50,305	22,426
Baselland .	54,026	59,171	61,922	4,842	48,847	12,961
Schaffhausen	37,642	38,241	37,798	5,074	32,890	4,813
Appenzell—						
(Ausser-Rhoden)	48,734	51,953	54,145	2,195	49,555	4,502
(Inner-Rhoden)	11,922	12,874	12,868	318	697	12,206
St. Gallen .	190,674	209,719	228,316	18,539	92,705	135,796
Grisons	92,103	93,864	94,686	8,932	52,842	43,320
Aargan	198,718	198,357	193,700	5,500	106,408	85,962
Thurgau .	93,202	99,231	104,816	10,339	74,282	30,337
Ticino	121,591	130,394	129,152	19,128	1,079	125,748
Vaud	229,588	235,349	247,569	19,867	227,467	22,428
Valais	96,722	100,190	102,320	2,993	865	101,013
Neuchâtel .	95,425	102,744	107,935	10,120	95,047	12,692
Geneva	88,791	99,712	105,966	40,967	51,669	52,817
	2,655,001	2,831,787	2,920,723	238,313	1,724,957	1,190,008

There are over 8000 Jews, and over 10,000 belonging to some other sect or to none at all. The German-speaking population exceed two millions; there are about 638,000 whose language is French, the remainder being mostly made up of those who speak Romansch and Ladin.

INDEX

www.ingramcontent.com/pod-product-compliance
Lightning Source LLC
Chambersburg PA
CBHW031034120726
47905CB00007B/2175